nF420995

Celestial Streams

Celestial Streams

Matthew Petchinsky

Celestial Streams: The Content Creator's Astrology Manual
By: Matthew Petchinsky

Introduction: Unveiling the Cosmic Blueprint for Content Creation

The universe has always been a source of mystery and wonder, its vast expanse offering a celestial map of influence that touches every aspect of our lives. Among its many gifts lies the ancient wisdom of astrology, a timeless framework for understanding the rhythms of the cosmos and their profound impact on human behavior, emotions, and decision-making. As we navigate the ever-evolving landscape of content creation, the intersection of astrology and creativity emerges as a compelling and transformative lens through which creators can unlock their full potential.

Content creation, in its essence, is an art that blends intuition, strategy, and self-expression. It is a process that requires not only skill but also a deep understanding of oneself, one's audience, and the timing of action. Astrology provides a powerful toolkit for creators, offering insights into personal strengths, optimal periods for productivity, and strategies for authentic audience engagement. By aligning creative efforts with astrological rhythms, content creators can elevate their craft, foster deeper connections with their audiences, and experience profound personal growth.

Astrology and Creativity: Unlocking Inner Potential

At its core, astrology is a study of cycles and energies, governed by the positions and movements of celestial bodies. Each planet, sign, and house in an astrological chart carries its own unique energy, influencing various facets of our lives. For content creators, understanding these influences can reveal invaluable insights into their creative processes.

For example, a person with a strong placement of Venus—the planet of beauty, art, and harmony—might naturally excel in visual storytelling or aesthetic-driven content. Meanwhile, a creator with a dominant Mercury—the planet of communication and intellect—may find their strength in writing, public speaking, or crafting persuasive narratives. By exploring their natal chart, creators can uncover hidden talents, understand their creative preferences, and align their content strategy with their natural strengths.

Moreover, astrology can shed light on potential creative blocks. Retrogrades, for instance, often inspire introspection and reevaluation, offering opportunities to refine existing projects rather than starting new ones. Similarly, understanding the influence of challenging planetary aspects can help creators navigate periods of self-doubt or stagnation with greater resilience.

Productivity in Harmony with the Cosmos

One of the most practical applications of astrology lies in its ability to optimize productivity. The Moon, with its rapid and cyclical phases, plays a pivotal role in influencing our energy levels and focus. By working in sync with the Moon's phases, creators can harness its energies for different stages of their projects.

- **New Moon:** A time for setting intentions and brainstorming new ideas. This phase encourages quiet reflection and planting seeds for future endeavors.
- **Waxing Moon:** Ideal for action, growth, and development. As the Moon's light increases, so does its supportive energy for building momentum.
- **Full Moon:** The culmination of efforts, this phase is perfect for launching new content, sharing bold ideas, or engaging with your audience on a larger scale.
- **Waning Moon:** A period for review, refinement, and letting go of what no longer serves your creative goals.

In addition to the Moon, other planetary transits—such as Jupiter's expansive influence or Saturn's disciplined guidance—can help creators identify the best times for launching projects, investing in skill development, or focusing on long-term growth.

Astrology and Audience Engagement

Astrology extends beyond the personal realm; it also offers insights into collective energies and audience behavior. Just as individuals are influenced by astrological transits, so too are groups and communities. By understanding the broader astrological climate, content creators can align their messaging with the moods and priorities of their audience.

For instance, during a Mercury retrograde, audiences might be more receptive to content that emphasizes reflection, nostalgia, or revisiting past ideas. On the other hand, a period influenced by fiery Mars might call for bold, action-oriented messaging that inspires motivation and drive. By crafting content that resonates with these cosmic themes, creators can foster deeper connections and build trust with their audience.

Astrology also enables creators to segment their audience more effectively. Knowing the astrological preferences or dominant signs of your target demographic can inform everything from branding choices to communication styles. A campaign designed to appeal to earthy, practical Taurus energy might emphasize reliability and value, while one aimed at adventurous Sagittarians might focus on exploration and innovation.

Personal Growth Through the Stars

Beyond its practical applications, astrology offers a transformative journey of self-discovery. For content creators, this journey is particularly meaningful, as their work often reflects their innermost thoughts, values, and aspirations. By exploring their astrological charts, creators can identify areas for personal growth and cultivate a deeper sense of purpose.

For instance, understanding one's North Node—the astrological marker of life purpose—can provide guidance on the themes and lessons that should shape one's creative journey. Similarly, exploring the influence of Chiron, the "wounded healer," can help creators address insecurities and channel their experiences into powerful, relatable content that resonates with their audience.

Astrology also encourages creators to embrace authenticity. In a digital world where trends and algorithms often dictate content strategies, astrology reminds us to honor our unique rhythms and creative voices. By aligning with the energies of the cosmos, creators can find balance between external demands and internal fulfillment.

The Cosmic Blueprint for Creative Success

The intersection of content creation and astrology is more than just a novel concept; it is a powerful framework for enhancing creativity, productivity, audience engagement, and personal growth. By integrating the wisdom of the stars into their creative processes, content creators can unlock new levels of inspiration, align their efforts with universal energies, and foster meaningful connections with their audiences.

In the chapters that follow, we will explore how to practically apply astrological insights to every aspect of content creation. From understanding your creative strengths to planning launches in sync with cosmic rhythms, this journey will empower you to not only create with purpose but also thrive in an ever-changing digital world. Let the stars guide your path as we embark on this exploration into the unique and transformative synergy between astrology and content creation.

Chapter 1: The Creator's Zodiac Map – Overview of All 12 Signs

Astrology begins with the twelve zodiac signs, each representing a distinct archetype and energy that shapes the way we approach life, creativity, and connection. For content creators, understanding the zodiac signs can provide invaluable insights into personal strengths, areas for growth, and ways to align with the cosmic flow. Each sign contributes its own flavor to the creative process, offering a blueprint for self-expression and productivity.

This chapter will provide an in-depth exploration of each zodiac sign, highlighting its core traits, creative strengths, potential challenges, and how these qualities influence content creation.

Aries: The Trailblazer (March 21 - April 19)

Element: Fire

Ruling Planet: Mars

Modality: Cardinal

Aries embodies boldness, passion, and initiative, making them natural leaders in the content creation space. Their pioneering spirit often leads them to tackle uncharted topics, setting trends rather than following them. They thrive on action and spontaneity, excelling in fast-paced environments where they can bring fresh, daring ideas to life.

- **Creative Strengths:** Courageous, innovative, and energetic, Aries creators are fearless when it comes to experimenting with new formats or addressing controversial topics.
- **Challenges:** Impulsivity can lead to burnout or unfinished projects. They may also struggle with patience, wanting immediate results.
- **Tips for Aries Creators:** Set realistic deadlines and learn to pace your efforts. While boldness is your strength, taking time for reflection will ensure your ideas reach their full potential.

Taurus: The Builder (April 20 - May 20)

Element: Earth

Ruling Planet: Venus

Modality: Fixed

Taurus creators are grounded and methodical, with a keen eye for beauty and aesthetics. Their content often feels rich and luxurious, reflecting their appreciation for the finer things in life. Consistency is their hallmark, and they excel at building long-term projects that stand the test of time.

- **Creative Strengths:** Patient, reliable, and resourceful, Taurus creators produce work that feels polished and professional. They have a natural talent for visual and sensory storytelling.
- **Challenges:** Resistance to change can lead to stagnation. They may also prioritize comfort over risk, missing opportunities for growth.
- **Tips for Taurus Creators:** Embrace innovation without abandoning your steady approach. Collaborate with more spontaneous individuals to balance your energy.

Gemini: The Communicator (May 21 - June 20)
Element: Air
Ruling Planet: Mercury
Modality: Mutable

Gemini creators are the ultimate storytellers, thriving in environments that allow for intellectual exploration and dynamic expression. They are versatile, curious, and masters of multitasking, often juggling multiple creative projects at once.

- **Creative Strengths:** Witty, adaptable, and engaging, Gemini excels in writing, podcasting, and other forms of communication that require quick thinking and versatility.
- **Challenges:** Scattered focus can lead to unfinished projects. Their need for variety may prevent them from delving deeply into one idea.
- **Tips for Gemini Creators:** Focus on honing one project at a time. Use your natural curiosity to explore niches in greater depth, creating richer content.

Cancer: The Nurturer (June 21 - July 22)
Element: Water
Ruling Planet: Moon
Modality: Cardinal

Cancer creators infuse their work with emotion, care, and a deep sense of connection. They excel at creating content that resonates on a personal level, often drawing from their own experiences to inspire others.

- **Creative Strengths:** Intuitive, empathetic, and emotionally intelligent, Cancer creators excel in content that nurtures, heals, or comforts their audience.
- **Challenges:** They may struggle with criticism or become overly attached to their work. Mood swings can impact their productivity.
- **Tips for Cancer Creators:** Develop a healthy detachment from your content. Use your natural emotional depth to create impactful and relatable material.

Leo: The Performer (July 23 - August 22)
Element: Fire
Ruling Planet: Sun
Modality: Fixed

Leo creators are charismatic and confident, often shining in the spotlight. Their work is bold, dramatic, and full of passion, capturing attention with its creative flair and storytelling prowess.

- **Creative Strengths:** Enthusiastic, entertaining, and inspiring, Leo creators excel in video content, public speaking, and theatrical storytelling.
- **Challenges:** A need for validation can hinder their creativity. They may also struggle with delegating tasks or sharing the spotlight.

- **Tips for Leo Creators:** Balance your confidence with humility. Seek constructive feedback to refine your work and strengthen your audience connections.

Virgo: The Perfectionist (August 23 - September 22)
Element: Earth
Ruling Planet: Mercury
Modality: Mutable

Virgo creators are detail-oriented and analytical, bringing a meticulous approach to their craft. They excel in creating highly organized, practical, and educational content that delivers value to their audience.

- **Creative Strengths:** Precise, organized, and resourceful, Virgo creators thrive in research-heavy projects and formats that require structure and clarity.
- **Challenges:** Over-perfectionism can lead to procrastination or burnout. They may also struggle with self-doubt.
- **Tips for Virgo Creators:** Embrace imperfection as part of the creative process. Set boundaries to prevent overworking and celebrate small wins.

Libra: The Harmonizer (September 23 - October 22)
Element: Air
Ruling Planet: Venus
Modality: Cardinal

Libra creators are natural mediators, seeking balance and harmony in their work. Their content often reflects beauty, fairness, and a desire to connect with others on a meaningful level.

- **Creative Strengths:** Diplomatic, artistic, and collaborative, Libra creators excel in partnerships and content that emphasizes aesthetics and relationships.
- **Challenges:** Indecision and people-pleasing tendencies can slow progress. They may also avoid conflict or controversial topics.
- **Tips for Libra Creators:** Trust your instincts when making decisions. Don't be afraid to tackle complex issues that resonate with your audience.

Scorpio: The Alchemist (October 23 - November 21)
Element: Water
Ruling Planet: Pluto
Modality: Fixed

Scorpio creators are intense and transformative, often delving into deep, taboo, or mysterious topics. Their work is powerful and emotionally charged, offering profound insights and transformative experiences.

- **Creative Strengths:** Passionate, resourceful, and magnetic, Scorpio creators excel in storytelling that challenges norms or explores hidden truths.
- **Challenges:** They may become overly secretive or struggle with trust, limiting collaboration. Intensity can lead to creative burnout.
- **Tips for Scorpio Creators:** Balance intensity with lighthearted moments. Open yourself to collaboration and trust the creative process.

Sagittarius: The Explorer (November 22 - December 21)
Element: Fire
Ruling Planet: Jupiter
Modality: Mutable

Sagittarius creators are adventurous and philosophical, thriving in content that explores new horizons. They excel in travel, education, and inspirational storytelling that broadens perspectives.

- **Creative Strengths:** Optimistic, curious, and visionary, Sagittarius creators inspire their audience with bold ideas and expansive storytelling.
- **Challenges:** A tendency to overcommit or lack focus can hinder productivity. They may also struggle with consistency.
- **Tips for Sagittarius Creators:** Ground your expansive ideas with practical steps. Focus on completing one project before moving to the next.

Capricorn: The Strategist (December 22 - January 19)
Element: Earth
Ruling Planet: Saturn
Modality: Cardinal

Capricorn creators are disciplined and goal-oriented, excelling in long-term projects that require strategy and perseverance. Their content often reflects professionalism, ambition, and practicality.

- **Creative Strengths:** Determined, reliable, and methodical, Capricorn creators thrive in business-oriented or educational content.
- **Challenges:** They may prioritize work over creativity, leading to rigidity. Fear of failure can also slow progress.
- **Tips for Capricorn Creators:** Embrace creativity as a strength, not a luxury. Allow yourself to experiment and take risks.

Aquarius: The Visionary (January 20 - February 18)
Element: Air
Ruling Planet: Uranus
Modality: Fixed

Aquarius creators are innovative and unconventional, often ahead of their time. Their work challenges norms and inspires progressive thinking, making them natural trailblazers in their fields.

- **Creative Strengths:** Original, idealistic, and future-focused, Aquarius creators excel in innovative projects that inspire change.
- **Challenges:** Detachment or over-intellectualizing can limit emotional resonance. They may also resist tradition even when it's beneficial.
- **Tips for Aquarius Creators:** Balance innovation with relatability. Build emotional connections to enhance the impact of your ideas.

Pisces: The Dreamer (February 19 - March 20)
Element: Water
Ruling Planet: Neptune
Modality: Mutable

Pisces creators are deeply imaginative and intuitive, often channeling their emotions and dreams into their work. Their content is often ethereal, poetic, and highly evocative.

- **Creative Strengths:** Compassionate, artistic, and visionary, Pisces creators excel in music, poetry, and storytelling that touches the soul.
- **Challenges:** Escapism and lack of structure can hinder productivity. They may struggle with boundaries.
- **Tips for Pisces Creators:** Ground your creativity with structure. Use your intuitive gifts to create meaningful, impactful content.

Understanding the zodiac signs allows content creators to navigate their unique creative energies while appreciating the diverse approaches of others. This cosmic map is not only a guide for self-awareness but also a tool for collaboration and innovation. In the following chapters, we'll delve deeper into how to harness these archetypes for specific aspects of content creation.

Chapter 2: Aries Creators – Unleashing Raw Energy in Digital Content

Aries, the first sign of the zodiac, is synonymous with action, ambition, and the fiery spark of creation. Ruled by Mars, the planet of passion and drive, Aries creators are natural trailblazers, brimming with energy and fearless in their pursuit of innovation. This chapter dives deep into the unique traits of Aries creators, exploring how their dynamic energy can be channeled into impactful digital content that captivates audiences and sets trends.

Understanding Aries Energy

As a cardinal fire sign, Aries is characterized by boldness, spontaneity, and a pioneering spirit. Aries creators are rarely content with the status quo; they thrive on initiating new projects, exploring uncharted territories, and pushing boundaries. Their approach to content creation is often fast-paced and instinctive, driven by their innate desire to make a mark on the world.

- **Key Traits of Aries Creators:**
    - **Passionate:** Their enthusiasm is infectious, bringing excitement and urgency to their work.
    - **Courageous:** They are unafraid to tackle controversial topics or experiment with unconventional ideas.
    - **Action-Oriented:** Aries creators prioritize execution over endless planning, making them prolific in producing content.
    - **Competitive:** Their desire to excel often motivates them to stay ahead of trends and deliver high-quality work.

While their energy is a powerful asset, it can also be a double-edged sword. Aries creators may struggle with impatience, impulsiveness, or burnout if they don't manage their fiery drive effectively.

The Aries Approach to Digital Content

Aries creators excel in dynamic, fast-moving digital spaces where their boldness and originality can shine. Whether it's crafting viral videos, launching groundbreaking campaigns, or engaging in real-time social media trends, Aries thrives in environments that reward quick thinking and decisive action.

1. Embracing Bold, Trendsetting Ideas

Aries creators are natural trendsetters. They have a knack for identifying emerging topics and injecting their unique perspective to create attention-grabbing content.

- **Example:** An Aries fashion influencer might lead the charge in showcasing unconventional styles, confidently breaking away from mainstream trends to inspire their audience.
- **Tip:** Focus on "first-mover advantage." Aries creators can excel by spotting trends early and creating content that establishes them as industry leaders.

2. High-Impact Visual Content

As a fire sign, Aries creators thrive on visual mediums that allow them to express their energy and enthusiasm. Platforms like Instagram, TikTok, and YouTube are ideal for Aries, who can use these spaces to create bold, visually stunning content.

- **Strengths:** High-energy videos, dynamic photo shoots, and action-oriented visuals resonate deeply with Aries' fiery nature.
- **Tip:** Use quick cuts, vibrant colors, and energetic music to reflect Aries' bold personality in video content.

3. Fearless Storytelling

Aries creators aren't afraid to share raw, authentic stories. Their courage allows them to tackle controversial or taboo subjects with honesty and conviction, creating a deep emotional connection with their audience.

- **Example:** An Aries blogger might write a deeply personal post about overcoming obstacles, inspiring others to face challenges head-on.
- **Tip:** Leverage personal experiences and bold perspectives to create emotionally impactful content that leaves a lasting impression.

4. Instant Engagement with Live and Real-Time Content

The fast-paced nature of live streaming, Twitter threads, and real-time audience interactions aligns perfectly with Aries' instinctive approach to communication. They thrive in spontaneous environments where they can showcase their wit and charisma.

- **Strengths:** Aries creators excel in Q&A sessions, live tutorials, and impromptu challenges that keep audiences engaged.
- **Tip:** Use live streams to connect with your audience authentically and showcase your unfiltered personality.

Overcoming Challenges as an Aries Creator

While Aries' fiery energy is their greatest strength, it can also present unique challenges. Recognizing and addressing these tendencies is key to maintaining balance and long-term success.

1. Avoiding Burnout

Aries creators often take on multiple projects simultaneously, driven by their boundless enthusiasm. However, this can lead to exhaustion and unfinished work.

- **Solution:** Practice mindful time management and set realistic deadlines. Prioritize rest and self-care to recharge your creative energy.

2. Managing Impulsiveness

Aries' go-getter attitude can sometimes result in impulsive decisions, such as launching content without proper research or planning.

- **Solution:** While spontaneity is a strength, balance it with thoughtful preparation. Collaborate with more detail-oriented individuals who can help refine your ideas.

3. Cultivating Patience

Aries creators may struggle with patience, especially when results aren't immediate. This can lead to frustration or abandoning projects prematurely.

- **Solution:** Focus on long-term goals and celebrate small milestones along the way. Remember that great content often takes time to build momentum.

The Aries Creator's Toolkit

To maximize their potential, Aries creators can adopt tools and strategies that align with their energetic, action-oriented nature.

1. Tools for Spontaneous Creativity

- **Mobile Content Creation Apps:** Tools like Canva, Adobe Spark, or InShot allow Aries creators to quickly produce high-quality content on the go.
- **Real-Time Engagement Platforms:** Use Twitter, Instagram Stories, or TikTok to stay connected with your audience in the moment.

2. Tools for Managing Workflow

- **Project Management Apps:** Tools like Trello or Asana can help Aries creators stay organized and ensure their projects stay on track.
- **Time-Blocking Techniques:** Allocate specific times for brainstorming, creation, and reflection to balance spontaneity with structure.

3. Tools for Tracking Trends

- **Social Listening Tools:** Platforms like BuzzSumo or Google Trends can help Aries creators identify emerging topics and tailor their content accordingly.
- **Analytics Dashboards:** Use analytics tools to monitor audience engagement and refine your strategies.

Aries Creators and Audience Connection

Aries creators have a magnetic quality that draws people in. Their boldness and authenticity inspire trust and loyalty among their audience. However, building a sustainable connection requires intentional effort.

- **Engagement Tips:**
    - Be authentic and transparent in your interactions.
    - Use your energy to motivate and uplift your audience.
    - Share behind-the-scenes moments to create a sense of intimacy and relatability.
- **Content Ideas:**
    - Inspirational stories about overcoming challenges.
    - Tutorials or how-to videos that showcase your expertise and energy.
    - Bold opinion pieces or hot takes on current trends.

Aries Success Stories

Aries creators have left an indelible mark on the digital landscape, their fearless energy driving them to achieve remarkable success. Take inspiration from well-known Aries personalities who embody the spirit of the Trailblazer.

- **Lady Gaga (March 28):** A musical icon known for her bold artistry and trendsetting performances.
- **Robert Downey Jr. (April 4):** A charismatic actor who redefined the superhero genre with his portrayal of Iron Man.

By channeling their innate boldness and passion, Aries creators can carve out a niche that sets them apart from the crowd.

Final Thoughts

Aries creators are the spark that ignites the digital content world. Their courage, energy, and pioneering spirit make them uniquely positioned to lead, innovate, and inspire. By embracing their natural strengths while addressing potential challenges, Aries creators can create impactful, trendsetting content that leaves a lasting legacy.

Chapter 3: Taurus Creators – Mastering Consistency and Luxury Aesthetics

Grounded, reliable, and attuned to beauty, Taurus creators bring a steady and methodical energy to content creation. As an earth sign ruled by Venus, the planet of love, beauty, and luxury, Taurus is naturally inclined toward aesthetics and sensory pleasures. Their ability to create timeless, high-quality content that appeals to the senses sets them apart as masters of consistency and elegance.

This chapter delves into the world of Taurus creators, exploring their unique strengths, challenges, and strategies for success in the digital landscape.

The Taurus Energy: Stability Meets Beauty

Taurus is a fixed earth sign, embodying steadfastness and an appreciation for the finer things in life. Taurus creators are known for their ability to focus deeply, produce high-quality work, and maintain a consistent creative output. They thrive in environments where they can take their time to perfect their craft, often prioritizing quality over speed.

- **Key Traits of Taurus Creators:**
  - **Practical:** They excel at creating content that is both beautiful and functional, blending artistic flair with utility.
  - **Persistent:** Taurus creators are not easily deterred. Once they commit to a project, they see it through with unwavering dedication.
  - **Sensory-Oriented:** With a heightened appreciation for beauty, Taurus creators often infuse their work with rich visuals, soothing sounds, or tactile experiences.
  - **Grounded:** They maintain a calm, stable presence, which translates into content that feels reliable and trustworthy.

While their strengths are undeniable, Taurus creators can sometimes become too fixed in their ways, resisting change or innovation. This tendency underscores the importance of balancing stability with flexibility.

The Taurus Approach to Digital Content

Taurus creators shine in projects that require patience, attention to detail, and a strong aesthetic sense. Whether curating an Instagram feed, crafting long-form blog posts, or producing high-quality videos, their work is a testament to their dedication and refined taste.

1. Excellence Through Consistency

Taurus creators are masters of consistency, a quality that is highly valued in the digital content space. They excel at building a recognizable brand identity and maintaining a regular posting schedule, fostering trust and loyalty among their audience.

- **Example:** A Taurus lifestyle blogger might post weekly updates featuring beautifully curated photographs, detailed product reviews, or practical tips for enhancing everyday life.
- **Tip:** Develop a content calendar that aligns with your strengths and allows for steady, manageable growth.

2. Luxury and Elegance in Aesthetics

Ruled by Venus, Taurus creators are naturally drawn to beauty and luxury. They have an innate ability to create visually stunning content that exudes sophistication, whether it's through photography, design, or writing.

- **Strengths:** Taurus excels in niches like fashion, interior design, gourmet food, and self-care, where elegance and attention to detail are paramount.
- **Tip:** Invest in high-quality tools and resources to ensure your visuals and content reflect the luxurious aesthetic Taurus is known for.

3. Sensory-Driven Content

Taurus creators have a deep connection to the senses, making their content particularly engaging. They excel in creating immersive experiences that evoke emotions and stimulate the senses.

- **Example:** A Taurus chef or food influencer might create recipe videos that showcase vibrant ingredients, soothing background music, and step-by-step instructions.
- **Tip:** Focus on sensory details that resonate with your audience, such as vivid imagery, rich textures, or evocative language.

4. Building Sustainable Content

Taurus creators prioritize longevity and sustainability in their projects. They focus on creating evergreen content—timeless material that remains relevant and valuable over time.

- **Example:** A Taurus travel blogger might craft in-depth guides to destinations, complete with practical tips, stunning visuals, and recommendations that remain useful for years.
- **Tip:** Invest time in research and development to produce content that will stand the test of time.

Overcoming Challenges as a Taurus Creator

While Taurus creators bring immense value through their persistence and aesthetic sensibilities, they also face challenges that can hinder their creative journey.

1. Resistance to Change

Taurus creators often prefer to stick with what's comfortable, which can make them hesitant to embrace new trends or technologies.

- **Solution:** Approach change as an opportunity to enhance, not disrupt, your process. Experiment with one small innovation at a time to integrate new ideas without feeling overwhelmed.

2. Risk Aversion

Taurus' practical nature can sometimes translate into reluctance to take risks, potentially leading to missed opportunities.

- **Solution:** Balance your cautious approach with calculated risks. Seek input from trusted collaborators to explore new directions confidently.

3. Perfectionism

The Taurus commitment to quality can sometimes lead to over-perfectionism, delaying project completion or stifling creativity.

- **Solution:** Set realistic deadlines and prioritize progress over perfection. Remember that authenticity often resonates more than flawless execution.

The Taurus Creator's Toolkit

To maximize their potential, Taurus creators can leverage tools and strategies that complement their methodical and aesthetic-driven approach.

1. Tools for Stunning Visuals

- **Design Tools:** Canva, Adobe Photoshop, and Lightroom are excellent for creating polished graphics and photos.
- **Photography Equipment:** Invest in a high-quality camera or smartphone with advanced photography features to elevate your visual content.

2. Tools for Organization

- **Content Management:** Platforms like Notion, Trello, or Monday.com can help Taurus creators organize their ideas and stay on top of their schedules.
- **Evergreen Planning:** Use tools like CoSchedule or Buffer to plan and automate the release of evergreen content.

3. Tools for Sensory Appeal

- **Video Editing Software:** Programs like Final Cut Pro or Adobe Premiere Pro allow Taurus creators to add professional touches to video content.
- **Sound Design:** Explore royalty-free music libraries or sound-editing tools like Audacity to enhance the auditory elements of your content.

Connecting with Your Audience

Taurus creators excel at building strong, loyal communities through their authenticity and reliability. Their calm and grounded energy naturally attracts audiences seeking stability and value.

- **Engagement Tips:**
  - Share your creative process to build trust and transparency with your audience.
  - Use storytelling to evoke emotions and deepen connections.
  - Focus on quality over quantity, ensuring every piece of content reflects your brand's aesthetic and values.
- **Content Ideas:**
  - Tutorials that teach practical skills with a touch of elegance.
  - Behind-the-scenes glimpses into your workflow or creative process.
  - Long-form content, such as blog posts or videos, that provides in-depth value.

Taurus Success Stories

Many successful creators embody Taurus energy, showcasing the beauty, persistence, and practicality that define this zodiac sign. Their work serves as inspiration for aspiring Taurus creators.

- **Adele (May 5):** Known for her soulful music and timeless appeal, Adele exemplifies the Taurus commitment to quality and authenticity.
- **David Beckham (May 2):** With his stylish branding and entrepreneurial ventures, Beckham reflects Taurus' refined taste and practicality.

By channeling their innate strengths, Taurus creators can achieve lasting success in the digital content space.

Final Thoughts

Taurus creators bring unparalleled stability, beauty, and dedication to the world of content creation. Their ability to produce consistent, high-quality work sets them apart as reliable and trustworthy voices in their niches. By embracing their natural talents while addressing challenges like resistance to change or perfectionism, Taurus creators can build a legacy of timeless, impactful content.

Chapter 4: Gemini Creators – Duality in Content and Communication Skills

Gemini, the third sign of the zodiac, is governed by Mercury, the planet of communication, intellect, and adaptability. Known as "The Twins," Gemini symbolizes duality, versatility, and a boundless thirst for knowledge. Gemini creators bring dynamic energy to content creation, thriving in their ability to juggle multiple ideas, adapt to various trends, and engage audiences with their wit and charm. This chapter explores the unique strengths, challenges, and strategies that Gemini creators can leverage to excel in their craft.

The Gemini Energy: The Power of Adaptability

As a mutable air sign, Gemini thrives on flexibility and intellectual curiosity. Gemini creators are quick thinkers who excel in fast-paced environments that reward innovation and variety. Their dual nature allows them to explore multiple perspectives, making their content layered, engaging, and thought-provoking.

- **Key Traits of Gemini Creators:**
    - **Communicative:** They have a natural talent for storytelling and connecting with audiences through words, whether in writing, speaking, or visual communication.
    - **Versatile:** Gemini creators can tackle diverse topics and switch between different creative styles with ease.
    - **Curious:** Their insatiable appetite for knowledge keeps their content fresh and relevant.
    - **Energetic:** They bring enthusiasm and vibrancy to their projects, often infusing humor or playful elements into their work.

However, Gemini's duality can sometimes manifest as indecision or scattered focus, making it essential for them to harness their energy in productive ways.

The Gemini Approach to Digital Content

Gemini creators shine in projects that require intellectual engagement, adaptability, and real-time interaction. Their ability to master various communication channels makes them versatile and impactful in the digital content landscape.

1. Engaging Through Storytelling and Humor

Gemini creators are natural storytellers who can captivate audiences with their wit and charm. They have an innate ability to turn ordinary experiences into compelling narratives, often infusing humor or relatability into their content.

- **Strengths:** Writing blogs, creating scripts for videos, or hosting podcasts are ideal platforms for Gemini creators to showcase their storytelling skills.
- **Example:** A Gemini lifestyle influencer might share humorous anecdotes about everyday life while weaving in practical advice or tips.
- **Tip:** Use humor and authentic storytelling to establish a strong emotional connection with your audience.

2. Mastering Multiple Formats

Gemini thrives on variety, making them skilled at experimenting with different content formats. From videos and blogs to social media posts and live streams, they can effortlessly pivot between mediums to keep their audience engaged.

- **Strengths:** Short-form content (like TikToks or Instagram Reels) and live interactions (such as Twitter Spaces or Clubhouse) align with Gemini's quick thinking and adaptability.
- **Tip:** Leverage your versatility to repurpose content across platforms. For example, turn a blog post into a podcast episode or a series of Instagram posts.

3. Exploring Diverse Topics

Gemini's curiosity enables them to cover a wide range of subjects, appealing to audiences with varied interests. They excel at blending entertainment with education, making their content both engaging and informative.

- **Example:** A Gemini tech blogger might create content that explains complex concepts in a fun, easy-to-understand manner.
- **Tip:** Tap into your curiosity by exploring niche topics that set you apart from competitors. Use your ability to simplify complex ideas to attract a broader audience.

4. Real-Time Engagement

Gemini creators excel in real-time interaction, whether through live streams, social media chats, or audience Q&A sessions. Their quick wit and ability to think on their feet make these formats highly effective.

- **Strengths:** Gemini's conversational style is perfect for hosting webinars, moderating discussions, or engaging with followers in comment sections.
- **Tip:** Schedule regular live sessions to foster a sense of community and keep your audience engaged.

The Gemini Creator's Toolkit

To optimize their creative potential, Gemini creators should embrace tools and strategies that align with their multifaceted nature and communication skills.

1. Tools for Multitasking and Organization

Gemini creators often juggle multiple projects at once, making organization key to their success.

- **Project Management Tools:** Trello, Asana, or Notion can help Gemini creators organize their ideas and manage deadlines effectively.
- **Content Scheduling Tools:** Platforms like Buffer, Hootsuite, or Later allow for consistent posting across social media.

2. Tools for Content Creation

- **Versatile Editing Software:** Canva and Adobe Premiere Pro are excellent for creating diverse content formats, from graphics to videos.
- **Writing and Editing Tools:** Grammarly or Hemingway can assist Gemini creators in crafting clear and engaging written content.

3. Tools for Real-Time Interaction

- **Live Streaming Platforms:** Instagram Live, TikTok Live, and YouTube Live are ideal for engaging with audiences in real-time.
- **Interactive Tools:** Polls, quizzes, and Q&A features on platforms like Instagram Stories or Twitter can keep Gemini creators connected with their audience.

Overcoming Challenges as a Gemini Creator

While Gemini creators possess remarkable strengths, their duality and need for variety can sometimes create obstacles. Recognizing and addressing these challenges is essential for sustained success.

1. Avoiding Scattered Focus

Gemini's tendency to jump between ideas can lead to unfinished projects or inconsistent content.

- **Solution:** Prioritize projects by setting clear goals and timelines. Use tools like time-blocking to dedicate specific periods to each task.

2. Managing Indecision

The duality of Gemini often results in difficulty making decisions, especially when faced with too many options.

- **Solution:** Simplify choices by narrowing your focus to what aligns most with your long-term goals. Seek feedback from trusted collaborators to gain clarity.

3. Maintaining Depth

While Gemini excels at covering a wide range of topics, this can sometimes come at the expense of depth.

- **Solution:** Commit to exploring a few key subjects in greater detail. Balance breadth with depth to establish yourself as an authority in your niche.

Connecting with Your Audience

Gemini's charm and adaptability make them natural audience magnets. Their ability to connect through humor, relatability, and quick thinking fosters strong relationships with their followers.

- **Engagement Tips:**
  - Share personal stories or behind-the-scenes moments to build intimacy.
  - Use interactive features like polls, quizzes, or live Q&A sessions to engage your audience directly.
  - Keep your content dynamic and varied to maintain interest and excitement.
- **Content Ideas:**
  - "Day in the Life" vlogs showcasing your multitasking abilities.
  - Explainer videos or blogs that simplify complex topics.
  - Collaborative projects that showcase your ability to work across different styles and mediums.

Gemini Success Stories

Many successful creators embody the dynamic and communicative energy of Gemini, showcasing how their adaptability and charisma can lead to remarkable achievements.

- **Kanye West (June 8):** Known for his versatility and constant reinvention, Kanye exemplifies Gemini's ability to push boundaries and stay ahead of trends.
- **Angelina Jolie (June 4):** A multifaceted actress and humanitarian, Jolie reflects Gemini's duality and intellectual depth.

By channeling their intellectual curiosity and communication skills, Gemini creators can leave a lasting impact on their audiences.

Final Thoughts

Gemini creators are the epitome of versatility and adaptability in the content creation world. Their ability to think quickly, engage dynamically, and explore diverse topics makes them invaluable in an ever-changing digital landscape. By harnessing their strengths while addressing challenges like scattered focus or indecision, Gemini creators can craft content that is both impactful and enduring.

Chapter 5: Cancer Creators – Emotional Resonance with Your Audience

Cancer, the fourth sign of the zodiac, is ruled by the Moon, symbolizing emotions, intuition, and the cycles of life. As a cardinal water sign, Cancer creators bring depth, empathy, and a nurturing energy to their content. Their ability to connect on an emotional level with their audience makes them powerful storytellers and relationship builders in the digital world.

In this chapter, we will explore how Cancer creators can leverage their emotional intelligence and natural empathy to create impactful content, foster meaningful connections, and build loyal communities.

The Cancer Energy: Intuitive and Nurturing

Cancer is often associated with the archetype of the caregiver or nurturer. These individuals are deeply in tune with their own emotions and those of others, allowing them to craft content that feels personal and relatable. They often draw inspiration from their own experiences, using vulnerability as a tool to connect authentically with their audience.

- **Key Traits of Cancer Creators:**
  - **Empathetic:** Cancer creators have an innate ability to understand and relate to their audience's emotions, crafting content that feels deeply personal.
  - **Intuitive:** Guided by their gut feelings, they often know what their audience needs before it's explicitly expressed.
  - **Nurturing:** Their content often provides comfort, support, and a sense of belonging, fostering loyal and engaged communities.
  - **Creative:** Ruled by the Moon, Cancer creators are naturally artistic and excel in storytelling, visual arts, and creating immersive emotional experiences.

However, Cancer's sensitivity can sometimes lead to challenges, such as difficulty handling criticism or becoming overly attached to their work. Understanding and addressing these tendencies is key to their growth.

The Cancer Approach to Digital Content

Cancer creators excel in content that prioritizes emotional connection, relatability, and storytelling. Their ability to balance creativity with authenticity makes them a valuable presence in any niche.

1. Building Emotional Connections

Cancer creators are masters of crafting emotionally resonant content. They excel in telling stories that make their audience feel seen, heard, and understood.

- **Strengths:** Personal blogs, memoir-style social media posts, and heartfelt videos are ideal formats for Cancer creators.
- **Example:** A Cancer mental health advocate might share personal experiences with overcoming challenges, offering hope and practical advice to their audience.
- **Tip:** Use your vulnerability as a strength. Sharing your authentic self helps establish trust and fosters a deeper connection with your audience.

2. Nurturing Through Supportive Content

Cancer's nurturing nature allows them to create content that feels like a safe space. Whether it's through advice, tutorials, or inspirational messages, their work often uplifts and comforts their audience.

- **Strengths:** Cancer creators thrive in niches like self-care, wellness, parenting, and mental health.
- **Example:** A Cancer creator focusing on self-care might develop guided meditations, soothing playlists, or calming affirmations.
- **Tip:** Create content that offers solutions or guidance, positioning yourself as a reliable and caring presence in your audience's life.

3. Storytelling with Visual and Emotional Depth

Cancer creators have a strong artistic streak, often excelling in visual storytelling that evokes emotion. Their content might include evocative photography, cinematic videos, or rich narratives.

- **Strengths:** Platforms like Instagram, Pinterest, and YouTube allow Cancer creators to showcase their artistic vision.
- **Example:** A Cancer travel vlogger might produce videos that highlight not just the destination but also the emotional journey of the experience.

- **Tip:** Use visuals to amplify your message. Pair emotional storytelling with imagery that evokes feelings of nostalgia, comfort, or wonder.

4. Creating a Sense of Community

Cancer creators excel at building tight-knit, supportive communities. Their ability to connect deeply with individuals makes their audience feel like part of a family.

- **Strengths:** Hosting online forums, creating membership groups, or fostering dialogue through comments are natural extensions of Cancer's energy.
- **Example:** A Cancer food blogger might create a Facebook group where followers share recipes, cooking tips, and personal stories.
- **Tip:** Focus on fostering engagement by responding thoughtfully to comments, hosting live Q&A sessions, or creating opportunities for collaboration within your community.

Overcoming Challenges as a Cancer Creator

While Cancer creators possess unique strengths, their emotional sensitivity can sometimes create obstacles. Learning to navigate these challenges is essential for long-term success.

1. Managing Sensitivity to Criticism

Cancer's emotional nature makes them deeply invested in their work, which can lead to difficulty handling criticism or negative feedback.

- **Solution:** Reframe criticism as an opportunity for growth. Develop a healthy detachment from your content to view feedback objectively.
- **Tip:** Practice self-compassion and remind yourself that constructive criticism is not a reflection of your worth.

2. Avoiding Emotional Burnout

Cancer creators often pour their hearts into their work, which can lead to emotional exhaustion or feeling overwhelmed.

- **Solution:** Set clear boundaries between your personal and professional life. Prioritize self-care and schedule regular breaks to recharge.
- **Tip:** Incorporate mindfulness practices, such as journaling or meditation, into your routine to maintain emotional balance.

3. Letting Go of Perfectionism

Cancer's attachment to their work can sometimes result in over-perfectionism or reluctance to release content.

- **Solution:** Embrace imperfection as part of the creative process. Focus on progress, not perfection, and trust that your authenticity will resonate more than flawless execution.

- **Tip:** Set deadlines to ensure you stay on track and avoid getting stuck in endless revisions.

The Cancer Creator's Toolkit

To amplify their creativity and emotional resonance, Cancer creators can adopt tools and strategies that align with their intuitive and nurturing approach.

1. Tools for Storytelling

- **Visual Platforms:** Use Instagram, Pinterest, or Canva to create visually compelling content that enhances your stories.
- **Writing Tools:** Grammarly, Hemingway, or Notion can help Cancer creators refine their writing for clarity and impact.

2. Tools for Engagement

- **Community-Building Platforms:** Use Facebook Groups, Discord, or Patreon to foster a sense of community and connection.
- **Interactive Features:** Polls, Q&A stickers, and comments on platforms like Instagram and TikTok help Cancer creators engage with their audience directly.

3. Tools for Emotional Well-Being

- **Mindfulness Apps:** Headspace or Calm can help Cancer creators maintain emotional balance.
- **Time Management Tools:** Trello or Asana can help organize projects and prevent overwhelm.

Connecting with Your Audience

Cancer creators excel in creating content that feels deeply personal and relatable. By leaning into their emotional intelligence, they can foster meaningful connections that inspire loyalty and engagement.

- **Engagement Tips:**
    - Share stories that highlight your vulnerability and humanity.
    - Create content that addresses your audience's emotions, such as affirmations, motivational messages, or heartfelt advice.
    - Encourage dialogue by asking open-ended questions and inviting your audience to share their experiences.
- **Content Ideas:**
    - Inspirational blogs or videos that offer hope and encouragement.
    - Tutorials or guides that provide comfort and practical solutions.
    - Visual storytelling projects that evoke nostalgia or emotional depth.

Cancer Success Stories

Many successful creators embody the nurturing and intuitive energy of Cancer, showcasing how their emotional resonance can lead to profound impact and success.

- **Princess Diana (July 1):** Known for her compassion and humanitarian work, Diana exemplified Cancer's ability to connect deeply with people on an emotional level.
- **Selena Gomez (July 22):** A singer and actress known for her vulnerability and relatability, Selena resonates with her audience by sharing her personal struggles and triumphs.

By channeling their empathy and creativity, Cancer creators can build content that not only engages but also inspires and heals.

Final Thoughts

Cancer creators are emotional alchemists, capable of transforming their experiences into meaningful, impactful content that resonates deeply with their audience. Their ability to nurture and connect makes them invaluable in the digital world, especially in niches that prioritize authenticity and support. By embracing their strengths while addressing challenges like emotional sensitivity or perfectionism, Cancer creators can cultivate lasting relationships and create content that truly matters.

Chapter 6: Leo Creators – The Art of Spotlight and Self-Promotion

Ruled by the Sun, Leo is the zodiac's most radiant and charismatic sign. As a fixed fire sign, Leo embodies confidence, creativity, and a natural flair for leadership. In the world of content creation, Leo creators excel at commanding attention, building personal brands, and inspiring audiences with their bold and passionate self-expression. Known for their charm and warmth, they thrive in the spotlight and have a unique ability to bring their ideas to life with flair and enthusiasm.

This chapter explores the strengths, strategies, and challenges of Leo creators, offering a roadmap for leveraging their natural talents to excel in the digital space.

The Leo Energy: Boldness Meets Creativity

Leo is associated with courage, generosity, and a love for self-expression. These creators bring a vibrant, magnetic energy to their work, making their content stand out in a crowded digital landscape. They are natural performers and storytellers, able to inspire and entertain audiences with their enthusiasm and creativity.

- **Key Traits of Leo Creators:**
    - **Charismatic:** Leo creators shine in front of an audience, drawing people in with their charm and confidence.
    - **Creative:** With a strong artistic streak, they excel in producing visually stunning and engaging content.
    - **Ambitious:** Driven by a desire to make an impact, Leos set high goals and work tirelessly to achieve them.
    - **Generous:** They often use their platform to uplift others, whether by promoting causes they care about or collaborating with other creators.

While Leo's energy is infectious, their strong focus on self-promotion can sometimes come across as ego-driven. Learning to balance confidence with humility is essential for sustained success.

The Leo Approach to Digital Content

Leo creators thrive in environments that reward boldness, visibility, and self-expression. They excel in personal branding, performance-based content, and projects that allow them to showcase their leadership and vision.

1. Owning the Spotlight

Leo creators are born to shine, making them ideal for roles that place them front and center. Whether they're hosting a podcast, leading a live stream, or creating video content, their confidence and charisma make them captivating performers.

- **Strengths:** Video platforms like YouTube, Instagram Reels, and TikTok are ideal for Leo creators to showcase their personality.
- **Example:** A Leo fitness influencer might create energetic workout videos paired with motivational speeches, inspiring their audience to achieve their goals.
- **Tip:** Lean into your natural charisma by choosing formats that allow your personality to shine. Focus on content that highlights your unique voice and perspective.

2. Building a Personal Brand

Leo creators excel at creating strong, recognizable personal brands. Their natural confidence and sense of style make them memorable and relatable to their audience.

- **Strengths:** Leo's ability to curate an authentic yet aspirational persona is ideal for building loyal followings across multiple platforms.
- **Example:** A Leo fashion blogger might combine bold outfits with personal stories about confidence and self-expression, building a brand that resonates deeply with their audience.
- **Tip:** Develop a cohesive aesthetic and message for your content. Use consistent visuals, tone, and storytelling to strengthen your personal brand.

3. Inspiring Through Storytelling

Leos are natural storytellers who excel at weaving compelling narratives into their content. Their passion and enthusiasm make their stories resonate deeply with audiences, inspiring action and engagement.

- **Strengths:** Leos shine in motivational or aspirational content, such as sharing personal journeys or highlighting success stories.
- **Example:** A Leo entrepreneur might create a video series about their journey from struggle to success, inspiring their audience to pursue their dreams.
- **Tip:** Use your storytelling skills to connect emotionally with your audience. Focus on authenticity and relatability to foster trust.

4. Creating High-Impact Visuals

Leos have a strong sense of aesthetics and a flair for the dramatic, making them skilled at producing visually striking content. From vibrant photos to cinematic videos, their work often feels larger-than-life.

- **Strengths:** Platforms like Instagram, Pinterest, and YouTube allow Leos to showcase their creativity through bold, eye-catching visuals.
- **Example:** A Leo travel vlogger might create breathtaking video montages of their adventures, paired with inspiring commentary.
- **Tip:** Invest in quality tools and resources to elevate the visual appeal of your content. Use bold colors, dynamic angles, and creative edits to make your work stand out.

Overcoming Challenges as a Leo Creator

While Leo creators possess remarkable strengths, their passion for the spotlight can sometimes lead to challenges. Understanding and addressing these tendencies is key to maintaining balance and authenticity.

1. Managing Ego and Overconfidence

Leos' love for recognition can sometimes be perceived as arrogance or self-centeredness, potentially alienating their audience.

- **Solution:** Practice humility and gratitude. Acknowledge the contributions of your team, collaborators, and audience to your success.
- **Tip:** Use your platform to uplift others. Highlighting other creators or engaging with your audience authentically can balance your self-promotion.

2. Handling Criticism

As a sign deeply connected to pride, Leo creators may struggle with handling criticism or negative feedback.

- **Solution:** Separate your work from your self-worth. View criticism as an opportunity to improve rather than a personal attack.
- **Tip:** Develop a thick skin by focusing on constructive feedback and ignoring baseless negativity.

3. Balancing Authenticity and Aspiration

Leos' tendency to focus on perfection or aspiration can sometimes create a disconnect with their audience, who may crave authenticity.

- **Solution:** Share both successes and struggles to create a more relatable narrative. Vulnerability can deepen your connection with your audience.
- **Tip:** Mix polished, aspirational content with behind-the-scenes glimpses or candid moments to maintain balance.

The Leo Creator's Toolkit

To amplify their creativity and impact, Leo creators can adopt tools and strategies that align with their bold, performance-driven approach.

1. Tools for High-Impact Visuals

- **Video Editing Software:** Adobe Premiere Pro or Final Cut Pro for creating cinematic, polished videos.
- **Photography Tools:** Invest in a high-quality DSLR camera or advanced smartphone for capturing stunning visuals.

2. Tools for Personal Branding

- **Design Tools:** Canva or Adobe Spark for creating consistent, branded graphics and promotional materials.
- **Social Media Management:** Platforms like Later or Hootsuite for planning and maintaining a cohesive online presence.

3. Tools for Engagement

- **Interactive Features:** Use Instagram Stories' Q&A, polls, and quizzes to connect with your audience.
- **Community Platforms:** Patreon or YouTube Memberships for building exclusive, engaged communities.

Connecting with Your Audience

Leos naturally attract followers with their warmth, enthusiasm, and authenticity. By leveraging these qualities, they can build loyal, engaged communities.

- **Engagement Tips:**
    - Use your charisma to inspire and motivate your audience.
    - Respond to comments and messages with genuine enthusiasm to strengthen relationships.
    - Highlight your audience's contributions by featuring fan art, testimonials, or shout-outs.
- **Content Ideas:**
    - Motivational speeches or videos that inspire action and confidence.
    - Behind-the-scenes content showcasing your creative process or daily life.
    - Bold campaigns or challenges that encourage audience participation.

Leo Success Stories

Many successful creators and public figures embody Leo's bold and radiant energy, showcasing how their confidence and charisma can lead to lasting success.

- **Jennifer Lopez (July 24):** A multitalented performer and entrepreneur, Lopez exemplifies Leo's ability to captivate audiences and build a strong personal brand.
- **Barack Obama (August 4):** Known for his charismatic leadership and inspirational speeches, Obama reflects Leo's ability to inspire and lead with vision.

By embracing their natural flair for self-promotion and storytelling, Leo creators can build powerful, influential platforms that leave a lasting impact.

Final Thoughts

Leo creators bring a unique combination of confidence, creativity, and leadership to the world of content creation. Their ability to command attention and inspire action makes them natural influencers and trendsetters. By leveraging their strengths while addressing challenges like handling criticism or balancing authenticity, Leo creators can create impactful content that resonates with their audience.

Chapter 7: Virgo Creators – Attention to Detail and Content Strategy

Virgo, the sixth sign of the zodiac, is ruled by Mercury, the planet of communication and intellect. Known for their analytical minds and meticulous nature, Virgo creators approach content creation with precision, practicality, and a focus on delivering value. As a mutable earth sign, Virgos are adaptable while maintaining a grounded and organized approach, making them masters of strategy and detail-oriented execution.

In this chapter, we'll explore how Virgo creators leverage their strengths to craft polished, meaningful content, build trust with their audience, and establish themselves as reliable authorities in their niches.

The Virgo Energy: Analytical and Methodical

Virgo is synonymous with perfectionism, organization, and a desire for improvement. Virgo creators are natural problem solvers who excel in creating content that educates, informs, and provides tangible benefits to their audience. They bring structure and strategy to their work, ensuring that every detail aligns with their vision.

- **Key Traits of Virgo Creators:**
    - **Detail-Oriented:** They focus on the finer points, ensuring their content is polished and professional.
    - **Practical:** Virgo creators prioritize functionality and utility, creating content that solves real-world problems.
    - **Organized:** They thrive on structure, often relying on schedules, outlines, and systems to manage their creative process.
    - **Self-Critical:** Their perfectionism drives them to continually refine their work, although this can sometimes lead to overthinking.

While Virgo creators' meticulousness is their greatest asset, it can also lead to challenges like procrastination or burnout. Balancing precision with flexibility is key to their creative success.

The Virgo Approach to Digital Content

Virgo creators shine in content that requires research, organization, and an educational or practical focus. Their ability to combine creativity with strategy makes them invaluable in any content space.

1. Creating High-Quality, Polished Content

Virgo creators are perfectionists who take pride in their work's quality. They excel in producing content that feels professional, thorough, and well-researched.

- **Strengths:** Blog posts, tutorials, and guides are ideal formats for Virgo creators who enjoy creating in-depth, actionable content.
- **Example:** A Virgo productivity coach might create a step-by-step guide to time management, complete with templates and detailed explanations.
- **Tip:** Use your attention to detail to craft evergreen content that remains valuable over time.

2. Structuring Content for Clarity and Value

Virgo creators have a knack for organizing information in a way that's easy to digest. Their content often follows a logical flow, making complex ideas accessible to their audience.

- **Strengths:** Virgo creators excel in creating structured content like how-to videos, educational infographics, or list-based articles.
- **Example:** A Virgo tech blogger might produce a series of tutorials on software tools, breaking down complicated processes into clear, actionable steps.
- **Tip:** Use outlines and templates to structure your content effectively. Focus on clarity and usability to maximize audience engagement.

3. Solving Problems Through Practicality

Virgo creators thrive in niches that prioritize utility and problem-solving. They excel at identifying their audience's pain points and providing solutions.

- **Strengths:** Content that offers tips, advice, or resources aligns perfectly with Virgo's practical nature.
- **Example:** A Virgo wellness influencer might create meal-planning guides tailored to specific dietary needs, offering both inspiration and practicality.
- **Tip:** Engage with your audience to understand their challenges, then tailor your content to address those needs.

4. Emphasizing Strategy and Consistency

Virgo creators approach content creation with a strategic mindset. They prioritize long-term planning and consistency, ensuring that their efforts align with their goals.

- **Strengths:** Virgo creators excel in building content calendars, developing SEO strategies, and maintaining a consistent posting schedule.
- **Example:** A Virgo marketing expert might design a year-long social media strategy, complete with content themes, posting schedules, and analytics tracking.
- **Tip:** Use analytics tools to measure your progress and refine your strategy over time.

Overcoming Challenges as a Virgo Creator

While Virgo creators' perfectionism and practicality are strengths, they can also lead to challenges that hinder their creative process. Recognizing and addressing these tendencies is essential for success.

1. Letting Go of Perfectionism

Virgo's desire for flawless work can sometimes lead to overthinking, procrastination, or reluctance to share content until it feels "perfect."

- **Solution:** Focus on progress over perfection. Set realistic deadlines to ensure your content gets published, even if it's not 100% perfect.
- **Tip:** Remember that your audience values authenticity and effort over unattainable perfection.

2. Avoiding Burnout

Virgo's work ethic often drives them to take on too much, leading to exhaustion or creative burnout.

- **Solution:** Establish boundaries and prioritize self-care. Schedule regular breaks and delegate tasks when possible.
- **Tip:** Use tools like time-blocking to manage your workload effectively and prevent overcommitting.

3. Embracing Creativity and Risk-Taking

Virgo's practical nature can sometimes make them hesitant to take risks or experiment with unconventional ideas.

- **Solution:** Challenge yourself to step out of your comfort zone. Collaborate with more spontaneous creators to balance your methodical approach.
- **Tip:** View experimentation as an opportunity to grow, even if the results aren't perfect.

The Virgo Creator's Toolkit

To maximize their potential, Virgo creators can adopt tools and strategies that enhance their organizational skills and attention to detail.

1. Tools for Organization and Strategy

- **Content Planning Tools:** Trello, Asana, or Notion for organizing content calendars, outlines, and workflows.
- **Analytics Tools:** Google Analytics or SEMrush to measure performance and refine strategies.

2. Tools for Polished Content Creation

- **Writing Tools:** Grammarly or Hemingway for refining written content to perfection.
- **Design Tools:** Canva or Adobe InDesign for creating clean, professional visuals.

3. Tools for Engagement and Community Building

- **Feedback Tools:** Use surveys or polls on platforms like Instagram or Google Forms to understand your audience's needs.
- **Automation Tools:** Platforms like Buffer or Hootsuite for maintaining a consistent posting schedule.

Connecting with Your Audience

Virgo creators excel at building trust with their audience through their reliability, professionalism, and dedication to delivering value. Their ability to address audience pain points makes them indispensable in their niches.

- **Engagement Tips:**
  - Share actionable advice, templates, or tools that solve specific problems.
  - Respond thoughtfully to comments and questions, showcasing your expertise and care.
  - Use storytelling to humanize your content and foster relatability.
- **Content Ideas:**
  - Tutorials or how-to guides that offer practical solutions.
  - Long-form blog posts or videos that dive deep into niche topics.
  - Interactive content like Q&A sessions or live demonstrations.

Virgo Success Stories

Many successful creators and public figures embody Virgo's meticulous and strategic energy, demonstrating how their attention to detail can lead to significant achievements.

- **Beyoncé (September 4):** Known for her perfectionism and work ethic, Beyoncé exemplifies Virgo's ability to produce polished, high-quality work while maintaining a strong personal brand.
- **Zendaya (September 1):** A multifaceted artist and advocate, Zendaya reflects Virgo's combination of creativity, intellect, and groundedness.

By channeling their precision and strategic mindset, Virgo creators can achieve long-lasting success in the digital world.

Final Thoughts

Virgo creators are the architects of the content creation world, bringing structure, strategy, and attention to detail to every project they undertake. Their ability to create polished, valuable content makes them reliable authorities in their niches. By embracing their strengths while addressing challenges like perfectionism or burnout, Virgo creators can craft meaningful, impactful content that resonates with their audience.

Chapter 8: Libra Creators – Balancing Creativity and Audience Engagement

Libra, the seventh sign of the zodiac, is ruled by Venus, the planet of love, beauty, and harmony. Represented by the scales, Libra embodies balance, fairness, and an innate desire for connection. Libra creators bring an artistic and diplomatic approach to content creation, excelling in crafting visually appealing work that resonates deeply with their audience. Known for their ability to see multiple perspectives, Libras have a natural talent for creating content that bridges gaps and fosters meaningful engagement.

This chapter delves into the strengths, challenges, and strategies of Libra creators, exploring how their artistic sensibilities and relational skills can lead to harmonious and impactful content.

The Libra Energy: Harmony and Connection

As a cardinal air sign, Libra thrives on communication, creativity, and collaboration. Libra creators are driven by the pursuit of beauty and balance, often striving to create content that not only looks great but also feels inclusive and equitable. Their natural charm and diplomatic nature make them adept at engaging with diverse audiences and building lasting connections.

- **Key Traits of Libra Creators:**
    - **Artistic:** With an eye for aesthetics, Libra creators excel in designing visually stunning and cohesive content.
    - **Diplomatic:** They have a gift for fostering harmony and resolving conflicts, which makes their content feel approachable and inclusive.
    - **Collaborative:** Libra creators thrive in partnerships and team settings, often bringing out the best in others.
    - **Relational:** They prioritize audience engagement, valuing meaningful connections over superficial interactions.

However, Libra's focus on balance can sometimes lead to indecision or people-pleasing tendencies, which may hinder their creative process. Understanding these challenges is essential for growth.

The Libra Approach to Digital Content

Libra creators shine in content that emphasizes beauty, storytelling, and relationship-building. Their ability to combine creativity with audience engagement makes them natural influencers and community builders.

1. Emphasizing Visual Aesthetics

Ruled by Venus, Libra creators have an exceptional sense of style and design. They excel in creating content that is not only visually appealing but also emotionally resonant.

- **Strengths:** Libra creators thrive on platforms that prioritize visuals, such as Instagram, Pinterest, and TikTok.
- **Example:** A Libra fashion influencer might curate a feed of perfectly coordinated outfits, complete with tips on achieving the same look.
- **Tip:** Invest in high-quality tools and resources, such as photography equipment and editing software, to enhance your visuals.

2. Fostering Audience Engagement

Libras are natural communicators who excel at building relationships. They are skilled at engaging their audience in meaningful conversations, whether through comments, direct messages, or interactive content.

- **Strengths:** Interactive formats like polls, Q&A sessions, and live streams are ideal for Libra creators who enjoy fostering dialogue.
- **Example:** A Libra wellness creator might host live meditation sessions, encouraging participants to share their experiences and ask questions.
- **Tip:** Focus on creating a welcoming and inclusive atmosphere that invites participation and feedback.

3. Collaborating for Mutual Growth

Libra's collaborative nature makes them excellent partners in content creation. They thrive in team settings and often excel in co-creating content that combines their artistic sensibilities with others' expertise.

- **Strengths:** Libra creators excel in joint projects, such as podcasts, interviews, or guest blog posts.
- **Example:** A Libra creator in the travel niche might collaborate with local guides to create content that highlights both personal experiences and cultural insights.
- **Tip:** Seek out partnerships with creators who complement your strengths, and focus on building mutually beneficial relationships.

4. Balancing Content Variety

Libras excel at blending different content styles and formats to create a harmonious brand. They have a natural ability to balance entertainment with education, making their content both engaging and informative.

- **Strengths:** Libra creators are versatile and can adapt their content to suit different platforms and audience preferences.
- **Example:** A Libra entrepreneur might balance business tips with personal anecdotes, creating a well-rounded and relatable brand.
- **Tip:** Use analytics to identify which content formats resonate most with your audience, and aim for a balanced mix.

Overcoming Challenges as a Libra Creator

While Libra creators possess unique strengths, their desire for balance and harmony can sometimes create obstacles. Recognizing and addressing these tendencies is key to maintaining creative momentum.

1. Managing Indecision

Libra's tendency to weigh all options can lead to decision paralysis, slowing down their creative process.

- **Solution:** Set clear priorities and deadlines to streamline decision-making. Trust your instincts and remember that not every choice needs to be perfect.
- **Tip:** Break large decisions into smaller, manageable steps to reduce overwhelm.

2. Avoiding People-Pleasing

Libra creators may struggle with people-pleasing tendencies, prioritizing audience approval over their authentic voice.

- **Solution:** Focus on staying true to your values and creative vision. While audience feedback is valuable, avoid compromising your authenticity to appease others.
- **Tip:** Set boundaries with your audience and collaborators to maintain creative integrity.

3. Balancing Collaboration with Independence

Libras' love for collaboration can sometimes lead to over-reliance on others or difficulty working independently.

- **Solution:** Cultivate confidence in your solo projects while continuing to seek collaborative opportunities.
- **Tip:** Allocate time for personal creative exploration to balance collaborative efforts.

The Libra Creator's Toolkit

To amplify their creativity and engagement, Libra creators can adopt tools and strategies that align with their artistic and relational approach.

1. Tools for Visual Design

- **Graphic Design:** Canva, Adobe Photoshop, or Lightroom for creating cohesive, visually appealing content.
- **Photography Tools:** Use a DSLR camera or smartphone with advanced photography features to enhance your visuals.

2. Tools for Engagement

- **Interactive Features:** Use Instagram Stories' polls, quizzes, and Q&A stickers to connect with your audience.
- **Community Platforms:** Build engaged communities through platforms like Patreon, Discord, or Facebook Groups.

3. Tools for Collaboration

- **Project Management:** Platforms like Trello, Asana, or Notion for coordinating collaborative projects.
- **Communication Tools:** Zoom or Slack for seamless communication with collaborators and teams.

Connecting with Your Audience

Libra creators excel at building meaningful connections with their audience, fostering loyalty and trust through their relational approach. By prioritizing engagement and inclusivity, they create content that feels personal and impactful.

- **Engagement Tips:**
    - Use storytelling to connect emotionally with your audience.
    - Respond to comments and messages thoughtfully, showing genuine interest in your audience's perspectives.
    - Encourage dialogue by asking open-ended questions or hosting community discussions.
- **Content Ideas:**
    - Collaborative projects that showcase diverse perspectives.
    - Tutorials or guides that combine style and substance, such as fashion tips or home decor advice.
    - Behind-the-scenes content that highlights your creative process.

Libra Success Stories

Many successful creators embody Libra's artistic and relational energy, demonstrating how balance and beauty can lead to impactful content.

- **Kim Kardashian (October 21):** Known for her strong personal brand and aesthetic, Kardashian reflects Libra's ability to balance beauty with business savvy.
- **John Lennon (October 9):** A musician and activist, Lennon exemplified Libra's commitment to harmony and collaboration.

By channeling their natural charm and creativity, Libra creators can build influential platforms that inspire and connect.

Final Thoughts

Libra creators are the bridge-builders of the content creation world, blending beauty, balance, and connection to create harmonious and engaging work. Their ability to foster relationships and adapt their content to suit diverse audiences makes them invaluable in any niche. By embracing their strengths while addressing challenges like indecision or people-pleasing, Libra creators can craft content that resonates deeply and builds lasting connections.

Chapter 9: Scorpio Creators – Delving into Deep, Intriguing Content

Scorpio, the eighth sign of the zodiac, is ruled by Pluto, the planet of transformation, and Mars, the planet of action and intensity. Known for their depth, mystery, and magnetism, Scorpio creators bring a unique intensity to the content creation world. They excel at exploring profound, taboo, or transformative topics, captivating audiences with their authenticity and raw emotional power. Scorpio creators are not afraid to venture into the shadows, uncovering hidden truths and delivering content that leaves a lasting impression.

This chapter explores the unique strengths, challenges, and strategies for Scorpio creators, highlighting how they can harness their intensity and depth to craft compelling, transformative content.

The Scorpio Energy: Depth and Transformation

Scorpio is a fixed water sign, symbolizing emotional depth, power, and the ability to transform. Scorpio creators are drawn to the unseen, the unspoken, and the transformative, often exploring topics that others shy away from. They are natural storytellers, uncovering layers of truth and emotion to create content that resonates on a deep, visceral level.

- **Key Traits of Scorpio Creators:**
  - **Intense:** Scorpio creators bring passion and focus to their projects, often diving deeply into their chosen topics.
  - **Mysterious:** They excel at cultivating intrigue, leaving audiences wanting more.
  - **Transformative:** Their content often inspires profound personal or societal change.
  - **Authentic:** Scorpio creators value truth and authenticity, often sharing raw and vulnerable stories.

However, Scorpio's intensity can sometimes lead to challenges, such as difficulty trusting others or becoming overly attached to their work. Balancing depth with lightness is key to their creative success.

The Scorpio Approach to Digital Content

Scorpio creators thrive in content that explores profound themes, challenges norms, or inspires transformation. Their ability to combine storytelling with emotional depth makes them powerful content creators in niches that demand authenticity and boldness.

1. Exploring Deep and Taboo Topics

Scorpio creators are not afraid to tackle difficult or controversial subjects. Their willingness to delve into the hidden or forbidden sets them apart from other creators.

- **Strengths:** Scorpio excels in niches like mental health, spirituality, true crime, or social justice, where depth and honesty are paramount.
- **Example:** A Scorpio creator might produce a documentary series uncovering untold stories of marginalized communities, combining research with emotional narratives.
- **Tip:** Use your natural curiosity to uncover unique angles on popular topics, ensuring your content stands out.

2. Creating Emotional Storytelling

Scorpio's emotional intelligence allows them to craft stories that resonate deeply with audiences. They excel at combining vulnerability with powerful imagery or language to evoke strong emotional responses.

- **Strengths:** Platforms like YouTube, podcasts, and blogs are ideal for Scorpio creators who enjoy long-form storytelling.
- **Example:** A Scorpio content creator might share their journey of overcoming personal trauma, inspiring others to embrace their own healing processes.
- **Tip:** Don't shy away from vulnerability. Sharing your personal experiences can create a powerful connection with your audience.

3. Capturing Audiences with Mystery

Scorpio creators are masters of intrigue, often using suspense or mystery to draw audiences in. They know how to craft content that keeps people guessing and coming back for more.

- **Strengths:** Scorpio creators excel in storytelling formats that allow for cliffhangers, such as serialized podcasts, video series, or mystery-themed blogs.
- **Example:** A Scorpio true crime podcaster might unravel cases episode by episode, layering suspense and emotional depth into their narratives.

- **Tip:** Use foreshadowing and strategic storytelling techniques to build suspense and keep your audience engaged.

4. Inspiring Transformation

Scorpio creators often use their platforms to inspire profound change, whether on a personal or societal level. They excel at content that challenges perceptions and encourages growth.

- **Strengths:** Scorpio's transformative energy makes them natural leaders in movements for self-improvement, activism, or healing.
- **Example:** A Scorpio spiritual influencer might create guided meditations or workshops focused on personal transformation and shadow work.
- **Tip:** Focus on actionable content that empowers your audience to take meaningful steps toward change.

Overcoming Challenges as a Scorpio Creator

While Scorpio creators possess unique strengths, their intensity and emotional depth can sometimes create obstacles. Recognizing and addressing these tendencies is essential for sustained success.

1. Managing Emotional Attachment

Scorpio's deep investment in their work can make it difficult for them to let go of projects or accept constructive criticism.

- **Solution:** Cultivate a sense of detachment by focusing on the bigger picture and viewing feedback as an opportunity for growth.
- **Tip:** Practice mindfulness to manage your emotional responses and maintain perspective.

2. Avoiding Burnout

Scorpio's all-or-nothing approach can lead to burnout if they don't balance their intensity with self-care.

- **Solution:** Set boundaries and prioritize rest. Schedule regular breaks to recharge your emotional and creative energy.
- **Tip:** Incorporate grounding practices, such as meditation or journaling, into your routine to maintain balance.

3. Building Trust in Collaboration

Scorpio's secretive nature can sometimes hinder collaboration, as they may struggle to trust others with their vision.

- **Solution:** Seek out collaborators who share your values and vision. Start with small projects to build trust and confidence.
- **Tip:** Use clear communication to set expectations and foster healthy working relationships.

The Scorpio Creator's Toolkit

To amplify their creativity and impact, Scorpio creators can adopt tools and strategies that align with their intense and transformative approach.

1. Tools for Storytelling

- **Video Editing Software:** Use Adobe Premiere Pro or Final Cut Pro to create cinematic, emotionally impactful videos.
- **Podcast Platforms:** Tools like Anchor or Audacity are ideal for creating serialized audio content that captivates listeners.

2. Tools for Research and Depth

- **Research Tools:** Platforms like Evernote or Zotero can help Scorpio creators organize detailed research for their projects.
- **Analytics Tools:** Use Google Analytics or YouTube Studio to understand audience behavior and refine your strategy.

3. Tools for Emotional Well-Being

- **Mindfulness Apps:** Apps like Calm or Insight Timer can help Scorpio creators manage stress and maintain emotional balance.
- **Time Management Tools:** Platforms like Trello or Asana can help Scorpio creators stay organized and prevent overwhelm.

Connecting with Your Audience

Scorpio creators excel at building deep, meaningful relationships with their audience. By prioritizing authenticity and emotional resonance, they can foster loyal and engaged communities.

- **Engagement Tips:**
    - Share personal stories or behind-the-scenes moments to build trust and relatability.
    - Encourage your audience to share their own experiences, creating a two-way dialogue.
    - Use storytelling techniques like cliffhangers or layered narratives to keep your audience engaged.
- **Content Ideas:**
    - In-depth explorations of niche or taboo topics.
    - Inspirational content focused on personal growth or transformation.
    - Serialized content, such as mystery podcasts or video series.

Scorpio Success Stories

Many successful creators embody Scorpio's depth and intensity, demonstrating how their transformative energy can lead to lasting impact and success.

- **Marie Curie (November 7):** A trailblazing scientist who transformed the field of radioactivity, Curie embodies Scorpio's passion for uncovering hidden truths.
- **Drake (October 24):** A musician known for his emotional depth and storytelling, Drake reflects Scorpio's ability to connect with audiences on a profound level.

By channeling their authenticity and intensity, Scorpio creators can create content that resonates deeply and inspires lasting change.

Final Thoughts

Scorpio creators are the deep divers of the content creation world, unearthing hidden truths and crafting transformative narratives that captivate and inspire. Their ability to explore profound topics and connect emotionally with their audience makes them invaluable in any niche. By embracing their strengths while addressing challenges like emotional attachment or burnout, Scorpio creators can craft impactful, unforgettable content.

Chapter 10: Sagittarius Creators – Infusing Adventure and Expansion into Work

Sagittarius, the ninth sign of the zodiac, is ruled by Jupiter, the planet of growth, abundance, and exploration. Symbolized by the Archer, Sagittarians are driven by a thirst for knowledge, adventure, and freedom. In the realm of content creation, Sagittarius creators shine as visionaries and storytellers, captivating their audience with bold ideas, global perspectives, and inspiring journeys. Their content often reflects their love for exploration—whether physical, intellectual, or spiritual—and their innate ability to motivate others.

This chapter explores the traits, strategies, and challenges of Sagittarius creators, offering insights into how they can harness their adventurous spirit to craft impactful and expansive content.

The Sagittarius Energy: Exploration and Optimism

Sagittarius is a mutable fire sign, characterized by curiosity, enthusiasm, and an unyielding desire for truth. Sagittarius creators bring a dynamic energy to their work, often seeking to inspire, educate, and entertain through their unique perspectives. Their optimism and open-mindedness make them ideal for tackling diverse topics and reaching broad audiences.

- **Key Traits of Sagittarius Creators:**
  - **Adventurous:** They are natural explorers, both in the physical world and in the realm of ideas, often bringing fresh perspectives to their content.
  - **Inspiring:** Sagittarius creators radiate positivity, motivating their audience to embrace new possibilities and expand their horizons.
  - **Visionary:** They excel at connecting the dots between seemingly unrelated concepts, offering innovative and forward-thinking ideas.
  - **Spontaneous:** Sagittarius creators thrive on spontaneity, often producing content that feels authentic and in-the-moment.

However, Sagittarius' restless nature can sometimes lead to scattered focus or difficulty completing projects. Balancing their big-picture thinking with attention to detail is essential for their creative success.

The Sagittarius Approach to Digital Content

Sagittarius creators thrive in content that emphasizes exploration, education, and inspiration. Their ability to weave storytelling with global or philosophical insights makes them powerful influencers in niches that celebrate curiosity and growth.

1. Storytelling Through Travel and Exploration

Sagittarius creators often gravitate toward travel and adventure content, sharing their journeys and experiences in a way that inspires wanderlust in their audience.

- **Strengths:** Platforms like YouTube, Instagram, and TikTok are ideal for Sagittarius creators who want to showcase their adventures through vivid imagery and storytelling.
- **Example:** A Sagittarius travel blogger might document their exploration of remote destinations, offering cultural insights and practical travel tips.
- **Tip:** Focus on creating immersive content that transports your audience to the places you explore. Use high-quality visuals and engaging narratives to enhance the experience.

2. Teaching and Sharing Knowledge

Ruled by Jupiter, the planet of higher learning, Sagittarius creators excel at educational content that broadens their audience's understanding of the world. They are natural teachers, often combining their love for learning with a desire to share wisdom.

- **Strengths:** Long-form content like podcasts, webinars, or online courses suits Sagittarius creators' intellectual depth and passion for education.
- **Example:** A Sagittarius wellness influencer might create a series of videos on holistic health practices from different cultures, blending storytelling with practical advice.
- **Tip:** Use your curiosity to research and present unique insights. Position yourself as a guide who helps your audience navigate new topics or perspectives.

3. Motivating Through Inspiration

Sagittarius creators have a gift for uplifting and motivating others. Their optimistic energy makes them ideal for content that inspires personal growth, adventure, or positive change.

- **Strengths:** Inspirational content, such as motivational speeches, quotes, or personal success stories, resonates deeply with Sagittarius' natural charisma.
- **Example:** A Sagittarius entrepreneur might share their journey of building a business, highlighting the lessons learned along the way to inspire others to take risks.
- **Tip:** Be authentic and relatable in your messaging. Share your challenges and triumphs to connect with your audience on a deeper level.

4. Tackling Big Ideas

Sagittarius thrives in content that explores philosophical, cultural, or global themes. Their ability to connect big-picture concepts with relatable narratives makes them compelling thought leaders.

- **Strengths:** Writing essays, hosting discussion panels, or creating documentaries are ideal for Sagittarius creators who enjoy diving into complex topics.
- **Example:** A Sagittarius content creator might produce a podcast exploring the intersection of technology, culture, and ethics, featuring interviews with experts from around the world.
- **Tip:** Balance your big-picture ideas with actionable takeaways to ensure your audience feels both inspired and empowered.

Overcoming Challenges as a Sagittarius Creator

While Sagittarius creators bring enthusiasm and vision to their work, their adventurous nature can sometimes lead to challenges. Addressing these tendencies is essential for sustained success.

1. Staying Focused

Sagittarius' restless energy can make it difficult to stay focused on long-term projects, leading to unfinished work or scattered content.

- **Solution:** Break projects into smaller, manageable tasks and set clear deadlines. Use tools like project management apps to stay organized.
- **Tip:** Align your projects with your passions to maintain motivation and interest over time.

2. Avoiding Overcommitment

Sagittarius creators often take on too much, driven by their love for exploration and new experiences. This can lead to burnout or diluted creative efforts.

- **Solution:** Prioritize quality over quantity by focusing on a few key projects that align with your goals.
- **Tip:** Practice saying "no" to opportunities that don't serve your vision or current workload.

3. Balancing Depth and Breadth

While Sagittarius excels at covering a wide range of topics, this can sometimes come at the expense of depth or consistency.

- **Solution:** Choose a few core themes or niches to focus on, ensuring your content remains cohesive and impactful.
- **Tip:** Use your curiosity to deepen your expertise in specific areas, building authority and trust with your audience.

The Sagittarius Creator's Toolkit

To amplify their creativity and impact, Sagittarius creators can adopt tools and strategies that support their adventurous, visionary approach.

1. Tools for Visual Storytelling

- **Photography Equipment:** Invest in a DSLR camera or advanced smartphone for capturing high-quality travel or lifestyle visuals.
- **Video Editing Software:** Use Adobe Premiere Pro or Final Cut Pro to create polished, cinematic videos.

2. Tools for Organization and Focus

- **Project Management:** Platforms like Asana or Trello can help Sagittarius creators stay organized and manage multiple projects effectively.
- **Time Management:** Use tools like Toggl or Google Calendar to balance spontaneity with structure.

3. Tools for Education and Outreach

- **Online Course Platforms:** Teachable or Kajabi are ideal for Sagittarius creators who want to share their knowledge through structured educational content.
- **Global Engagement:** Use tools like Google Translate or multi-language subtitles to connect with a global audience.

Connecting with Your Audience

Sagittarius creators excel at building enthusiastic and loyal communities through their authenticity, optimism, and relatability. Their ability to inspire and educate makes them natural leaders and motivators.

- **Engagement Tips:**
    - Use storytelling to share your adventures, lessons, and insights in an authentic way.
    - Encourage audience participation by asking questions or inviting them to share their own stories and experiences.
    - Be approachable and responsive, fostering a sense of connection and camaraderie.
- **Content Ideas:**
    - Travel vlogs or blogs highlighting cultural insights and personal anecdotes.
    - Motivational videos or speeches that inspire action and growth.
    - Educational content exploring global or philosophical themes.

Sagittarius Success Stories

Many successful creators and influencers embody Sagittarius' adventurous and visionary energy, demonstrating how their passion for exploration can lead to profound impact.

- **Taylor Swift (December 13):** Known for her storytelling and ability to connect deeply with her audience, Swift reflects Sagittarius' talent for inspiring others through personal narratives.
- **Walt Disney (December 5):** A pioneer in entertainment and innovation, Disney exemplified Sagittarius' visionary spirit and ability to inspire global audiences.

By channeling their curiosity, enthusiasm, and big-picture thinking, Sagittarius creators can craft content that resonates deeply and inspires positive change.

Final Thoughts

Sagittarius creators are the explorers and visionaries of the content creation world, bringing bold ideas, global perspectives, and inspiring energy to their work. Their ability to infuse adventure and expansion into their content makes them invaluable in niches that celebrate curiosity and growth. By embracing their strengths while addressing challenges like scattered focus or overcommitment, Sagittarius creators can craft impactful, transformative content that motivates and educates their audience.

Chapter 11: Capricorn Creators – Building a Legacy with Structured Content

Capricorn, the tenth sign of the zodiac, is ruled by Saturn, the planet of discipline, structure, and ambition. Represented by the mountain goat, Capricorns are known for their determination, resilience, and long-term vision. Capricorn creators bring a disciplined, methodical approach to their craft, striving to build lasting legacies through structured and impactful content. Their ability to focus on the bigger picture while mastering the details sets them apart as strategic and results-driven innovators.

In this chapter, we'll explore the strengths, challenges, and strategies that define Capricorn creators, offering insights into how they can create content that stands the test of time while achieving their lofty goals.

The Capricorn Energy: Discipline and Ambition

As a cardinal earth sign, Capricorn embodies practicality, ambition, and a strong sense of responsibility. Capricorn creators are natural planners and strategists who excel at turning ideas into actionable plans. They are driven by the desire to achieve greatness, often prioritizing long-term success over short-term gains.

- **Key Traits of Capricorn Creators:**
    - **Disciplined:** They are highly organized and committed, ensuring their content is consistent and of high quality.
    - **Ambitious:** Capricorn creators are goal-oriented, focusing on content that contributes to their overarching vision and purpose.
    - **Resilient:** They excel at overcoming challenges, using setbacks as opportunities for growth and improvement.
    - **Professional:** Their work often reflects a polished, sophisticated style that conveys credibility and authority.

However, Capricorn's focus on structure and success can sometimes lead to overworking or an overly rigid mindset. Balancing ambition with creativity and flexibility is key to their success.

The Capricorn Approach to Digital Content

Capricorn creators thrive in content that emphasizes structure, strategy, and value. Their ability to combine creativity with a business-oriented mindset makes them natural leaders in niches that require professionalism and expertise.

1. Crafting Long-Form, Evergreen Content

Capricorn creators excel at producing comprehensive, high-quality content that remains relevant over time. Their focus on thoroughness and accuracy ensures their work is a valuable resource for their audience.

- **Strengths:** Capricorn creators thrive in blogs, podcasts, or YouTube channels that provide in-depth tutorials, guides, or analyses.
- **Example:** A Capricorn business coach might create a series of long-form blog posts on building a sustainable company, complete with step-by-step instructions and case studies.
- **Tip:** Invest time in research and planning to ensure your content offers lasting value and can be repurposed across multiple platforms.

2. Building a Strategic Content Plan

Capricorn creators are masters of strategy, often creating detailed content calendars and long-term plans to achieve their goals. They prioritize consistency and alignment with their overarching vision.

- **Strengths:** Capricorns excel in creating content series, courses, or campaigns that are well-structured and aligned with their brand identity.
- **Example:** A Capricorn fitness influencer might design a 12-month workout program with clear milestones, offering subscribers a step-by-step roadmap to achieving their fitness goals.
- **Tip:** Use project management tools to organize your ideas and track your progress. Break large projects into manageable steps to maintain momentum.

3. Showcasing Professionalism and Expertise

Capricorn creators bring a polished, professional approach to their content, often positioning themselves as authorities in their field. Their work reflects their commitment to quality and credibility.

- **Strengths:** Platforms like LinkedIn, professional blogs, and webinars suit Capricorn creators who want to establish themselves as thought leaders.
- **Example:** A Capricorn tech influencer might create a series of in-depth tutorials on software development, complete with industry insights and practical tips.
- **Tip:** Focus on building trust with your audience by sharing your expertise and backing up your claims with research or evidence.

4. Combining Business Savvy with Creativity

Capricorn creators are adept at monetizing their content while maintaining its artistic integrity. Their practical mindset allows them to balance creativity with financial sustainability.

- **Strengths:** Capricorn creators excel in creating eBooks, online courses, or subscription-based models that generate consistent income.
- **Example:** A Capricorn artist might create a membership program offering exclusive tutorials, behind-the-scenes content, and one-on-one coaching sessions.
- **Tip:** Diversify your income streams to build a stable, scalable business around your content.

Overcoming Challenges as a Capricorn Creator

While Capricorn creators' discipline and ambition are strengths, these qualities can also create challenges that hinder their creative process. Recognizing and addressing these tendencies is essential for long-term success.

1. Avoiding Overworking

Capricorns' drive for success can lead to overworking or neglecting self-care, resulting in burnout.

- **Solution:** Set boundaries around your work schedule and prioritize time for rest and relaxation.
- **Tip:** Incorporate mindfulness practices, such as meditation or journaling, to maintain balance and recharge your energy.

2. Embracing Flexibility

Capricorn's focus on structure can sometimes make them resistant to change or new ideas, limiting their creative potential.

- **Solution:** Experiment with different formats, styles, or platforms to expand your creative horizons. View flexibility as an opportunity for growth.
- **Tip:** Collaborate with more spontaneous creators to balance your structured approach with fresh perspectives.

3. Overcoming Perfectionism

Capricorns' commitment to excellence can sometimes result in perfectionism, delaying projects or creating unnecessary stress.

- **Solution:** Set realistic goals and deadlines to ensure your content gets published. Remember that done is better than perfect.
- **Tip:** Focus on the impact of your content rather than its flaws, trusting that your audience values effort and authenticity.

The Capricorn Creator's Toolkit

To amplify their creativity and productivity, Capricorn creators can adopt tools and strategies that support their structured, goal-oriented approach.

1. Tools for Organization and Planning

- **Project Management Tools:** Platforms like Trello, Asana, or Notion help Capricorn creators organize their ideas and track progress.
- **Content Scheduling Tools:** Use Buffer, Hootsuite, or CoSchedule to maintain a consistent posting schedule.

2. Tools for Professional Content Creation

- **Design Tools:** Canva or Adobe InDesign for creating polished graphics and branded materials.
- **Video Editing Software:** Use Final Cut Pro or DaVinci Resolve to produce professional-quality videos.

3. Tools for Monetization

- **eCommerce Platforms:** Use Patreon, Gumroad, or Shopify to sell products or offer subscription-based content.
- **Online Course Platforms:** Platforms like Teachable or Thinkific are ideal for creating and selling educational content.

Connecting with Your Audience

Capricorn creators excel at building trust and loyalty with their audience through their professionalism, reliability, and value-driven content. Their ability to create structured, actionable content makes them indispensable in their niches.

- **Engagement Tips:**
  - Share behind-the-scenes glimpses of your planning or creative process to build transparency.
  - Use storytelling to connect emotionally with your audience while showcasing your expertise.
  - Offer practical takeaways, such as templates, worksheets, or action plans, to enhance audience engagement.
- **Content Ideas:**
  - Step-by-step guides or tutorials that address specific challenges.
  - Long-term programs or series that help your audience achieve measurable results.
  - Thought leadership pieces exploring trends, challenges, or innovations in your industry.

Capricorn Success Stories

Many successful creators embody Capricorn's disciplined and ambitious energy, showcasing how structure and vision can lead to lasting success.

- **Michelle Obama (January 17):** Known for her poise, resilience, and impactful initiatives, Obama exemplifies Capricorn's ability to combine discipline with a commitment to legacy-building.
- **LeBron James (December 30):** A basketball legend and entrepreneur, James reflects Capricorn's determination, professionalism, and long-term vision.

By channeling their ambition and structured mindset, Capricorn creators can achieve their goals while leaving a lasting legacy.

Final Thoughts

Capricorn creators are the builders of the content creation world, combining discipline, strategy, and ambition to craft impactful, long-lasting work. Their ability to balance creativity with professionalism makes them invaluable in niches that prioritize expertise and reliability. By embracing their strengths while addressing challenges like overworking or perfectionism, Capricorn creators can build content that not only resonates but also endures.

Chapter 12: Aquarius Creators – Innovating in the Digital Age

Aquarius, the eleventh sign of the zodiac, is ruled by Uranus, the planet of innovation, technology, and rebellion, as well as Saturn, which brings structure and discipline. Represented by the Water Bearer, Aquarius symbolizes the sharing of knowledge and the flow of progressive ideas. In the realm of content creation, Aquarius creators are the trailblazers—boldly pushing boundaries, experimenting with new formats, and embracing technology to redefine what's possible. Their content often challenges norms, inspires change, and connects diverse communities.

In this chapter, we'll explore the unique strengths, strategies, and challenges of Aquarius creators, uncovering how they can harness their forward-thinking energy to thrive in the ever-evolving digital age.

The Aquarius Energy: Innovation and Vision

As a fixed air sign, Aquarius combines intellectual depth with unwavering commitment to progress and transformation. Aquarius creators are known for their unconventional ideas, collaborative spirit, and ability to think ahead of their time. Their work often reflects a desire to educate, inspire, and unite others while embracing the latest trends and technologies.

- **Key Traits of Aquarius Creators:**
    - **Innovative:** Aquarius creators excel at thinking outside the box, often leading the way in adopting new tools and formats.
    - **Visionary:** They are future-focused, crafting content that addresses emerging trends and global challenges.
    - **Collaborative:** Aquarius creators value community and often use their platforms to amplify diverse voices and foster dialogue.
    - **Rebellious:** They are unafraid to challenge conventions and embrace bold, unconventional approaches.

However, Aquarius' focus on innovation can sometimes lead to detachment or difficulty connecting emotionally with their audience. Striking a balance between intellect and relatability is key to their success.

The Aquarius Approach to Digital Content

Aquarius creators thrive in content that emphasizes innovation, education, and community. Their ability to leverage technology and explore unconventional ideas makes them leaders in the digital space, especially in niches that celebrate creativity and progress.

1. Embracing Emerging Technologies

Aquarius creators are natural early adopters, often among the first to explore new platforms, tools, and technologies. Their willingness to experiment helps them stay ahead of trends and stand out in a crowded market.

- **Strengths:** Aquarius creators excel in digital art, virtual reality (VR), augmented reality (AR), and other tech-driven formats.
- **Example:** An Aquarius digital artist might create immersive VR experiences or NFTs that push the boundaries of traditional art.
- **Tip:** Stay updated on technological advancements in your niche and don't hesitate to experiment with cutting-edge tools.

2. Crafting Content with a Cause

Aquarius creators are deeply driven by social and global issues. Their content often reflects their commitment to education, activism, and positive change, making them powerful advocates in the digital space.

- **Strengths:** Educational videos, podcasts, or social media campaigns allow Aquarius creators to share knowledge and spark meaningful conversations.
- **Example:** An Aquarius environmental advocate might create a YouTube series exploring innovative solutions to climate change, combining research with actionable tips.
- **Tip:** Align your content with causes you're passionate about, using your platform to inspire and mobilize your audience.

3. Fostering Online Communities

Community-building comes naturally to Aquarius creators, who thrive on collaboration and connection. They often use their platforms to unite people around shared interests or goals.

- **Strengths:** Aquarius creators excel at hosting forums, live events, or interactive content that fosters dialogue and participation.
- **Example:** An Aquarius content creator in the tech niche might host weekly live streams discussing emerging technologies, encouraging audience input and collaboration.

- **Tip:** Use interactive features like polls, Q&A sessions, or live chats to engage your audience and create a sense of belonging.

4. Breaking Creative Boundaries

Aquarius creators are unafraid to challenge conventions and experiment with unconventional ideas. Their content often feels fresh, surprising, and thought-provoking.

- **Strengths:** Aquarius thrives in niches like experimental filmmaking, avant-garde fashion, or conceptual art that reward originality and boldness.
- **Example:** An Aquarius filmmaker might produce a short film using entirely AI-generated visuals, exploring the intersection of technology and creativity.
- **Tip:** Let your curiosity guide you. Don't be afraid to take risks or explore unconventional formats that reflect your unique vision.

Overcoming Challenges as an Aquarius Creator

While Aquarius creators bring remarkable innovation and vision to their work, their unconventional nature can sometimes create challenges. Addressing these tendencies is essential for sustained success.

1. Staying Grounded

Aquarius' focus on the future can sometimes lead to a lack of follow-through or difficulty finishing projects.

- **Solution:** Set clear goals and timelines to ensure your ideas are realized. Use project management tools to stay organized and accountable.
- **Tip:** Balance your big-picture thinking with actionable steps, focusing on progress over perfection.

2. Connecting Emotionally

Aquarius creators' intellectual approach can sometimes make their content feel detached or overly analytical, limiting audience connection.

- **Solution:** Incorporate personal stories or relatable anecdotes into your content to create an emotional connection with your audience.
- **Tip:** Use your storytelling skills to humanize complex topics, making them accessible and engaging.

3. Managing Collaboration Challenges

While Aquarius thrives on collaboration, their independent streak can sometimes lead to clashes or difficulties working within rigid structures.

- **Solution:** Approach collaborations with flexibility and open communication. Seek out partners who share your values and vision.
- **Tip:** Use your natural diplomacy to navigate challenges and build harmonious working relationships.

The Aquarius Creator's Toolkit

To amplify their creativity and impact, Aquarius creators can adopt tools and strategies that align with their innovative and collaborative approach.

1. Tools for Innovation

- **Digital Art Platforms:** Tools like Procreate or Adobe Creative Cloud for exploring digital design and animation.
- **VR/AR Creation Tools:** Platforms like Unity or Spark AR for developing immersive experiences and interactive content.

2. Tools for Community Building

- **Community Platforms:** Use Discord, Reddit, or Patreon to foster online communities around shared interests.
- **Interactive Features:** Platforms like YouTube Live, Instagram Stories, or Twitter Spaces for real-time audience engagement.

3. Tools for Organization and Research

- **Project Management Tools:** Trello, Asana, or ClickUp to organize ideas and manage collaborative projects.
- **Research Tools:** Use Feedly or Pocket to stay informed on emerging trends and topics in your niche.

Connecting with Your Audience

Aquarius creators excel at building loyal, engaged communities through their innovation and inclusivity. By fostering dialogue and embracing diversity, they can create content that resonates deeply and inspires action.

- **Engagement Tips:**
  - Use your platform to amplify diverse voices and perspectives, fostering inclusivity and collaboration.
  - Encourage audience participation through polls, challenges, or interactive events.
  - Share your creative process or the inspiration behind your work to build transparency and trust.
- **Content Ideas:**
  - Experimental projects that challenge conventions or explore new technologies.
  - Educational content that simplifies complex ideas or highlights global issues.
  - Collaborative series featuring guest experts or co-creators from different fields.

Aquarius Success Stories

Many successful creators and innovators embody Aquarius' forward-thinking and visionary energy, showcasing how their unique approach can lead to transformative impact.

- **Oprah Winfrey (January 29):** Known for her groundbreaking talk show and philanthropic initiatives, Oprah reflects Aquarius' ability to inspire change and build inclusive communities.
- **Elon Musk (June 28, with strong Aquarian traits):** A trailblazer in technology and innovation, Musk exemplifies Aquarius' passion for exploring new frontiers and challenging norms.

By channeling their creativity and intellect, Aquarius creators can redefine industries and inspire global audiences.

Final Thoughts

Aquarius creators are the innovators and disruptors of the content creation world, pushing boundaries and embracing technology to craft content that challenges and inspires. Their ability to balance intellectual depth with collaborative energy makes them invaluable in niches that value progress and inclusivity. By addressing challenges like detachment or unfinished projects, Aquarius creators can create content that not only resonates but also transforms the digital landscape.

Chapter 13: Pisces Creators – The Power of Imagination and Intuition

Pisces, the twelfth sign of the zodiac, is ruled by Neptune, the planet of dreams, creativity, and spirituality, and Jupiter, which brings expansion and vision. Represented by two fish swimming in opposite directions, Pisces embodies the duality of the dream world and reality, making them deeply imaginative and emotionally intuitive. In the realm of content creation, Pisces creators stand out for their ability to evoke emotion, craft mesmerizing visuals, and connect with their audience on a profoundly empathetic level. Their work often carries an ethereal quality, blending fantasy with authenticity.

This chapter explores the strengths, challenges, and strategies of Pisces creators, highlighting how they can harness their imagination and intuition to create compelling, transformative content.

The Pisces Energy: Dreamy and Intuitive

As a mutable water sign, Pisces is fluid, adaptable, and deeply connected to their emotions and the collective energy around them. Pisces creators often have a natural talent for storytelling and art, weaving their inner world into their work in a way that resonates deeply with others. Their creativity knows no bounds, making them masters of imaginative and emotionally engaging content.

- **Key Traits of Pisces Creators:**
    - **Creative:** Pisces creators excel in visual arts, music, poetry, and storytelling, often blending mediums to produce unique, multidimensional content.
    - **Intuitive:** They have a knack for understanding their audience's needs and emotions, crafting content that feels deeply personal and relatable.
    - **Empathetic:** Their ability to tap into universal emotions makes their work resonate across diverse audiences.
    - **Spiritual:** Pisces often infuse their content with themes of mysticism, healing, or higher purpose, creating work that inspires and uplifts.

However, Pisces' dreamy nature can sometimes lead to challenges like procrastination, overidealism, or difficulty staying grounded. Finding a balance between creativity and practicality is crucial for their success.

The Pisces Approach to Digital Content

Pisces creators thrive in content that emphasizes storytelling, emotion, and visual beauty. Their ability to blend imagination with authenticity makes them stand out in niches that value creativity and connection.

1. Crafting Emotional Storytelling

Pisces creators are natural storytellers who excel at creating narratives that evoke deep emotions. Their work often feels personal, poetic, and profoundly moving, drawing their audience into a shared emotional experience.

- **Strengths:** Platforms like YouTube, podcasts, and Instagram are ideal for Pisces creators to share heartfelt stories or visually stunning narratives.
- **Example:** A Pisces lifestyle vlogger might document their journey of self-discovery through candid videos, blending raw emotion with artistic visuals.
- **Tip:** Lean into your vulnerability and use it to connect with your audience on a personal level. Don't be afraid to share your inner world.

2. Excelling in Visual and Artistic Content

Ruled by Neptune, the planet of dreams and illusions, Pisces creators often have an unparalleled eye for beauty and artistry. They excel in creating content that feels ethereal, dreamlike, or other-worldly.

- **Strengths:** Pisces creators shine in visual mediums like photography, filmmaking, or digital art.
- **Example:** A Pisces digital artist might create surreal, fantasy-inspired illustrations that transport their audience to another realm.
- **Tip:** Use tools like photo or video editing software to enhance the dreamlike quality of your content. Experiment with colors, textures, and lighting to evoke specific emotions.

3. Infusing Spirituality and Healing

Pisces creators are often drawn to spiritual or healing themes, creating content that inspires introspection, growth, and connection to something greater.

- **Strengths:** Niches like meditation, tarot, astrology, and mindfulness align perfectly with Pisces' intuitive and spiritual nature.
- **Example:** A Pisces wellness influencer might produce guided meditations or affirmations designed to help their audience relax, heal, or manifest their goals.
- **Tip:** Tap into your natural intuition to create content that feels meaningful and transformative. Share tools or practices that have helped you in your own journey.

4. Creating Escapist Experiences

Pisces creators excel at crafting content that offers their audience an escape from reality, whether through fantastical stories, immersive visuals, or calming environments.

- **Strengths:** Pisces thrive in niches like fantasy writing, ASMR videos, or virtual reality (VR) experiences.
- **Example:** A Pisces writer might publish serialized fantasy stories that transport readers to magical worlds, blending relatable characters with imaginative settings.
- **Tip:** Use your imagination to design immersive experiences that captivate your audience. Think beyond conventional formats to create something truly unique.

Overcoming Challenges as a Pisces Creator

While Pisces creators bring unparalleled creativity and emotional depth to their work, their dreamy nature can sometimes create obstacles. Addressing these tendencies is essential for building a sustainable creative practice.

1. Staying Grounded

Pisces' tendency to get lost in their imagination or emotions can make it difficult to stay focused on practical goals.

- **Solution:** Establish clear routines and use tools like to-do lists or planners to stay organized.
- **Tip:** Set aside specific times for brainstorming and creating, balancing free-flowing creativity with structured action.

2. Managing Sensitivity

Pisces creators' deep empathy can make them vulnerable to criticism or burnout, especially if they take on too much emotional labor.

- **Solution:** Develop a healthy detachment from your work and practice self-care to maintain emotional balance.
- **Tip:** Surround yourself with supportive collaborators or communities that encourage and uplift you.

3. Avoiding Overidealism

Pisces' idealistic nature can sometimes lead to unrealistic expectations or difficulty finishing projects.

- **Solution:** Break large projects into smaller, achievable steps and celebrate progress along the way.
- **Tip:** Balance your vision with practicality by setting realistic goals and timelines for your work.

The Pisces Creator's Toolkit

To amplify their creativity and productivity, Pisces creators can adopt tools and strategies that support their imaginative and intuitive approach.

1. Tools for Visual Storytelling

- **Photo and Video Editing:** Use Adobe Photoshop, Lightroom, or Final Cut Pro to enhance the aesthetic quality of your visuals.
- **Digital Art Platforms:** Tools like Procreate or Canva are ideal for creating ethereal, dream-like designs.

2. Tools for Emotional Engagement

- **Music and Sound Design:** Incorporate soothing or atmospheric audio using tools like GarageBand or Audacity.
- **Interactive Features:** Use Instagram Stories or YouTube polls to engage with your audience and understand their needs.

3. Tools for Organization and Focus

- **Time Management Tools:** Platforms like Trello or Asana can help Pisces creators stay on track and meet deadlines.
- **Mindfulness Apps:** Use Calm or Insight Timer to recharge and maintain emotional balance.

Connecting with Your Audience

Pisces creators excel at building loyal and engaged communities through their empathy, authenticity, and creativity. By sharing their emotions and inner world, they create content that feels deeply personal and impactful.

- **Engagement Tips:**
  - Respond thoughtfully to comments and messages, showing genuine care and interest in your audience's experiences.
  - Use storytelling to connect emotionally, weaving universal themes into your content.
  - Offer tools or practices, such as journaling prompts or meditation guides, that help your audience navigate their own emotional journeys.
- **Content Ideas:**
  - Personal blogs or vlogs that explore themes of growth, healing, or self-discovery.
  - Artistic projects, such as short films or digital illustrations, that evoke emotion and spark imagination.
  - Spiritual or mindfulness content, such as guided meditations or tarot readings.

Pisces Success Stories

Many successful creators embody Pisces' imaginative and intuitive energy, showcasing how their emotional depth and creativity can lead to lasting impact.

- **Rihanna (February 20):** A multi-talented artist and entrepreneur, Rihanna reflects Pisces' ability to blend creativity with emotional connection, building an empire that resonates globally.
- **Albert Einstein (March 14):** Known for his imaginative thinking and groundbreaking discoveries, Einstein exemplified Pisces' visionary and dreamlike approach to problem-solving.

By channeling their artistic vision and empathetic nature, Pisces creators can craft content that inspires, heals, and captivates.

Final Thoughts

Pisces creators are the dreamers and healers of the content creation world, bringing unparalleled imagination and emotional depth to their work. Their ability to blend artistry with intuition makes them uniquely suited for crafting transformative, impactful content. By addressing challenges like staying grounded or managing sensitivity, Pisces creators can harness their full potential and build a meaningful legacy in the digital age.

Chapter 14: Planetary Alignments – How They Influence Content Creation

In astrology, planetary alignments play a crucial role in shaping energy, creativity, and decision-making. Each planet governs specific aspects of life, and its alignment with other celestial bodies can influence emotions, productivity, and inspiration. For content creators, understanding planetary alignments offers valuable insights into how cosmic shifts might impact their creative processes, audience engagement, and the timing of their projects.

This chapter explores the influence of planetary alignments on content creation, detailing how creators can harness these celestial events to maximize their impact, align with their goals, and connect with their audience on a deeper level.

Understanding Planetary Alignments

Planetary alignments occur when celestial bodies form specific angles or positions relative to one another in the sky. These alignments—whether harmonious or challenging—create unique energy that influences collective and individual experiences.

- **Conjunction:** When two planets align in the same sign, their energies merge, amplifying their combined influence.
    - Example: A Sun-Mercury conjunction enhances clarity in communication and creativity.
- **Opposition:** When two planets are opposite each other, their energies create tension, urging balance and compromise.
    - Example: A Sun-Moon opposition can create emotional conflict but also inspire personal growth.
- **Trine:** When planets are 120° apart, they form a harmonious aspect, fostering flow and ease.
    - Example: A Venus-Mars trine supports creativity and passionate self-expression.
- **Square:** A 90° angle between planets creates tension and challenge, pushing for growth.
    - Example: A Saturn-Uranus square can disrupt routines but inspire innovative solutions.
- **Sextile:** A 60° angle brings opportunities for growth through effort and collaboration.
    - Example: A Jupiter-Neptune sextile enhances imagination and spiritual creativity.

Each alignment brings unique energy, and understanding these aspects allows content creators to align their workflows and projects with cosmic rhythms.

Key Planetary Influences on Content Creation

Each planet governs specific energies that influence creativity, communication, motivation, and strategy. Here's how they play a role in content creation:

1. The Sun: Self-Expression and Vitality

The Sun represents identity, vitality, and creative expression. Its position and alignments influence confidence, motivation, and the ability to shine in one's work.

- **Content Impact:** During positive Sun alignments, creators may feel inspired and energized, excelling in self-promotional activities and bold content.
- **Tip:** Use Sun transits through fire signs (Aries, Leo, Sagittarius) to launch new projects or assert your unique voice.

2. The Moon: Emotions and Intuition

The Moon governs emotions, intuition, and subconscious drives. Its phases and alignments influence creativity, mood, and the ability to connect with audiences on an emotional level.

- **Content Impact:** During a Full Moon, emotions peak, making it a powerful time for content that resonates deeply. The New Moon is ideal for setting intentions and brainstorming new ideas.
- **Tip:** Plan emotionally driven content, such as storytelling or personal reflections, during Moon alignments.

3. Mercury: Communication and Strategy

Mercury rules communication, intellect, and technology. Its alignments influence writing, speaking, and planning.

- **Content Impact:** Positive Mercury alignments enhance clarity and productivity in content creation, while Mercury retrogrades may cause delays or miscommunications.
- **Tip:** During retrogrades, focus on reviewing and refining existing projects rather than launching new ones.

4. Venus: Creativity and Aesthetics

Venus governs beauty, harmony, and relationships. Its alignments influence design, branding, and collaborative projects.

- **Content Impact:** Venus alignments enhance visual creativity, making them ideal for content related to fashion, art, or relationships.
- **Tip:** Use Venus transits to refresh your branding, launch visually stunning campaigns, or connect with collaborators.

5. Mars: Drive and Motivation

Mars represents action, ambition, and passion. Its alignments influence energy levels and the ability to take initiative.

- **Content Impact:** Positive Mars alignments boost productivity and focus, while challenging alignments may bring frustration or burnout.
- **Tip:** Align high-energy tasks, such as video production or event planning, with Mars transits for optimal results.

6. Jupiter: Growth and Expansion

Jupiter governs luck, growth, and abundance. Its alignments influence vision, learning, and the ability to connect with a wider audience.

- **Content Impact:** Jupiter alignments inspire big-picture thinking and expansive content, such as launching new projects or scaling existing ones.
- **Tip:** Use Jupiter transits to focus on long-term goals, educational content, or collaborations with influencers.

7. Saturn: Discipline and Structure

Saturn rules discipline, structure, and responsibility. Its alignments influence planning, strategy, and perseverance.

- **Content Impact:** Positive Saturn alignments help creators establish systems and routines, while challenging aspects test resilience.
- **Tip:** Use Saturn transits to refine your workflow, implement new strategies, or tackle long-term projects.

8. Uranus: Innovation and Change

Uranus governs innovation, disruption, and technology. Its alignments influence creativity, adaptability, and the ability to embrace new trends.

- **Content Impact:** Positive Uranus alignments encourage experimentation, while challenging aspects may bring unexpected changes.
- **Tip:** Embrace Uranus transits to explore unconventional ideas, pivot strategies, or adopt cutting-edge tools.

9. Neptune: Imagination and Spirituality

Neptune represents dreams, intuition, and artistic inspiration. Its alignments influence creativity, empathy, and the ability to inspire.

- **Content Impact:** Positive Neptune alignments enhance artistic vision and storytelling, while challenging aspects may cloud focus.
- **Tip:** Use Neptune transits to craft emotionally resonant or spiritual content that connects deeply with your audience.

10. Pluto: Transformation and Power

Pluto governs transformation, power, and rebirth. Its alignments influence the ability to tackle profound topics and inspire change.

- **Content Impact:** Positive Pluto alignments support deep, impactful content, while challenging aspects encourage growth through introspection.
- **Tip:** Align transformative content, such as personal journeys or social justice topics, with Pluto transits.

Using Planetary Alignments to Optimize Content Creation

Astrology provides a roadmap for aligning your content strategy with planetary energies. Here's how to harness these alignments effectively:

1. Track Key Alignments

Use an astrology calendar or app to monitor planetary transits and alignments. Note significant aspects that align with your creative goals.

- **Example:** Plan content launches during Jupiter alignments for maximum growth potential or utilize Venus alignments for rebranding efforts.

2. Align Tasks with Planetary Energies

Match your tasks with the energy of the planets. For instance, use Mars transits for high-energy tasks or Mercury transits for communication-heavy work.

3. Embrace Retrogrades as Opportunities

While retrogrades are often viewed as challenging, they are ideal for reviewing, revising, and refining your content. Use these periods to address unresolved projects or enhance your skills.

4. Plan Around Moon Phases

The Moon's phases influence energy levels and creativity. Use the Waxing Moon for growth-oriented tasks, the Full Moon for high-impact content, and the Waning Moon for reflection and closure.

Real-Life Applications of Planetary Alignments

Many successful creators have unknowingly aligned their projects with planetary energies, reflecting the power of astrological timing.

- **Example 1:** A filmmaker launched a crowdfunding campaign during a Jupiter-Venus trine, attracting widespread support and exceeding their funding goals.
- **Example 2:** A content creator revamped their website during a Mercury retrograde, using the energy for reflection and refinement to create a more polished platform.

Final Thoughts

Planetary alignments offer profound insights into the ebb and flow of creative energy, productivity, and audience engagement. By understanding and aligning with these cosmic rhythms, content creators can harness the power of the planets to optimize their work, connect with their audience, and achieve their goals. Whether you're planning a major launch or reflecting on your creative journey, the stars provide guidance and inspiration for every step of the process.

Chapter 15: Mercury Retrograde – Navigating Communication Challenges

Mercury retrograde is one of the most well-known astrological phenomena, often associated with miscommunications, technical glitches, and delays. For content creators, Mercury retrograde can feel like a minefield, as it rules over key areas like communication, technology, and planning. However, while this cosmic event is often viewed as disruptive, it also offers opportunities for reflection, review, and refining existing work.

In this chapter, we will explore the mechanics of Mercury retrograde, its impact on content creation, and actionable strategies to navigate this period effectively. With the right approach, Mercury retrograde can be transformed from a source of frustration into a catalyst for growth and creativity.

What Is Mercury Retrograde?

In astronomy, Mercury retrograde is an optical illusion that occurs when Mercury appears to move backward in its orbit relative to Earth. In astrology, this phenomenon is believed to create disruptions in areas governed by Mercury, including:

- **Communication:** Misunderstandings, unclear messages, or forgotten details.
- **Technology:** Software glitches, hardware failures, and issues with digital tools.
- **Travel and Scheduling:** Delays, missed deadlines, and logistical mix-ups.
- **Contracts and Agreements:** Misinterpretations or overlooked details in legal or business dealings.

Mercury retrograde occurs approximately three to four times a year, lasting about three weeks each time. While its effects can feel chaotic, understanding its influence allows creators to work with this energy rather than against it.

How Mercury Retrograde Impacts Content Creation

Mercury retrograde directly influences processes that are integral to content creation. Understanding these effects can help you anticipate and adapt to potential challenges.

1. Communication Breakdowns

- **Impact:** Emails might go unanswered, social media posts could be misinterpreted, or collaborations may experience misunderstandings.
- **Example:** A content creator schedules a live stream, but due to a miscommunication, their co-host misses the event.

2. Technical Issues

- **Impact:** Software crashes, data loss, or hardware malfunctions can disrupt workflows.
- **Example:** A podcaster loses a recorded episode due to a corrupted file.

3. Delays in Projects

- **Impact:** Launch dates may be postponed, or shipments of merchandise may be delayed.
- **Example:** A creator plans to release a new eBook, but formatting errors push the release date back.

4. Challenges in Planning

- **Impact:** Misaligned schedules, overlooked details, or miscommunications can complicate project management.
- **Example:** A marketing campaign is launched without realizing a key element was omitted.

While these disruptions can be frustrating, Mercury retrograde also encourages introspection and offers opportunities to revisit and refine past work.

Opportunities During Mercury Retrograde

Contrary to its reputation, Mercury retrograde can be a productive time if approached with the right mindset. Its reflective energy supports activities such as:

1. Reviewing Existing Content

- **Opportunity:** Revisit old projects to identify areas for improvement or repurpose successful content for new formats.
- **Example:** A blogger updates high-performing posts with fresh insights and SEO optimization.

2. Refining Strategies

- **Opportunity:** Assess the effectiveness of current workflows, branding, or audience engagement strategies.
- **Example:** A creator uses this time to audit their social media analytics and refine their posting schedule.

3. Resolving Unfinished Projects

- **Opportunity:** Complete drafts or ideas that have been left on the backburner.
- **Example:** A YouTuber revisits an abandoned video series, bringing it to completion.

4. Strengthening Communication

- **Opportunity:** Use the period to clarify expectations and improve communication with collaborators or audiences.
- **Example:** A creator schedules check-ins with team members to ensure alignment on shared goals.

Strategies for Navigating Mercury Retrograde

With preparation and adaptability, content creators can minimize disruptions and harness the reflective energy of Mercury retrograde. Here's how:

1. Double-Check Everything

Mercury retrograde often brings overlooked details to light. Take extra time to review all aspects of your work.

- **Action:** Proofread emails, double-check deadlines, and ensure that all assets (like graphics or captions) are accurate.
- **Example:** Before launching a product, a creator tests the payment system and reviews the landing page for errors.

2. Back Up Your Work

Technical issues are a hallmark of Mercury retrograde, making it essential to safeguard your projects.

- **Action:** Regularly back up files, save drafts frequently, and use cloud storage for critical data.
- **Example:** A photographer duplicates their edited photos on an external hard drive to avoid losing progress.

3. Avoid Major Launches

While Mercury retrograde is great for refining existing ideas, it's not ideal for launching new projects.

- **Action:** Delay launches or announcements until after the retrograde period if possible.
- **Example:** A creator postpones the release of a new podcast series to ensure all elements are polished and aligned.

4. Communicate Clearly

Miscommunications are common during Mercury retrograde, so prioritize clarity in all interactions.

- **Action:** Confirm details in writing, repeat key points during meetings, and seek feedback to ensure mutual understanding.
- **Example:** A graphic designer clarifies client expectations with a detailed project brief and scheduled check-ins.

5. Embrace Flexibility

Plans may change unexpectedly, so adopt a flexible mindset to navigate disruptions gracefully.

- **Action:** Build buffer time into your schedule to accommodate delays or revisions.
- **Example:** A live streamer has a backup activity prepared in case of technical difficulties during their event.

Harnessing Mercury Retrograde for Creativity

Mercury retrograde's introspective energy can spark creativity and offer unique insights. Here are ways to leverage its potential:

1. Reconnect with Inspiration

- **Action:** Revisit old notebooks, mood boards, or brainstorming sessions to rediscover forgotten ideas.
- **Example:** A writer revisits drafts of unfinished short stories, finding inspiration to complete them.

2. Experiment with Formats

- **Action:** Use this period to experiment with new content formats or revisit ideas that didn't work before.
- **Example:** A video creator tries converting long-form videos into bite-sized TikToks.

3. Build Deeper Connections

- **Action:** Use Mercury retrograde to connect with your audience through personal or reflective content.
- **Example:** A blogger shares their journey of overcoming setbacks, resonating deeply with their readers.

The Post-Retrograde Shadow Period

Even after Mercury retrograde ends, the "shadow period" (lasting about two weeks) can still carry residual energy. Use this time to:

- Finalize projects that began during retrograde.
- Reflect on lessons learned and apply them to future work.
- Reassess long-term goals and adjust strategies as needed.

Real-Life Examples of Mercury Retrograde Success

Many creators and brands have turned Mercury retrograde into a period of reflection and reinvention:

- **Example 1:** A content creator uses the retrograde to revamp their website, fixing navigation issues and optimizing for mobile users.
- **Example 2:** A team experiencing project delays takes the opportunity to revisit their strategy, resulting in a stronger, more cohesive campaign.

Final Thoughts

Mercury retrograde, while challenging, is a valuable time for reflection, revision, and growth. By approaching this period with patience, preparation, and adaptability, content creators can navigate its challenges and uncover new opportunities for success. Instead of fearing its disruptions, embrace Mercury retrograde as a chance to slow down, reassess, and refine your creative journey.

Chapter 16: Venus Phases – Enhancing Content with Beauty and Aesthetic Appeal

In astrology, Venus is the planet of love, beauty, harmony, and creativity. Beyond its associations with relationships, Venus governs the principles of aesthetics, art, and the appreciation of beauty. For content creators, understanding Venus and its phases provides a powerful tool for enhancing the visual and emotional appeal of their work. By aligning with Venusian energy, creators can refine their branding, foster collaboration, and produce content that resonates deeply with their audience.

This chapter delves into the phases of Venus, how they influence creativity and aesthetics, and actionable strategies for incorporating Venusian principles into your content.

The Role of Venus in Content Creation

Venus rules over the realms of beauty, values, and connection, all of which are central to creating engaging content. Its influence encourages creators to prioritize visual appeal, harmony, and emotional resonance.

- **Beauty:** Venus inspires elegance and design, making it a guiding force for creators in visual arts, fashion, and branding.
- **Connection:** Venusian energy fosters relationships, both with collaborators and audiences, emphasizing content that builds trust and rapport.
- **Pleasure:** Venus reminds creators to infuse joy and passion into their work, making the creative process fulfilling and the content more appealing.

By understanding Venus' phases and alignments, creators can time their efforts to maximize the planet's influence, creating content that is not only visually stunning but also emotionally engaging.

Understanding the Phases of Venus

Venus moves through a cycle similar to the Moon, alternating between its evening star (waning) and morning star (waxing) phases. Each phase offers unique energy that can be harnessed for different aspects of content creation.

1. Morning Star Phase (Waxing Venus)

- **Symbolism:** New beginnings, inspiration, and the emergence of creative ideas.
- **Energy:** This phase is ideal for brainstorming, conceptualizing, and exploring fresh ideas.
- **Content Focus:**
    ◦ Develop new branding elements or concepts.
    ◦ Experiment with visual styles or color palettes.
    ◦ Focus on personal growth and self-expression.

2. Full Venus

- **Symbolism:** Peak beauty, abundance, and creative flow.
- **Energy:** This phase amplifies Venusian themes, making it the perfect time for high-impact, visually striking content.
- **Content Focus:**
    ◦ Launch new projects, campaigns, or collaborations.
    ◦ Focus on aesthetics, such as photo shoots or website redesigns.
    ◦ Release visually captivating content, such as art or videos.

3. Evening Star Phase (Waning Venus)

- **Symbolism:** Reflection, refinement, and deeper connections.
- **Energy:** This phase supports reviewing and enhancing existing work while fostering emotional resonance.
- **Content Focus:**
    ◦ Revisit and refine past projects or visuals.
    ◦ Strengthen relationships with your audience or collaborators.
    ◦ Share introspective or behind-the-scenes content.

4. Venus Retrograde

- **Symbolism:** Introspection, revaluation, and rediscovery.
- **Energy:** During Venus retrograde, creators are encouraged to revisit and refine their aesthetic, values, and connections.
- **Content Focus:**
  - Reflect on your brand's identity and adjust where necessary.
  - Rethink your visual style or engagement strategies.
  - Focus on rebuilding relationships or addressing feedback.

How Venus Influences Aesthetic Appeal

The principles of Venus provide a framework for elevating the aesthetic quality of your content. Here's how Venus inspires beauty and harmony across various creative elements:

1. Visual Design

Venus rules over balance, symmetry, and elegance, making it a critical influence on design choices.

- **Applications:**
    - Focus on cohesive branding with harmonious color schemes, typography, and layouts.
    - Embrace minimalism or maximalism, depending on your aesthetic, but ensure elements feel balanced.
    - Use tools like Canva or Adobe Creative Cloud to refine the visual aspects of your content.

2. Storytelling

Venus enhances the emotional and narrative aspects of storytelling, emphasizing connection and resonance.

- **Applications:**
    - Craft narratives that evoke joy, love, or inspiration.
    - Use poetic or visually descriptive language to draw your audience in.
    - Explore themes of beauty, relationships, or self-discovery in your content.

3. Branding

Venus supports the creation of a brand identity that feels authentic, attractive, and aligned with your values.

- **Applications:**
    - Develop a visual style guide to ensure consistency across platforms.
    - Highlight your unique strengths and passions in your branding.
    - Incorporate design elements that reflect your personal or brand values.

4. Collaboration

Venus fosters harmony in relationships, making it an ideal influence for partnerships and team-work.

- **Applications:**
    - ◦ Collaborate with creators or brands that align with your aesthetic and values.
    - ◦ Use Venus' energy to build trust and rapport with collaborators.
    - ◦ Focus on joint projects that emphasize shared creativity and mutual benefit.

Harnessing Venus Phases for Content Creation

Understanding Venus' cycles allows creators to align their efforts with its energy, maximizing creativity, productivity, and impact.

1. Plan Around Venus Transits

Monitor Venus' transits and alignments to identify optimal times for specific creative tasks.

- **Example:** Use a Venus-Jupiter conjunction to launch visually stunning campaigns, as this alignment enhances beauty and abundance.

2. Prioritize Aesthetics and Harmony

Make aesthetic appeal a cornerstone of your creative process.

- **Tip:** Focus on small details, such as typography, layout, and color coordination, to elevate your content's visual quality.

3. Infuse Emotion and Connection

Create content that resonates emotionally with your audience, drawing on Venusian themes like love, joy, and harmony.

- **Example:** A lifestyle influencer could share personal stories about relationships or self-love, connecting with their audience on a deeper level.

4. Reflect and Refine During Venus Retrograde

Use Venus retrograde to assess and enhance your content, branding, and audience relationships.

- **Example:** A graphic designer could revisit their portfolio, refining older projects to align with their current aesthetic.

Real-Life Applications of Venus Energy

Many creators have intuitively harnessed Venusian principles to enhance their content:

- **Example 1:** A fashion influencer plans a photo shoot during Venus' Full Phase, capturing visually stunning images that boost engagement.
- **Example 2:** A digital artist revamps their branding during Venus retrograde, creating a cohesive style that aligns with their evolving vision.

Tools to Elevate Venus-Inspired Content

1. Visual Creation Tools

- Canva, Adobe Creative Cloud, Procreate for designing visually appealing graphics and illustrations.

2. Branding Platforms

- Squarespace or Wix for creating aesthetically pleasing websites.

3. Social Media Tools

- Instagram and Pinterest for showcasing visual content and engaging with aesthetically driven audiences.

Final Thoughts

The phases of Venus offer a roadmap for enhancing the beauty, emotional resonance, and aesthetic quality of your content. By aligning with Venus' energy, creators can elevate their work, foster deeper connections with their audience, and create a brand that exudes harmony and authenticity. Whether you're refining your visual style, collaborating with others, or crafting emotionally resonant content, Venus provides the inspiration and guidance to succeed.

Chapter 17: Mars Transits – Using Energy and Action in Content Launches

Mars, the planet of energy, drive, and action, governs ambition, passion, and the ability to take initiative. Known as the warrior planet, Mars embodies a dynamic, fiery force that motivates creators to push boundaries, take risks, and transform ideas into action. For content creators, understanding Mars transits provides a powerful framework for timing launches, tackling high-energy tasks, and maintaining momentum in their projects.

In this chapter, we'll explore the influence of Mars transits on content creation, diving into how its energy can be harnessed to boost productivity, drive impactful launches, and sustain motivation.

The Role of Mars in Content Creation

Mars influences the active, goal-oriented aspects of content creation. Its energy is bold, assertive, and proactive, encouraging creators to move forward with confidence and determination. Mars governs several key areas that are crucial for creators:

- **Initiative:** Mars helps creators take the first step in launching new projects or exploring uncharted territories.
- **Courage:** Its fiery nature encourages risk-taking and embracing challenges.
- **Focus:** Mars provides the stamina and discipline needed to see projects through to completion.
- **Productivity:** It drives high-energy tasks, ensuring efficiency and effectiveness.

When aligned with Mars transits, content creators can amplify their output and ensure their work is action-oriented and impactful.

Understanding Mars Transits

Mars moves through the zodiac every two years, spending about six to seven weeks in each sign. Its energy shifts based on its position, influencing how creators approach their work during that time. Additionally, aspects Mars forms with other planets create unique opportunities and challenges.

Mars in Fire Signs (Aries, Leo, Sagittarius)

- **Energy:** Bold, creative, and adventurous.
- **Focus:** Perfect for initiating new projects, taking bold risks, and building momentum.
- **Content Ideas:** Launch campaigns, create energetic videos, or explore new creative directions.

Mars in Earth Signs (Taurus, Virgo, Capricorn)

- **Energy:** Practical, disciplined, and methodical.
- **Focus:** Ideal for organizing, planning, and executing long-term strategies.
- **Content Ideas:** Build systems for consistent posting, refine branding, or develop educational resources.

Mars in Air Signs (Gemini, Libra, Aquarius)

- **Energy:** Intellectual, collaborative, and communicative.
- **Focus:** Great for brainstorming, networking, and creating engaging dialogue with audiences.
- **Content Ideas:** Host live Q&A sessions, collaborate with other creators, or focus on storytelling.

Mars in Water Signs (Cancer, Scorpio, Pisces)

- **Energy:** Emotional, intuitive, and transformative.
- **Focus:** Best for emotionally driven content or addressing deeper themes.
- **Content Ideas:** Share personal stories, create content about healing or transformation, or explore spiritual topics.

How Mars Transits Influence Content Launches

Mars is most powerful when it's driving action and results. Content creators can use its transits to plan impactful launches and energize their projects. Below are specific ways Mars transits can enhance your efforts:

1. Building Momentum

Mars transits provide the energy needed to start and maintain momentum in your projects. Its fiery nature helps you overcome inertia and push through barriers.

- **Example:** A creator launching a new YouTube channel during Mars in Aries capitalizes on the transit's pioneering energy to generate excitement and establish a strong foundation.
- **Action Tip:** Use Mars transits to set clear goals and take bold first steps in your projects.

2. Timing for Impact

Mars governs timing and execution, making its transits ideal for planning high-energy tasks such as content launches, major campaigns, or events.

- **Example:** A content creator schedules the launch of their new product during a Mars-Jupiter trine, aligning Mars' drive with Jupiter's expansive energy to maximize visibility and success.
- **Action Tip:** Plan launches during Mars in fire or air signs for maximum dynamism and audience engagement.

3. Sustaining Productivity

Mars transits help creators stay focused and disciplined, especially when working on long-term projects or handling demanding workloads.

- **Example:** A blogger uses Mars in Capricorn to organize a year-long content calendar, ensuring consistency and efficiency in their output.
- **Action Tip:** Break large tasks into smaller, actionable steps and use Mars' energy to tackle them with determination.

4. Embracing Risk and Bold Moves

Mars encourages creators to step out of their comfort zones and take risks that could yield significant rewards.

- **Example:** A content creator collaborates with a high-profile influencer during Mars in Leo, leveraging the transit's confident energy to expand their audience.

• **Action Tip:** Use Mars transits to experiment with new formats, partnerships, or marketing strategies.

Harnessing Mars' Energy in Content Creation

To fully leverage Mars transits, creators must align their actions with the planet's fiery, proactive energy. Here's how to make the most of its influence:

1. Channel Your Passion

Mars thrives on enthusiasm and drive. Focus on projects that ignite your passion and reflect your core values.

- **Example:** A creator passionate about environmental advocacy launches a content series on sustainable living during Mars in Sagittarius.
- **Action Tip:** Identify topics or projects that excite you and commit to pursuing them with energy and purpose.

2. Set Clear Goals

Mars operates best when there's a clear direction. Use its energy to define your objectives and create actionable plans.

- **Example:** A podcaster sets a goal to release 10 episodes during Mars in Virgo, breaking the process into manageable milestones.
- **Action Tip:** Write down your goals and map out a timeline to keep yourself accountable.

3. Take Decisive Action

Mars rewards boldness and initiative. Avoid overthinking and trust your instincts when making decisions.

- **Example:** A creator uses Mars in Aries to pitch a new idea to a potential collaborator, securing an opportunity for growth.
- **Action Tip:** Prioritize decisive actions over hesitation. If an idea excites you, act on it.

4. Overcome Challenges with Resilience

Mars transits can bring friction, but they also provide the determination to push through obstacles.

- **Example:** A content creator experiences technical setbacks during a Mars-Saturn square but uses the transit's disciplined energy to troubleshoot and stay on track.
- **Action Tip:** Embrace challenges as opportunities for growth and use Mars' energy to find solutions.

Navigating Mars Retrograde

Mars retrograde, which occurs approximately every two years, is a period where Mars' forward momentum slows, encouraging introspection and strategic reassessment.

- **Challenges:** Energy may feel scattered, and progress could slow. Frustrations or conflicts may arise.
- **Opportunities:** Reflect on past actions, refine strategies, and tackle unfinished projects.
- **Example:** A creator uses Mars retrograde to revisit an abandoned content series, updating it with fresh ideas and a renewed focus.

Tools to Maximize Mars Energy
1. Productivity Tools

- **Asana or Trello:** Use these tools to break down tasks and maintain focus on your goals.
- **Pomodoro Technique:** Leverage short bursts of focused work to align with Mars' active energy.

2. Content Creation Tools

- **Canva or Adobe Premiere Pro:** Create visually impactful content with bold designs and dynamic visuals.
- **Social Media Schedulers (Buffer, Hootsuite):** Plan posts in advance to maintain momentum during high-energy transits.

3. Analytics Tools

- **Google Analytics or YouTube Studio:** Use data to measure the impact of your efforts and adjust your strategy during Mars transits.

Real-Life Examples of Mars Energy in Action

- **Example 1:** A fitness influencer launches a high-energy workout program during Mars in Aries, attracting a wave of new subscribers with their bold and dynamic approach.
- **Example 2:** A motivational speaker uses Mars in Leo to plan a virtual summit, channeling the transit's confidence and charisma to engage attendees.

Final Thoughts

Mars transits provide a powerful surge of energy, motivation, and focus, making them ideal for content creators seeking to take bold action, launch impactful projects, and sustain productivity. By understanding the unique energies of Mars in each sign and aligning their efforts accordingly, creators can harness the planet's fiery drive to achieve their goals and make a lasting impact.

Chapter 18: Jupiter's Influence – Expanding Reach and Growth Opportunities

Jupiter, known as the "Great Benefic" in astrology, is the planet of expansion, abundance, and higher learning. Representing growth and opportunity, Jupiter encourages creators to think big, take bold steps, and explore uncharted territories. It governs themes of luck, optimism, wisdom, and vision, making it a powerful influence for content creators looking to expand their reach and maximize their impact.

In this chapter, we will explore how Jupiter's transits and alignments influence content creation, uncovering strategies to leverage its energy for growth, abundance, and long-term success.

The Role of Jupiter in Content Creation

Jupiter's energy inspires creators to push boundaries, take risks, and embrace opportunities that lead to growth. Its influence is expansive, helping creators broaden their audience, diversify their offerings, and explore new creative directions. Key themes associated with Jupiter include:

- **Expansion:** Jupiter encourages growth in all areas, whether it's audience reach, brand visibility, or creative exploration.
- **Optimism:** Its influence inspires confidence and a positive outlook, helping creators take bold steps forward.
- **Knowledge:** Jupiter governs wisdom and learning, making it ideal for creators focused on education or thought leadership.
- **Luck:** Jupiter's benevolent energy brings opportunities that align with personal and professional goals.

By understanding Jupiter's cycles and aligning their efforts with its energy, creators can unlock new possibilities and scale their success.

Understanding Jupiter's Transits

Jupiter takes approximately 12 years to complete a full journey through the zodiac, spending about a year in each sign. Its placement influences how its expansive energy manifests during that period. Additionally, Jupiter's aspects to other planets create unique opportunities and challenges for growth.

Jupiter in Fire Signs (Aries, Leo, Sagittarius)

- **Energy:** Bold, visionary, and high-energy.
- **Focus:** Ideal for launching big projects, expanding visibility, and pursuing creative risks.
- **Example:** A content creator uses Jupiter in Leo to focus on personal branding and leadership, establishing themselves as a thought leader.

Jupiter in Earth Signs (Taurus, Virgo, Capricorn)

- **Energy:** Practical, grounded, and resource-driven.
- **Focus:** Perfect for building sustainable systems, scaling businesses, and monetizing content.
- **Example:** A blogger uses Jupiter in Capricorn to develop a long-term strategy for monetizing their platform through courses and sponsorships.

Jupiter in Air Signs (Gemini, Libra, Aquarius)

- **Energy:** Intellectual, innovative, and network-oriented.
- **Focus:** Best for exploring collaborative opportunities, diversifying content, and expanding global reach.
- **Example:** A podcaster uses Jupiter in Aquarius to collaborate with international guests, growing their audience across new markets.

Jupiter in Water Signs (Cancer, Scorpio, Pisces)

- **Energy:** Intuitive, emotional, and imaginative.
- **Focus:** Ideal for creating emotionally resonant content, exploring spirituality, and building deep audience connections.
- **Example:** A spiritual influencer uses Jupiter in Pisces to expand their offerings with guided meditations and emotional healing content.

Jupiter Alignments and Their Impact

The aspects Jupiter forms with other planets during its transits create distinct opportunities for content creators:

- **Jupiter-Sun Alignments:** Amplifies confidence, visibility, and leadership. Great for personal branding and high-profile launches.
- **Jupiter-Mercury Alignments:** Enhances communication and intellectual pursuits. Ideal for writing, teaching, or launching courses.
- **Jupiter-Venus Alignments:** Brings beauty, creativity, and abundance. Excellent for rebranding, collaborations, or aesthetic-focused projects.
- **Jupiter-Mars Alignments:** Fuels ambition and action. Perfect for initiating bold projects or expanding existing ones.

How Jupiter Influences Growth Opportunities

Jupiter's expansive energy directly impacts key areas of content creation, offering numerous ways to scale and grow your efforts.

1. Growing Your Audience

Jupiter's influence makes it an ideal time to focus on increasing your visibility and connecting with a wider audience.

- **Strategies:**
    - Invest in targeted ads or social media campaigns to reach new demographics.
    - Collaborate with influencers or creators who align with your niche.
    - Expand into new platforms or explore international audiences.
- **Example:** A content creator uses Jupiter in Gemini to launch a multilingual blog, attracting readers from different cultural backgrounds.

2. Launching Big Projects

Jupiter's energy is expansive and optimistic, making it a powerful force for initiating ambitious projects.

- **Strategies:**
    - Plan launches during positive Jupiter alignments to maximize visibility and impact.
    - Focus on projects that reflect your long-term goals and vision.
    - Use Jupiter's influence to pitch ideas to sponsors or collaborators.
- **Example:** An artist launches a crowdfunding campaign for a large-scale exhibition during Jupiter in Sagittarius, using its adventurous energy to attract widespread support.

3. Expanding Offerings

Jupiter encourages diversification, making it a great time to explore new content formats, products, or services.

- **Strategies:**
    - Experiment with different mediums, such as podcasts, video series, or live events.
    - Create premium offerings, such as online courses, workshops, or exclusive memberships.
    - Develop a tiered monetization strategy to cater to different audience segments.
- **Example:** A fitness influencer uses Jupiter in Taurus to expand their offerings with a subscription-based meal-planning app.

4. Investing in Education and Skill-Building

Jupiter's association with higher learning makes its transits ideal for acquiring new skills or knowledge that elevate your content.

- **Strategies:**
    - Enroll in courses or workshops to enhance your expertise.
    - Invest in tools or software that improve your production quality.
    - Share your learning journey with your audience, creating educational content.
- **Example:** A video creator uses Jupiter in Virgo to learn advanced editing techniques, elevating the quality of their projects.

5. Exploring Long-Term Vision

Jupiter encourages creators to think big and align their efforts with their overarching purpose.

- **Strategies:**
    - Reflect on your long-term goals and how your current projects support them.
    - Use Jupiter's energy to create a vision board or strategic plan for the next year.
    - Seek opportunities that align with your personal values and passions.
- **Example:** A sustainability advocate uses Jupiter in Aquarius to develop a 5-year plan for creating content that educates and empowers global audiences.

Harnessing Jupiter Energy in Content Creation

To fully leverage Jupiter's influence, creators must align their actions with its expansive and optimistic energy. Here's how:

1. Take Calculated Risks

Jupiter rewards bold moves, but it also encourages thoughtful planning.

- **Tip:** Identify opportunities that feel ambitious but align with your long-term goals. Avoid overextending yourself by focusing on quality over quantity.

2. Collaborate and Network

Jupiter thrives on connection and shared vision, making collaboration a key theme.

- **Tip:** Reach out to like-minded creators or brands for partnerships that amplify both your audiences.

3. Stay Open to Opportunities

Jupiter's influence often brings unexpected opportunities that align with your growth.

- **Tip:** Keep an open mind and remain flexible. Say "yes" to opportunities that feel aligned, even if they push you out of your comfort zone.

4. Reflect and Refine

While Jupiter is associated with expansion, it also encourages creators to reflect on what's working and refine their approach.

- **Tip:** Use Jupiter retrogrades (when its energy turns inward) to revisit and improve existing projects or strategies.

Tools to Leverage Jupiter's Energy
1. Analytics and Insights

- Use tools like Google Analytics, YouTube Studio, or Instagram Insights to identify growth patterns and audience preferences.

2. Productivity Platforms

- Trello or Notion can help you organize ambitious projects and maintain focus during periods of rapid growth.

3. Learning Platforms

- Enroll in Skillshare or Coursera to expand your knowledge and skills during Jupiter's transits.

Real-Life Applications of Jupiter Energy

- **Example 1:** A wellness coach uses Jupiter in Libra to partner with influencers, creating a viral campaign that doubles their audience size.
- **Example 2:** A filmmaker launches an independent documentary during Jupiter in Sagittarius, receiving critical acclaim and international recognition.

Final Thoughts

Jupiter's transits offer unparalleled opportunities for expansion, growth, and abundance. By aligning with its optimistic energy, content creators can take bold steps to scale their platforms, connect with new audiences, and achieve long-term success. Whether it's launching a big project, diversifying offerings, or investing in education, Jupiter encourages creators to dream big and embrace the possibilities.

Chapter 19: Saturn's Guidance — Mastering Discipline and Scheduling

Saturn, often referred to as the "Taskmaster of the Zodiac," is the planet of structure, discipline, responsibility, and long-term growth. While its energy can feel heavy or restrictive, Saturn's influence is essential for mastering the art of planning, time management, and sustained success. For content creators, Saturn provides the guidance needed to establish routines, maintain consistency, and build a foundation for lasting achievements.

In this chapter, we'll explore Saturn's role in content creation, detailing how its disciplined energy can be harnessed to create effective schedules, overcome procrastination, and develop sustainable practices.

The Role of Saturn in Content Creation

Saturn governs the structures and systems that support long-term goals. Its influence challenges creators to approach their work with discipline, responsibility, and maturity. Key themes associated with Saturn include:

- **Structure:** Saturn encourages the creation of systems and schedules that enhance productivity.
- **Discipline:** Its energy helps creators overcome distractions and focus on their goals.
- **Responsibility:** Saturn emphasizes accountability, urging creators to take ownership of their work.
- **Longevity:** It supports the development of strategies that ensure sustained success over time.

While Saturn's lessons may feel challenging, they ultimately empower creators to build strong, reliable foundations for their content and careers.

Understanding Saturn's Transits

Saturn takes about 29.5 years to complete its journey through the zodiac, spending approximately 2.5 years in each sign. Its transits highlight areas of life where discipline, responsibility, and effort are required. These periods often bring challenges, but they also offer opportunities for growth and mastery.

Saturn in Fire Signs (Aries, Leo, Sagittarius)

- **Energy:** Focused on leadership, creativity, and self-expression.
- **Content Focus:** Build confidence in personal branding and refine your creative vision.
- **Example:** A content creator uses Saturn in Leo to develop a strong personal brand that aligns with their long-term goals.

Saturn in Earth Signs (Taurus, Virgo, Capricorn)

- **Energy:** Grounded, practical, and resource-oriented.
- **Content Focus:** Focus on monetization strategies, building sustainable workflows, and refining technical skills.
- **Example:** A creator uses Saturn in Capricorn to establish a detailed business plan for scaling their platform.

Saturn in Air Signs (Gemini, Libra, Aquarius)

- **Energy:** Intellectual, network-oriented, and collaborative.
- **Content Focus:** Strengthen communication strategies, build partnerships, and refine audience engagement.
- **Example:** A writer uses Saturn in Gemini to hone their craft and establish a consistent publishing schedule.

Saturn in Water Signs (Cancer, Scorpio, Pisces)

- **Energy:** Emotional, intuitive, and reflective.
- **Content Focus:** Focus on content that resonates deeply with your audience and aligns with your values.
- **Example:** A wellness influencer uses Saturn in Pisces to create a series of guided meditations, developing a consistent release schedule.

Saturn's Influence on Discipline and Scheduling

Saturn's energy helps creators establish the habits and systems needed to stay organized, meet deadlines, and maintain consistency. Here's how its influence manifests in content creation:

1. Building Effective Schedules

Saturn emphasizes the importance of planning and time management. Its energy supports the creation of structured schedules that align with your goals.

- **Strategies:**
  - Use project management tools to organize your workflow and set deadlines.
  - Break large tasks into smaller, manageable steps.
  - Prioritize tasks based on urgency and importance.
- **Example:** A YouTuber creates a monthly content calendar, outlining filming, editing, and publishing dates to ensure consistency.

2. Overcoming Procrastination

Saturn's disciplined energy encourages creators to tackle tasks head-on, even when motivation is low.

- **Strategies:**
  - Establish routines that reinforce productivity, such as setting specific work hours or using the Pomodoro Technique.
  - Break tasks into smaller segments to reduce overwhelm.
  - Hold yourself accountable by tracking your progress.
- **Example:** A writer sets a daily goal of 500 words, using Saturn's energy to maintain momentum on their manuscript.

3. Establishing Consistency

Saturn values reliability and consistency, making it a powerful influence for creators seeking to build trust and loyalty with their audience.

- **Strategies:**
  - Develop a posting schedule that aligns with your audience's preferences.
  - Maintain consistency in branding, tone, and content style.
  - Use analytics to track performance and refine your approach.
- **Example:** A social media influencer posts three times a week on Instagram, ensuring their content aligns with their brand aesthetic and messaging.

4. Creating Long-Term Strategies

Saturn encourages creators to think beyond short-term goals, focusing on strategies that ensure sustainability and growth.

- **Strategies:**
    - Set SMART (Specific, Measurable, Achievable, Relevant, Time-bound) goals for your content.
    - Develop a vision for where you want your platform to be in 1, 5, or 10 years.
    - Invest time in skills or tools that will support your long-term goals.
- **Example:** A blogger develops a 5-year plan to grow their platform, incorporating milestones for audience growth, monetization, and collaborations.

Harnessing Saturn's Energy in Content Creation

To fully leverage Saturn's disciplined energy, creators must embrace its lessons and apply them to their workflows and strategies. Here's how to make the most of its influence:

1. Embrace Hard Work

Saturn rewards effort and perseverance. Approach your projects with a commitment to excellence and a willingness to tackle challenges.

- **Tip:** Focus on quality over quantity, prioritizing thoughtful, impactful content.

2. Set Boundaries

Saturn encourages responsibility and accountability, but it also reminds creators to set boundaries to avoid burnout.

- **Tip:** Define clear work-life boundaries, ensuring you have time for rest and self-care.

3. Learn from Challenges

Saturn's energy often brings obstacles, but these challenges are opportunities for growth and refinement.

- **Tip:** Reflect on setbacks and use them as learning experiences to improve your processes.

4. Create Systems for Success

Saturn supports the development of systems and routines that enhance efficiency and productivity.

- **Tip:** Automate repetitive tasks using tools like social media schedulers or email marketing platforms.

Tools to Support Saturn's Energy
1. Project Management Tools

- **Asana or Trello:** Organize tasks, set deadlines, and track progress.

2. Time Management Apps

- **Toggl or Clockify:** Track how much time you spend on tasks and optimize your workflow.

3. Content Planning Tools

- **Google Calendar or Notion:** Develop detailed content calendars and plan your projects.

4. Analytics Platforms

- **Google Analytics or YouTube Studio:** Use data to measure performance and refine strategies.

Real-Life Applications of Saturn Energy

- **Example 1:** A content creator experiencing Saturn's transit in Virgo creates a comprehensive workflow for producing weekly blog posts, ensuring consistency and quality.
- **Example 2:** A filmmaker uses Saturn in Capricorn to plan a crowdfunding campaign, outlining a clear budget and timeline to meet their goals.

Saturn Retrograde: Reflection and Refinement
During Saturn retrograde, its energy turns inward, encouraging creators to reflect on their goals and refine their strategies. Use this time to:

- Assess your progress and identify areas for improvement.
- Revisit old projects or ideas that were left unfinished.
- Reflect on whether your current efforts align with your long-term vision.

Final Thoughts
Saturn's influence is a powerful ally for content creators seeking to master discipline, establish effective schedules, and achieve long-term success. By embracing its lessons and aligning with its energy, creators can build strong foundations for their work, ensuring consistency, sustainability, and growth. While Saturn's demands may feel challenging, they ultimately pave the way for achievements that stand the test of time.

Chapter 20: Uranus – Embracing Unexpected Creativity and Change

Uranus, the planet of innovation, disruption, and sudden change, is often referred to as the "Great Awakener" in astrology. It represents breakthroughs, rebellion against convention, and the pursuit of originality. For content creators, Uranus' influence sparks bold, unconventional ideas and challenges them to step outside their comfort zones. Its energy encourages embracing change and experimenting with fresh approaches, making it a powerful force for creators seeking to break boundaries and redefine their niches.

In this chapter, we will explore how Uranus influences creativity and change, offering strategies for leveraging its innovative energy to enhance content creation and thrive in a rapidly evolving digital landscape.

The Role of Uranus in Content Creation

Uranus governs originality, technology, and the willingness to disrupt traditional norms. It inspires creators to think differently, take creative risks, and embrace new tools or trends. Key themes associated with Uranus include:

- **Innovation:** Encouraging creators to adopt cutting-edge technology or pioneering ideas.
- **Disruption:** Breaking free from outdated methods or restrictive routines.
- **Unpredictability:** Navigating sudden changes or unexpected opportunities with agility.
- **Independence:** Empowering creators to carve their own paths and embrace authenticity.

By understanding Uranus' influence, creators can harness its energy to stand out in competitive spaces, develop unique content strategies, and adapt to changing trends.

Understanding Uranus' Transits

Uranus takes approximately 84 years to complete its journey through the zodiac, spending about 7 years in each sign. Its position during these transits highlights areas of life and creativity that are ripe for innovation and transformation.

Uranus in Fire Signs (Aries, Leo, Sagittarius)

- **Energy:** Bold, dramatic, and action-oriented.
- **Focus:** Perfect for taking creative risks, exploring personal expression, and launching ambitious projects.
- **Example:** A content creator uses Uranus in Aries to develop a dynamic, interactive series that encourages audience participation.

Uranus in Earth Signs (Taurus, Virgo, Capricorn)

- **Energy:** Groundbreaking, practical, and resourceful.
- **Focus:** Ideal for innovating in sustainable practices, monetization strategies, or digital tools.
- **Example:** A lifestyle influencer explores eco-friendly content during Uranus in Taurus, blending creativity with sustainability.

Uranus in Air Signs (Gemini, Libra, Aquarius)

- **Energy:** Intellectual, communicative, and collaborative.
- **Focus:** Perfect for networking, exploring emerging platforms, or fostering global communities.
- **Example:** A creator leverages Uranus in Aquarius to launch a cutting-edge app that connects creators with audiences worldwide.

Uranus in Water Signs (Cancer, Scorpio, Pisces)

- **Energy:** Intuitive, emotional, and imaginative.
- **Focus:** Ideal for exploring deep, transformative themes or using creative storytelling to connect emotionally with audiences.
- **Example:** A filmmaker experiments with surreal narratives and dreamlike visuals during Uranus in Pisces, creating content that challenges conventional storytelling.

Uranus' Influence on Content Creation

Uranus' energy encourages creators to embrace change, take bold risks, and push boundaries. Here's how its influence manifests in content creation:

1. Inspiring Originality

Uranus fuels innovative thinking, encouraging creators to explore unconventional ideas and break free from traditional norms.

- **Strategies:**
  - Brainstorm outside-the-box concepts that challenge industry standards.
  - Experiment with new formats or visual styles that set your content apart.
  - Draw inspiration from unexpected sources, such as art movements, subcultures, or emerging technologies.
- **Example:** A photographer uses Uranus' influence to create a series of AI-generated art, blending traditional photography with futuristic elements.

2. Adapting to Change

Uranus governs unpredictability, often bringing sudden shifts or opportunities that require quick thinking and adaptability.

- **Strategies:**
  - Stay informed about emerging trends or platforms that could benefit your niche.
  - Embrace flexibility in your content strategy to respond to sudden changes or opportunities.
  - Use challenges as a chance to pivot or refine your approach.
- **Example:** A content creator seizes the opportunity to collaborate with a trending influencer, adapting their schedule to accommodate the partnership.

3. Leveraging Technology

Uranus rules over technology and innovation, making it a prime influence for creators who want to explore new tools or platforms.

- **Strategies:**
  - Invest in cutting-edge tools or software to enhance your production quality.
  - Explore emerging platforms like VR, AR, or blockchain for unique content opportunities.
  - Experiment with automation or AI-driven tools to streamline your workflow.

- **Example:** A digital artist creates a series of NFTs, leveraging blockchain technology to reach a new audience and monetize their work.

4. Breaking Free from Routine

Uranus encourages creators to challenge routines or methods that feel restrictive, fostering a sense of freedom and exploration.

- **Strategies:**
    - Reevaluate your workflow to identify areas where you can experiment or innovate.
    - Step outside your comfort zone by exploring new genres or themes.
    - Take creative breaks to recharge and spark fresh ideas.
- **Example:** A podcaster revamps their format, incorporating live audience interactions and unscripted episodes to create a more dynamic listening experience.

Harnessing Uranus' Energy in Content Creation

To fully leverage Uranus' influence, creators must embrace its disruptive energy and use it as a catalyst for innovation and growth. Here's how to make the most of its impact:

1. Stay Open to Experimentation

Uranus thrives on novelty and exploration. Use its energy to test new ideas, formats, or platforms.

- **Tip:** Treat experiments as learning experiences, even if they don't produce immediate results.

2. Embrace Collaboration

Uranus values community and collective innovation. Seek opportunities to collaborate with like-minded creators or audiences.

- **Tip:** Use technology like virtual events or live streaming to connect with collaborators and audiences worldwide.

3. Prepare for the Unexpected

Uranus often brings sudden changes or challenges. Stay adaptable and ready to pivot when needed.

- **Tip:** Build flexibility into your schedule and approach unexpected events with a problem-solving mindset.

4. Innovate with Technology

Leverage Uranus' association with technology to enhance your content and streamline your workflow.

- **Tip:** Explore tools like AI-generated content, AR filters, or cutting-edge editing software to elevate your projects.

Tools to Support Uranus' Energy
1. Innovation Platforms

- **Canva, Procreate, or Adobe Premiere Pro:** Explore bold new designs or editing techniques.

2. Emerging Tech Tools

- **Unity or Spark AR:** Dive into VR or AR content creation to stay ahead of trends.

3. Analytics and Feedback

- **Google Trends or BuzzSumo:** Identify emerging topics and trends to guide your experiments.

4. Collaboration Tools

- **Zoom or Slack:** Foster connections with collaborators or audiences in real time.

Real-Life Applications of Uranus Energy

- **Example 1:** A fashion designer uses Uranus in Aquarius to create a virtual runway show, blending futuristic designs with AR technology.
- **Example 2:** A gamer leverages Uranus' energy to start a Twitch channel during a trend boom, quickly gaining followers through innovative gameplay.

Final Thoughts
Uranus' energy offers unparalleled opportunities for innovation, creativity, and transformation. By embracing its disruptive influence, content creators can break free from conventions, explore bold new ideas, and adapt to the ever-changing digital landscape. Whether you're experimenting with new tools, tackling unexpected challenges, or pushing the boundaries of your niche, Uranus encourages you to think fearlessly and embrace the unknown.

Chapter 21: Neptune's Illusions – Maintaining Authenticity

Neptune, the planet of dreams, illusions, and intuition, is often associated with creativity, spirituality, and the unseen. It governs imagination, empathy, and the pursuit of higher ideals, making it a significant influence for creators who thrive on storytelling, emotional resonance, and artistic expression. However, Neptune's energy can also blur the lines between reality and fantasy, leading to challenges like overidealism, misrepresentation, or disconnection from one's authentic voice.

In this chapter, we'll explore how Neptune influences content creation, highlighting the balance between embracing its imaginative energy and maintaining authenticity. With the right approach, creators can use Neptune's energy to craft deeply meaningful and inspiring content while staying grounded in their truth.

The Role of Neptune in Content Creation

Neptune inspires creators to dream big, connect emotionally, and explore themes of spirituality and compassion. Its influence encourages creators to craft content that resonates on a deeper level, transcending the superficial. Key themes associated with Neptune include:

- **Creativity:** Neptune enhances artistic expression and imaginative storytelling.
- **Intuition:** It fosters emotional intelligence, helping creators connect with their audience's feelings.
- **Empathy:** Neptune's energy encourages the exploration of universal themes like love, healing, and connection.
- **Illusion:** It challenges creators to discern between fantasy and reality, ensuring their work remains authentic and grounded.

While Neptune's energy can spark inspiration and emotional depth, it also requires vigilance to avoid pitfalls like idealization, escapism, or misrepresentation.

Understanding Neptune's Transits

Neptune takes approximately 165 years to complete its journey through the zodiac, spending about 14 years in each sign. Its long transits influence generational shifts in creativity, spirituality, and collective consciousness. For content creators, these transits highlight periods of heightened inspiration and emotional resonance.

Neptune in Fire Signs (Aries, Leo, Sagittarius)

- **Energy:** Passionate, visionary, and dramatic.
- **Focus:** Ideal for exploring bold, creative ideas that inspire and uplift.
- **Example:** A filmmaker uses Neptune in Leo to produce a visually stunning movie that celebrates individuality and self-expression.

Neptune in Earth Signs (Taurus, Virgo, Capricorn)

- **Energy:** Grounded, sensual, and practical.
- **Focus:** Encourages blending imagination with tangible results, such as sustainable creativity or resource-based projects.
- **Example:** A lifestyle influencer uses Neptune in Taurus to create content about sustainable living, blending beauty with practicality.

Neptune in Air Signs (Gemini, Libra, Aquarius)

- **Energy:** Intellectual, communicative, and collaborative.
- **Focus:** Inspires creators to explore abstract ideas, technology, and social justice themes.
- **Example:** A podcaster uses Neptune in Aquarius to launch a series on ethical innovation and technology.

Neptune in Water Signs (Cancer, Scorpio, Pisces)

- **Energy:** Emotional, intuitive, and mystical.
- **Focus:** Perfect for exploring themes of healing, spirituality, and deep emotional connections.
- **Example:** A wellness creator uses Neptune in Pisces to share guided meditations and emotional healing practices.

Neptune's Influence on Authenticity

While Neptune fuels creativity and emotional depth, its energy can sometimes obscure clarity or lead to inauthentic expression. Here's how its influence impacts content creation:

1. Enhancing Creativity and Storytelling

Neptune encourages creators to push boundaries in storytelling, crafting content that feels immersive, poetic, and deeply emotional.

- **Strategies:**
    - Use symbolism and metaphors to convey complex emotions or themes.
    - Incorporate dreamy, surreal elements into your visuals or narratives.
    - Explore universal themes like love, compassion, or the human condition.
- **Example:** A writer uses Neptune's energy to craft a novel that weaves magical realism with relatable human experiences.

2. Deepening Emotional Connections

Neptune enhances empathy, making it easier for creators to connect with their audience on a personal level.

- **Strategies:**
    - Share personal stories that resonate with your audience's struggles or dreams.
    - Use visual or auditory elements that evoke strong emotions, such as music or color schemes.
    - Engage with your audience authentically, fostering trust and vulnerability.
- **Example:** A content creator produces a video series on mental health, combining personal anecdotes with practical advice.

3. Navigating Illusions and Misrepresentation

While Neptune inspires imagination, it can also blur boundaries between truth and fiction, leading to potential pitfalls in authenticity.

- **Challenges:**
    - Overidealizing your projects or creating unrealistic expectations.
    - Misrepresenting yourself or your content to appeal to trends or audiences.
    - Escaping into fantasy, avoiding the realities of content creation.
- **Strategies:**
    - Ground your creative vision with practical steps and achievable goals.
    - Be transparent with your audience about your process, values, and intentions.
    - Regularly reflect on whether your content aligns with your authentic voice.

- **Example:** An influencer avoids using excessive filters or editing in their posts, ensuring their content reflects reality while maintaining aesthetic appeal.

Balancing Neptune's Energy with Authenticity

To harness Neptune's imaginative energy without losing authenticity, creators must strike a balance between inspiration and practicality. Here's how:

1. Embrace Vulnerability

Neptune encourages creators to share their emotions and experiences, fostering a deeper connection with their audience.

- **Tip:** Use storytelling to reveal your personal journey, struggles, and growth. Authenticity comes from being open and honest, even about challenges.

2. Set Realistic Goals

Ground Neptune's dreamy energy with actionable steps to ensure your ideas are achievable.

- **Tip:** Break larger projects into smaller milestones, tracking progress along the way.

3. Maintain Transparency

Be honest with your audience about your intentions, values, and creative process.

- **Tip:** Share behind-the-scenes content or candid moments that highlight your journey and challenges.

4. Stay Grounded

Balance Neptune's ethereal energy with practices that keep you connected to reality.

- **Tip:** Use mindfulness or journaling to stay present and reflective, ensuring your work aligns with your authentic self.

Harnessing Neptune's Energy in Content Creation

To fully leverage Neptune's influence, creators must embrace its imaginative and empathetic energy while remaining true to their values. Here's how to align with its energy:

1. Explore Spiritual and Emotional Themes

Neptune thrives in content that delves into the deeper aspects of life, such as spirituality, healing, or human connection.

- **Example:** A content creator develops a series on mindfulness practices, blending serene visuals with calming narration.

2. Use Symbolism and Visual Storytelling

Neptune inspires creators to incorporate symbolic or surreal elements into their work, enhancing its emotional impact.

- **Example:** A filmmaker uses water imagery to represent emotional growth, creating a visually compelling narrative.

3. Create Immersive Experiences

Neptune's energy supports content that feels immersive and transportive, whether through visuals, sound, or storytelling.

- **Example:** A musician creates an album that tells a story, complete with music videos that visually bring the narrative to life.

4. Engage with Your Audience Intuitively

Use Neptune's empathetic energy to understand and respond to your audience's needs and emotions.

- **Example:** A creator hosts live Q&A sessions, addressing their audience's questions with compassion and insight.

Tools to Support Neptune's Energy
1. Visual and Artistic Tools

- **Canva or Adobe Premiere Pro:** Enhance the dreamlike quality of your visuals or videos.
- **Procreate:** Create surreal or symbolic illustrations.

2. Mindfulness and Reflection Tools

- **Calm or Insight Timer:** Use these tools to stay centered and aligned with your authentic self.

3. Audience Engagement Tools

- **Instagram Live or YouTube Comments:** Foster meaningful interactions with your audience.

Real-Life Applications of Neptune Energy

- **Example 1:** A wellness influencer uses Neptune in Pisces to launch a podcast series exploring emotional resilience, blending personal stories with expert interviews.
- **Example 2:** An artist creates a series of paintings inspired by dreams, using surreal imagery to evoke deep emotional responses.

Final Thoughts

Neptune's energy offers unparalleled opportunities for creativity, emotional depth, and storytelling. By embracing its intuitive and imaginative qualities, content creators can craft work that resonates deeply with their audience. However, maintaining authenticity is crucial to ensure that Neptune's illusions do not lead to misrepresentation or disconnection. With a grounded and reflective approach, creators can use Neptune's influence to inspire, heal, and connect.

Chapter 22: Pluto's Power – Transforming Your Content Strategy

Pluto, the planet of transformation, rebirth, and power, governs profound change and regeneration. In astrology, Pluto represents cycles of destruction and creation, urging individuals and creators to confront their deepest truths and evolve. For content creators, Pluto's influence encourages a deep dive into their strategy, branding, and message, dismantling what no longer serves and rebuilding something more impactful, authentic, and aligned.

This chapter explores how Pluto's transformative energy can revolutionize content creation strategies, helping creators navigate challenges, embrace change, and build a foundation for long-lasting success.

The Role of Pluto in Content Creation

Pluto's energy pushes creators to go beyond surface-level trends, urging them to uncover their core purpose and align their work with their deepest values. Its themes include:

- **Transformation:** Pluto encourages the reimagining of content strategies, from branding to messaging.
- **Authenticity:** Its influence calls for confronting and shedding inauthentic practices.
- **Empowerment:** Pluto inspires creators to step into their power, building content that reflects their strengths and passions.
- **Depth:** It supports the exploration of complex, often overlooked themes, creating work that resonates deeply.

Pluto's transformative energy is intense, but it offers unparalleled opportunities for growth and reinvention when embraced with intention.

Understanding Pluto's Transits

Pluto takes approximately 248 years to complete its orbit, spending 12–30 years in each sign. Its long transits influence generational shifts and highlight profound changes in the collective consciousness. On a personal level, Pluto's transits mark periods of transformation and rebirth.

Pluto in Fire Signs (Aries, Leo, Sagittarius)

- **Energy:** Bold, passionate, and assertive.
- **Focus:** Ideal for exploring themes of personal empowerment, leadership, and creative expression.
- **Example:** A content creator uses Pluto in Leo to embrace their unique voice, developing a personal brand that exudes confidence and authenticity.

Pluto in Earth Signs (Taurus, Virgo, Capricorn)

- **Energy:** Grounded, resourceful, and practical.
- **Focus:** Encourages the restructuring of workflows, monetization strategies, and long-term planning.
- **Example:** A blogger uses Pluto in Capricorn to rebuild their content calendar, prioritizing quality over quantity and aligning with their core values.

Pluto in Air Signs (Gemini, Libra, Aquarius)

- **Energy:** Intellectual, collaborative, and innovative.
- **Focus:** Inspires creators to rethink communication strategies and foster meaningful connections.
- **Example:** A podcaster uses Pluto in Gemini to create deep, insightful conversations about social change.

Pluto in Water Signs (Cancer, Scorpio, Pisces)

- **Energy:** Emotional, intuitive, and healing.
- **Focus:** Supports the exploration of vulnerability, emotional depth, and transformative storytelling.
- **Example:** A filmmaker uses Pluto in Scorpio to create a documentary that addresses taboo topics with sensitivity and courage.

How Pluto Influences Content Strategy

Pluto's influence challenges creators to confront their current strategies, shed what no longer aligns, and embrace new approaches that are deeply impactful and sustainable. Here's how its transformative energy manifests in content creation:

1. Reassessing Your Purpose

Pluto urges creators to connect with their core purpose, shedding superficial motivations and focusing on work that aligns with their values and vision.

- **Strategies:**
    - Reflect on why you started creating content and whether your current strategy aligns with that purpose.
    - Identify areas where you may have strayed from your vision due to external pressures or trends.
    - Focus on long-term impact rather than short-term gains.
- **Example:** A wellness influencer shifts their focus from trending challenges to creating content that promotes deep, sustainable well-being.

2. Letting Go of What No Longer Serves

Pluto's energy supports the process of releasing outdated practices, platforms, or strategies that no longer align with your goals.

- **Strategies:**
    - Audit your content library to identify outdated or underperforming pieces and either refresh or archive them.
    - Reevaluate your platforms and focus on those that resonate most with your audience and strengths.
    - Streamline your workflow to eliminate unnecessary steps or tools.
- **Example:** A YouTuber discontinues a series that no longer excites them, redirecting their energy toward a new, more fulfilling project.

3. Embracing Transformation

Pluto encourages creators to embrace significant changes, whether it's rebranding, exploring a new niche, or pivoting their business model.

- **Strategies:**
    - Use Pluto transits to plan major shifts, such as a brand overhaul or new product launch.
    - Embrace feedback from your audience to inform your transformation.
    - Approach change with curiosity and an open mind, viewing it as an opportunity for growth.

- **Example:** A lifestyle blogger rebrands as a sustainability advocate, shifting their focus to content that aligns with their personal values.

4. Exploring Depth and Authenticity

Pluto inspires creators to go beyond surface-level content, addressing deeper themes that resonate on an emotional or intellectual level.

- **Strategies:**
    - Create content that tackles complex or underrepresented topics in your niche.
    - Use storytelling to share personal experiences, challenges, or growth journeys.
    - Focus on quality over quantity, producing fewer but more impactful pieces.
- **Example:** A writer publishes a series of essays exploring the intersection of creativity and mental health, sharing their own experiences with vulnerability and insight.

Harnessing Pluto's Energy in Content Creation

To fully leverage Pluto's transformative energy, creators must embrace its intensity and use it as a catalyst for meaningful change. Here's how:

1. Conduct a Content Audit

Pluto's influence encourages deep reflection. Use this energy to evaluate your existing content and identify areas for improvement or transformation.

- **Tip:** Analyze your metrics to determine which pieces resonate most with your audience and why. Use these insights to refine your strategy.

2. Focus on Depth and Impact

Pluto thrives on depth and transformation. Prioritize content that challenges norms, sparks conversation, or inspires change.

- **Tip:** Experiment with formats like long-form articles, documentaries, or in-depth podcasts to explore complex themes.

3. Embrace Vulnerability

Pluto's energy supports authenticity and honesty. Share your personal growth, challenges, or lessons learned to foster a deeper connection with your audience.

- **Tip:** Use storytelling to humanize your brand and build trust with your audience.

4. Prepare for Challenges

Pluto's transformative process often involves confronting challenges or setbacks. Approach these moments as opportunities for growth.

- **Tip:** Practice resilience and adaptability, using obstacles as stepping stones toward greater clarity and alignment.

Tools to Support Pluto's Energy
1. Analytics Platforms

- **Google Analytics or YouTube Studio:** Evaluate your content's performance and identify trends that inform your strategy.

2. Content Management Tools

- **Notion or Trello:** Organize your content audit, plan new projects, and track your transformation process.

3. Reflection Tools

- **Journaling Apps or Notebooks:** Document your creative journey, noting areas of growth and transformation.

Real-Life Applications of Pluto Energy

- **Example 1:** A fashion influencer experiencing a Pluto transit in Capricorn rebrands as a sustainable fashion advocate, aligning their content with their values and audience interests.
- **Example 2:** A filmmaker uses Pluto in Scorpio to produce a groundbreaking documentary on social justice, combining personal narratives with powerful visuals.

Final Thoughts
Pluto's transformative energy offers content creators the opportunity to evolve, align with their purpose, and create work that resonates deeply. By embracing its lessons, letting go of outdated strategies, and exploring new approaches, creators can build a foundation for long-term success and impact. While Pluto's influence may feel intense, its power lies in its ability to guide creators toward their most authentic and empowered selves.

Chapter 23: Eclipses – Harnessing Powerful Shifts for Content Releases

Eclipses are some of the most powerful celestial events in astrology, marking periods of significant transformation, revelation, and redirection. Often seen as cosmic resets, eclipses magnify the energy of the New Moon (solar eclipse) or Full Moon (lunar eclipse), accelerating changes and pushing individuals and creators to realign with their true path. For content creators, eclipses offer unique opportunities to release outdated strategies, embrace fresh perspectives, and make impactful launches that align with their audience's needs and desires.

This chapter explores the influence of eclipses on content creation, offering insights into how to harness their potent energy for innovative releases, transformative rebranding, and strategic resets.

Understanding Eclipses in Astrology

Eclipses occur when the Sun, Moon, and Earth align, blocking light and creating a powerful energetic shift. Their astrological significance stems from their ability to illuminate hidden truths, catalyze transformation, and set the stage for new beginnings or closures.

Solar Eclipses (New Moon Eclipses)

- **Energy:** Fresh starts, opportunities, and new directions.
- **Focus:** Ideal for launching projects, setting intentions, and embracing new beginnings.
- **Example:** A content creator uses a solar eclipse to debut a new series or product line, aligning with the eclipse's energizing and forward-focused energy.

Lunar Eclipses (Full Moon Eclipses)

- **Energy:** Culminations, revelations, and emotional breakthroughs.
- **Focus:** Perfect for releasing outdated practices, gaining clarity, and wrapping up significant projects.
- **Example:** A creator uses a lunar eclipse to reflect on their content strategy, letting go of what no longer aligns and making space for growth.

Eclipse Seasons

Eclipses occur in pairs or trios over a period of a few weeks, known as an **eclipse season**, which happens twice a year. These periods amplify the energy of transformation, making them pivotal for creators seeking to pivot or level up.

The Role of Eclipses in Content Creation

Eclipses challenge creators to embrace change, confront what isn't working, and take bold steps toward alignment and authenticity. Key themes include:

- **Revelation:** Eclipses uncover hidden truths, helping creators identify blind spots or untapped opportunities.
- **Realignment:** They push creators to pivot or refine their strategies to align with their purpose and audience.
- **Momentum:** Eclipses often create a sense of urgency, accelerating timelines and bringing significant shifts.
- **Emotional Resonance:** Their heightened energy fosters deep emotional connections, making content more impactful.

How Eclipses Influence Content Releases

Eclipses magnify the energy of new beginnings or closures, making them ideal for strategically timed content launches or resets. Here's how they can enhance specific aspects of content creation:

1. Launching New Projects (Solar Eclipses)

Solar eclipses are like cosmic doorways, inviting creators to embrace bold ideas and take action on new opportunities.

- **Strategies:**
    - Plan launches that signify a fresh start, such as rebranding, introducing a new series, or debuting a product line.
    - Use the eclipse's energy to set ambitious goals and take decisive action.
    - Focus on projects that align with your long-term vision and values.
- **Example:** A fitness influencer launches a wellness program during a solar eclipse, capitalizing on the energy of renewal and growth.

2. Reflecting and Releasing (Lunar Eclipses)

Lunar eclipses encourage introspection and closure, making them perfect for evaluating strategies and releasing outdated practices.

- **Strategies:**
    - Conduct a content audit to identify underperforming pieces and decide whether to refresh, repurpose, or retire them.
    - Reflect on your audience's evolving needs and adjust your approach accordingly.
    - Use the eclipse's emotional energy to share vulnerable or reflective content, fostering deeper connections.
- **Example:** A blogger writes a heartfelt farewell post to an outdated niche, signaling their transition to a new focus area.

3. Embracing Transformation

Eclipses often bring unexpected shifts, challenging creators to adapt and grow. Their energy supports bold pivots and transformative changes.

- **Strategies:**
    - Rebrand or revamp your platform to reflect your current goals and vision.
    - Experiment with new formats, themes, or platforms to expand your reach.
    - Use eclipse seasons to embrace risks that push your creative boundaries.
- **Example:** A content creator transitions from short-form videos to long-form documentaries during an eclipse season, signaling their commitment to deeper storytelling.

4. Amplifying Emotional Impact

The heightened energy of eclipses fosters deep emotional resonance, making it a powerful time for storytelling and audience engagement.

- **Strategies:**
  - Share personal stories or content that reflects the collective themes of the eclipse (e.g., transformation, closure, or new beginnings).
  - Use visuals and narratives that evoke strong emotions, such as hope, resilience, or reflection.
  - Engage your audience with interactive content, such as live Q&A sessions or polls.
- **Example:** A creator releases a video series on overcoming challenges during a lunar eclipse, tapping into the eclipse's emotionally charged energy.

Harnessing Eclipse Energy in Content Creation

To align with the transformative energy of eclipses, creators should approach these periods with intention, reflection, and flexibility. Here's how to make the most of their influence:

1. Plan Strategically

Eclipses are not random; they follow predictable cycles in pairs or trios. Use an astrology calendar to identify upcoming eclipses and plan key projects or evaluations around them.

- **Tip:** Reserve solar eclipses for beginnings and lunar eclipses for closures or reflections.

2. Stay Flexible

Eclipses often bring surprises, so approach these periods with adaptability and openness to change.

- **Tip:** Build buffer time into your schedule to accommodate unexpected shifts or opportunities.

3. Reflect and Realign

Eclipses provide clarity, making them ideal for reevaluating your goals and strategies.

- **Tip:** Journal or meditate during eclipse seasons to gain insights into what needs to change or evolve in your work.

4. Take Bold Steps

Eclipses encourage decisive action. Use their energy to make courageous choices that align with your long-term vision.

- **Tip:** Don't shy away from risks if they feel aligned with your values and goals.

Tools to Leverage Eclipse Energy
1. Planning Tools

- **Astrology Calendars:** Track eclipse dates and their astrological significance.
- **Project Management Tools (Trello, Notion):** Plan launches or evaluations around eclipse seasons.

2. Reflection Tools

- **Journaling Apps or Notebooks:** Document your insights and shifts during eclipse seasons.
- **Meditation Apps (Calm, Insight Timer):** Use guided meditations to connect with your intuition.

3. Analytics Platforms

- **Google Analytics, YouTube Studio:** Evaluate performance metrics during lunar eclipses to inform future strategies.

Real-Life Applications of Eclipse Energy

- **Example 1:** A lifestyle blogger uses a solar eclipse to launch a sustainability-focused rebrand, aligning with their evolving values and audience interests.
- **Example 2:** A filmmaker reflects on their body of work during a lunar eclipse, identifying themes to explore in future projects.

Final Thoughts
Eclipses are powerful cosmic events that offer content creators opportunities for transformation, growth, and alignment. By understanding their influence and timing key actions with their energy, creators can harness these celestial shifts to refresh their strategies, deepen their impact, and align with their highest vision. Whether launching a new project, reflecting on your journey, or embracing bold changes, eclipses remind us of the power of transformation and the importance of staying true to our authentic path.

Chapter 24: Solar Flares – Maximizing Periods of High Energy

Solar flares are powerful bursts of energy released from the Sun's surface, often accompanied by coronal mass ejections (CMEs) that send charged particles hurtling through space. In astrology and metaphysics, solar flares are considered catalysts of high-energy surges, impacting human emotions, thought processes, and creativity. For content creators, these periods can bring heightened energy, bursts of inspiration, and opportunities to push forward on major projects—if properly harnessed.

In this chapter, we explore the astrological and symbolic significance of solar flares, their effects on creativity and focus, and how content creators can align their strategies to maximize productivity and innovation during these high-energy periods.

The Significance of Solar Flares

Solar flares represent a surge of solar energy that affects not only Earth's electromagnetic field but also human biofields and mental states. Metaphorically, they signify heightened activity, rapid transformation, and bursts of inspiration. These periods are ideal for creative breakthroughs, rapid action, and energizing your projects.

Key Themes of Solar Flares:

1. **Increased Energy:** Solar flares bring a sense of urgency, motivation, and drive, making them ideal for high-intensity work.
2. **Clarity and Focus:** The energy can clear mental blocks, offering fresh perspectives and insights.
3. **Emotional Intensity:** While solar flares can heighten creativity, they may also amplify emotions, requiring balance and grounding.
4. **Rapid Transformation:** These periods encourage quick decisions, adaptability, and embracing new opportunities.

How Solar Flares Impact Content Creation

The intense energy of solar flares can amplify productivity and creativity when channeled effectively. However, their influence can also overwhelm or scatter focus if not managed properly. Here's how they manifest in content creation:

1. Heightened Creativity and Inspiration

Solar flares ignite bursts of creative energy, making them ideal for brainstorming, generating ideas, or experimenting with new formats.

- **Example:** A content creator suddenly gets an inspired idea for a unique series during a solar flare event, quickly drafting a plan and executing the first piece.

2. Increased Drive and Productivity

The high-energy atmosphere encourages action, making it easier to tackle ambitious projects or complete tasks with urgency.

- **Example:** A blogger uses the momentum of a solar flare to write and schedule multiple posts in one sitting, completing weeks' worth of content in a single day.

3. Emotional Amplification

While solar flares can bring clarity, they may also amplify emotions, potentially leading to impulsivity or overreaction.

- **Example:** A creator feels frustrated by minor setbacks during a solar flare but channels that intensity into creating a powerful, emotionally charged video.

4. Rapid Shifts and Transformations

Solar flares often bring sudden opportunities or changes, requiring flexibility and quick decision-making.

- **Example:** A brand reaches out with a last-minute collaboration offer, and the creator uses the solar flare energy to pivot their schedule and deliver high-quality results.

Strategies for Maximizing Solar Flare Energy

To fully harness the energy of solar flares, content creators must strike a balance between productivity and mindfulness. Here are actionable strategies:

1. Plan High-Energy Tasks

Leverage solar flare periods for tasks that require focus, creativity, or physical energy, such as brainstorming, video production, or launching campaigns.

- **Action Plan:**
  - Prioritize your most ambitious or time-sensitive tasks during these periods.
  - Break larger projects into manageable segments to avoid feeling overwhelmed.
  - Use time-blocking techniques to stay organized and maintain focus.

2. Embrace Spontaneity

Solar flares often spark unexpected ideas or opportunities. Be open to pivoting your plans and experimenting with fresh approaches.

- **Action Plan:**
  - Keep a notebook or digital app handy to capture spontaneous ideas.
  - Allow flexibility in your schedule for impromptu creative sessions.
  - Test new formats, platforms, or collaborations during this high-energy phase.

3. Ground Your Energy

The intensity of solar flares can sometimes lead to burnout or scattered focus. Grounding practices help maintain balance and channel energy productively.

- **Action Plan:**
  - Incorporate mindfulness practices, such as meditation or deep breathing, to stay centered.
  - Use physical activity, like yoga or walking, to release excess energy.
  - Limit multitasking to avoid overwhelm.

4. Monitor Emotional Responses

While solar flares can fuel creativity, they may also amplify emotions. Awareness of your emotional state can help you navigate challenges constructively.

- **Action Plan:**
  - Pause before reacting to setbacks or challenges, ensuring your responses are thoughtful.
  - Channel heightened emotions into creative outlets, such as storytelling, journaling, or art.

    ◦ Communicate openly and clearly with collaborators to avoid misunderstandings.

5. Optimize Timing for Engagement

Solar flares may also affect collective energy, increasing audience receptivity to emotionally charged or innovative content.

- **Action Plan:**
  - ◦ Time major content releases during solar flare periods to align with heightened audience engagement.
  - ◦ Focus on content that inspires or energizes your audience, such as motivational messages or bold visuals.
  - ◦ Use analytics tools to track audience responses and refine your strategy.

Content Ideas for Solar Flare Periods

Harness the creative momentum of solar flares by focusing on impactful, high-energy content. Here are some ideas:

1. **Inspirational Posts:** Share stories of resilience, growth, or transformation to resonate with heightened emotions.
2. **Interactive Content:** Host live Q&A sessions, polls, or challenges to engage with your energized audience.
3. **Innovative Projects:** Experiment with new formats, such as AR filters, immersive storytelling, or collaborative campaigns.
4. **Empowering Messages:** Create motivational videos or graphics that uplift and inspire your community.

Tools to Support High-Energy Productivity

1. Productivity Tools

- **Trello or Notion:** Organize your tasks and ideas during solar flare surges.
- **Pomodoro Timers:** Maintain focus and avoid burnout with structured work intervals.

2. Creative Tools

- **Procreate or Adobe Creative Suite:** Bring your spontaneous ideas to life with advanced design and editing tools.
- **Brainstorming Apps (Miro, MindMeister):** Capture and organize ideas during bursts of creativity.

3. Mindfulness Tools

- **Calm or Insight Timer:** Incorporate grounding practices to stay balanced.
- **Movement Apps (Yoga Studio, Strava):** Channel excess energy into physical activity.

Real-Life Applications of Solar Flare Energy

- **Example 1:** A fitness influencer uses a solar flare event to shoot a week's worth of workout videos, channeling the high-energy atmosphere into dynamic and engaging content.
- **Example 2:** A digital artist leverages the clarity of a solar flare to complete an ambitious series of illustrations, bringing a long-standing project to fruition.

Potential Challenges and How to Navigate Them
1. Overwhelm
The intensity of solar flares may lead to overstimulation or difficulty focusing.

- **Solution:** Break tasks into smaller steps and take regular breaks to reset your energy.

2. Impulsivity
Heightened emotions during solar flares may lead to rushed decisions.

- **Solution:** Pause and reflect before making major choices, ensuring they align with your goals.

3. Burnout
Prolonged high-energy activity can deplete your resources.

- **Solution:** Balance productivity with self-care, prioritizing rest and rejuvenation.

Final Thoughts
Solar flares are potent periods of high energy, offering content creators unique opportunities for creativity, productivity, and transformation. By aligning with their influence, creators can harness bursts of inspiration, tackle ambitious projects, and connect more deeply with their audience. While their intensity may bring challenges, grounding practices and mindful strategies can help channel this energy into impactful, high-quality work.

Chapter 25: Moon Phases – Timing Content for Optimal Engagement

The Moon, with its rhythmic waxing and waning, exerts a profound influence on our emotions, energy levels, and decision-making. In astrology, the Moon governs intuition, creativity, and cycles of growth and release. For content creators, aligning with the Moon's phases provides a natural framework for planning, creating, and launching content that resonates deeply with their audience. Each phase of the Moon offers unique energies that can be harnessed to optimize engagement, enhance creativity, and align with the rhythms of both personal and collective energy.

This chapter explores the significance of the Moon's phases in content creation, detailing how to leverage each phase for maximum impact, emotional resonance, and productivity.

Understanding the Moon's Phases

The Moon completes its cycle approximately every 29.5 days, moving through eight distinct phases, each carrying unique energetic qualities. These phases are divided into two primary cycles:

1. **Waxing Cycle (New Moon to Full Moon):** A period of growth, expansion, and action.
2. **Waning Cycle (Full Moon to New Moon):** A time for reflection, refinement, and release.

The Eight Moon Phases:

1. **New Moon:** A time of beginnings and setting intentions.
2. **Waxing Crescent:** Building momentum and nurturing ideas.
3. **First Quarter:** Taking decisive action and overcoming challenges.
4. **Waxing Gibbous:** Refining and preparing for culmination.
5. **Full Moon:** Culmination, visibility, and heightened emotions.
6. **Waning Gibbous:** Sharing insights and reflecting on achievements.
7. **Last Quarter:** Releasing what no longer serves and reassessing goals.
8. **Waning Crescent:** Resting, restoring, and preparing for the next cycle.

How Moon Phases Influence Content Creation

Each phase of the Moon offers specific energies that can guide the content creation process. By aligning your efforts with these phases, you can optimize your workflow, connect more deeply with your audience, and enhance engagement.

1. New Moon: Setting Intentions

The New Moon marks the beginning of the lunar cycle, representing new beginnings and fresh ideas. This phase is ideal for planning and setting intentions for upcoming projects.

- **Content Strategy:**
    - Brainstorm ideas and outline your content calendar.
    - Set goals for the month or upcoming cycle.
    - Introduce new themes, campaigns, or projects.
- **Example:** A creator launches a teaser campaign for an upcoming product, building anticipation during this phase of quiet intention-setting.

2. Waxing Crescent: Building Momentum

As the Moon begins to grow, the Waxing Crescent phase brings energy and focus. This is the time to nurture your ideas and start taking action.

- **Content Strategy:**
    - Begin creating content, such as drafting blog posts or recording videos.
    - Lay the groundwork for larger projects, focusing on foundational tasks.
    - Engage your audience with hints or previews of what's to come.
- **Example:** A content creator shares behind-the-scenes footage of an upcoming series, sparking curiosity and building excitement.

3. First Quarter: Taking Action

The First Quarter Moon is a time of decisive action and overcoming obstacles. It encourages creators to push forward with confidence and address challenges head-on.

- **Content Strategy:**
    - Execute your plans and publish your first major pieces of content.
    - Address any roadblocks or refine your approach as needed.
    - Use bold, impactful messaging to capture attention.
- **Example:** A social media influencer debuts the first post of a new campaign, using bold visuals and clear calls to action to engage their audience.

4. Waxing Gibbous: Refining and Perfecting

As the Moon approaches fullness, the Waxing Gibbous phase is a time for refinement and preparation. This phase is about perfecting your content and ensuring it's ready for maximum impact.

- **Content Strategy:**
  - Finalize and polish content, such as editing videos or proofreading articles.
  - Test your strategies, gathering feedback from collaborators or small groups.
  - Plan the details of your major launches or releases.
- **Example:** A podcaster finalizes their episode schedule and ensures all promotional materials are ready ahead of a major release.

5. Full Moon: Culmination and Visibility

The Full Moon is the peak of the lunar cycle, symbolizing culmination, visibility, and heightened emotions. This is the ideal time for launching major projects, sharing impactful content, and engaging with your audience.

- **Content Strategy:**
  - Release your most important or visible content, such as a product launch or major campaign.
  - Host live events, webinars, or Q&A sessions to maximize engagement.
  - Share content that evokes strong emotions or tells a compelling story.
- **Example:** A creator releases a highly anticipated eBook, hosting a live launch event to connect with their audience and celebrate the culmination of their efforts.

6. Waning Gibbous: Reflecting and Sharing

As the Moon begins to wane, the Waning Gibbous phase encourages reflection and the sharing of insights. It's a time to assess your successes and gather feedback.

- **Content Strategy:**
  - Share educational or reflective content, such as tutorials or case studies.
  - Engage your audience by asking for feedback or testimonials.
  - Analyze performance metrics and identify areas for improvement.
- **Example:** A YouTuber posts a "lessons learned" video, reflecting on their recent project and inviting audience interaction.

7. Last Quarter: Releasing and Reassessing

The Last Quarter Moon is about letting go and reassessing your goals. It's a time for decluttering, simplifying, and preparing for the next cycle.

- **Content Strategy:**
    - Archive or retire outdated content that no longer aligns with your vision.
    - Reevaluate your strategies and identify areas for growth.
    - Focus on smaller, maintenance tasks, such as updating your website or organizing files.
- **Example:** A creator conducts a content audit, removing posts that no longer reflect their brand and updating older pieces with fresh insights.

8. Waning Crescent: Resting and Restoring

The Waning Crescent Moon signals the end of the cycle, encouraging rest, restoration, and introspection. This is a time to recharge and prepare for the next New Moon.

- **Content Strategy:**
    - Take a break from creating new content and focus on self-care.
    - Reflect on your progress and celebrate your achievements.
    - Plan for the upcoming cycle, revisiting your goals and vision.
- **Example:** A content creator shares a gratitude post, thanking their audience for their support and hinting at what's to come in the next cycle.

Tips for Aligning with Moon Phases

1. **Track the Moon Cycle:** Use an astrology app or lunar calendar to track the Moon's phases and plan your content accordingly.
2. **Set Intentions Regularly:** Align your monthly goals with the New Moon, using this phase to establish your focus for the cycle.
3. **Use the Moon's Energy:** Plan high-energy tasks, like launches or events, during the Full Moon, and reserve reflective tasks for the waning phases.
4. **Engage Your Audience:** Share content that resonates with the collective energy of the Moon phase, such as motivational posts during the waxing cycle or reflective pieces during the waning cycle.

Tools to Support Moon-Phase Planning

1. **Lunar Apps:** Use apps like Moon Phase Calendar or The Moon Calendar to track phases and plan accordingly.
2. **Project Management Tools:** Use Notion or Asana to align your content calendar with the Moon's cycles.
3. **Analytics Platforms:** Track audience engagement patterns to determine which phases resonate most with your community.

Real-Life Applications of Moon Phases

- **Example 1:** A fitness influencer launches a 30-day challenge during the New Moon, capitalizing on the collective energy of new beginnings.
- **Example 2:** A blogger reflects on their year during the Waning Crescent, sharing personal insights and setting intentions for the next cycle.

Final Thoughts

The Moon's phases offer a natural rhythm for content creation, guiding creators through cycles of growth, reflection, and renewal. By aligning with these phases, you can optimize your workflow, deepen your connection with your audience, and create content that resonates on a more intuitive level. Whether you're brainstorming during the New Moon, launching during the Full Moon, or reflecting during the waning phases, the Moon provides a cosmic framework for consistent and impactful content creation.

Chapter 26: The New Moon – Initiating Fresh Content Ideas

The New Moon marks the beginning of the lunar cycle, symbolizing new beginnings, fresh energy, and the setting of intentions. In astrology, this phase represents a clean slate—a time to plant seeds for the future and focus on growth. For content creators, the New Moon is the perfect opportunity to brainstorm innovative ideas, outline new projects, and align their efforts with long-term goals. It is a period of quiet energy, ideal for introspection and strategic planning.

This chapter explores the significance of the New Moon in content creation, detailing how to harness its energy to initiate fresh ideas, build momentum, and lay the groundwork for impactful and aligned content.

The Astrological Significance of the New Moon

The New Moon occurs when the Sun and Moon align in the same zodiac sign, blending their energies to create a powerful moment of synergy. In astrology, the New Moon's qualities include:

- **Beginnings:** It represents a starting point, making it ideal for setting intentions.
- **Clarity:** The absence of moonlight allows for introspection and focus.
- **Potential:** The energy is fertile, supporting the growth of new ideas and projects.
- **Zodiac Influence:** Each New Moon is flavored by the traits of the zodiac sign in which it occurs, adding a unique layer to its energy.

For content creators, the New Moon offers a chance to reset, reflect, and strategize, ensuring that their efforts are intentional and aligned with their goals.

How the New Moon Influences Content Creation

The New Moon's energy is subtle but powerful, supporting creators in the early stages of their projects. Here's how it impacts key aspects of content creation:

1. Brainstorming New Ideas

The New Moon's fresh energy inspires creativity and innovation, making it an excellent time to generate ideas for content.

- **Example:** A creator uses the New Moon to brainstorm a new podcast series, focusing on unique themes and episode structures.
- **Tip:** Dedicate time to freewriting or mind mapping to explore different angles and perspectives.

2. Setting Intentions

The New Moon encourages creators to establish clear intentions and goals for the coming month or cycle.

- **Example:** A social media manager sets an intention to increase audience engagement by focusing on interactive posts and live Q&A sessions.
- **Tip:** Write down your goals for the lunar cycle, including specific metrics or milestones you want to achieve.

3. Aligning with Your Vision

This phase supports introspection, helping creators realign their work with their values and long-term objectives.

- **Example:** A lifestyle influencer uses the New Moon to revisit their content pillars, ensuring they align with their brand identity.
- **Tip:** Reflect on your overarching vision and how your current projects contribute to it.

4. Planning and Outlining Projects

The New Moon's quiet energy is ideal for strategic planning and organizing your ideas into actionable steps.

- **Example:** A writer outlines a new eBook during the New Moon, breaking it into chapters and setting a writing schedule.
- **Tip:** Use this phase to create content calendars or project plans, focusing on high-level strategies.

Steps to Harness New Moon Energy for Content Creation

To fully leverage the New Moon's potential, creators should approach this phase with intention, focus, and creativity. Here are actionable steps:

1. Create a Ritual for Brainstorming

The New Moon is a time for quiet reflection and creativity. Set the mood for brainstorming by creating a ritual that enhances focus and inspiration.

- **Action Plan:**
    - Choose a calming environment, free from distractions.
    - Use tools like a notebook, whiteboard, or brainstorming app.
    - Set a timer for uninterrupted creative exploration.
- **Example:** Light a candle or play instrumental music to create a serene atmosphere while brainstorming.

2. Set Clear Intentions

Use the New Moon's energy to define your goals and align them with your overall vision.

- **Action Plan:**
    - Write down three to five intentions for the lunar cycle.
    - Focus on goals that are specific, measurable, and achievable.
    - Keep your intentions visible, such as on your desk or in a journal.
- **Example:** A content creator sets the intention to grow their YouTube channel by publishing four high-quality videos in the next month.

3. Outline Your Content Calendar

The New Moon is the ideal time to map out your projects for the month, aligning your efforts with your goals.

- **Action Plan:**
    - Use project management tools like Notion, Asana, or Trello to organize your ideas.
    - Schedule key tasks, such as brainstorming, production, and publishing, throughout the lunar cycle.
    - Highlight important dates, such as launches or collaborations.
- **Example:** A blogger plans weekly themes for their posts, ensuring each aligns with their monthly goals.

4. Reflect on Your Audience

The New Moon's introspective energy is perfect for reconnecting with your audience's needs and preferences.

- **Action Plan:**
    - Review audience analytics to identify trends or gaps in engagement.
    - Conduct polls or surveys to gather insights into what your audience wants to see.
    - Use the feedback to shape your content strategy for the coming weeks.
- **Example:** A creator sends a survey to their newsletter subscribers, asking for input on upcoming topics or formats.

5. Experiment with New Formats

This phase is ideal for exploring new content formats or platforms that align with your goals.

- **Action Plan:**
    - Test a new content type, such as live streams, short videos, or interactive posts.
    - Focus on projects that excite you or challenge your creative boundaries.
    - Monitor audience responses to gauge the format's effectiveness.
- **Example:** A digital artist experiments with time-lapse videos of their work, sharing them on TikTok to reach a new audience.

Content Ideas for the New Moon

1. **Goal-Setting Posts:** Share your intentions for the month, inspiring your audience to set their own.
2. **Behind-the-Scenes Content:** Give a sneak peek into upcoming projects or processes.
3. **Motivational Messages:** Create posts or videos that encourage fresh starts and new beginnings.
4. **Interactive Content:** Engage your audience with polls, Q&A sessions, or discussions about their goals.
5. **Personal Reflections:** Share your creative journey and how you plan to grow in the coming weeks.

Tools to Enhance Your New Moon Workflow

1. **Brainstorming Tools:** Use apps like Miro or MindMeister for idea mapping.
2. **Project Management Platforms:** Organize your plans with tools like Trello, Notion, or Monday.com.
3. **Lunar Apps:** Track New Moon dates and their zodiac influences using apps like Moon Phase Calendar or The Moon Calendar.

Real-Life Applications of New Moon Energy

- **Example 1:** A wellness influencer uses the New Moon to launch a new yoga series, aligning each session with themes of intention and renewal.
- **Example 2:** A business coach outlines a month-long social media campaign during the New Moon, focusing on empowering entrepreneurs to embrace change.

Potential Challenges and How to Overcome Them

1. Lack of Clarity

The quiet energy of the New Moon may feel unfocused or overwhelming.

- **Solution:** Break your brainstorming into smaller sessions, focusing on one goal or theme at a time.

2. Overambition

The excitement of fresh starts can lead to setting too many goals.

- **Solution:** Prioritize a few key intentions that align with your long-term vision and values.

3. Resistance to Change

Starting something new can feel daunting or uncertain.

- **Solution:** Focus on small, actionable steps that build confidence and momentum.

Final Thoughts

The New Moon offers a powerful opportunity to initiate fresh content ideas, set meaningful intentions, and align your efforts with your long-term goals. By embracing its energy, content creators can approach their projects with renewed focus, creativity, and purpose. Whether brainstorming innovative concepts, planning your calendar, or reflecting on your audience's needs, the New Moon is the perfect time to plant seeds for future growth and success.

Chapter 27: The Full Moon – Reaping Rewards and Peak Visibility

The Full Moon represents the culmination of the lunar cycle, symbolizing completion, celebration, and heightened energy. In astrology, it is a time of illumination, visibility, and emotional intensity, as the Moon's light brings clarity and amplifies both successes and challenges. For content creators, the Full Moon is a powerful phase for releasing impactful content, engaging with audiences, and reflecting on accomplishments. It's a time to celebrate your progress, reap the rewards of your efforts, and gain maximum visibility.

In this chapter, we explore how to harness the Full Moon's energy to amplify your content, connect with your audience, and achieve peak engagement. We also examine how to use this phase for reflection and planning your next steps.

The Astrological Significance of the Full Moon

The Full Moon occurs when the Sun and Moon are in opposition, creating a perfect balance between light and dark. This alignment brings heightened energy, emotional clarity, and opportunities to bring your intentions to fruition. Key qualities of the Full Moon include:

- **Culmination:** The Full Moon marks the peak of the lunar cycle, making it ideal for celebrating achievements and sharing results.
- **Illumination:** It brings clarity, highlighting both successes and areas for improvement.
- **Visibility:** The Full Moon's energy amplifies attention and engagement, making it a powerful time for launches and announcements.
- **Emotional Intensity:** This phase can heighten emotions, making it a time for authentic and vulnerable content.

For content creators, the Full Moon offers a unique opportunity to maximize their impact, connect with their audience, and showcase their best work.

How the Full Moon Influences Content Creation

The Full Moon's energy encourages creators to step into the spotlight, embrace their successes, and share their work with the world. Here's how this phase impacts content creation:

1. Amplified Visibility and Engagement

The Full Moon's heightened energy draws attention, making it an ideal time to release high-impact content or launch major projects.

- **Example:** A creator times the release of a long-anticipated video during the Full Moon, leveraging its energy to maximize views and shares.
- **Tip:** Plan your most visible and engaging posts or campaigns for this phase.

2. Celebrating Achievements

The Full Moon is a time of culmination and celebration, offering an opportunity to reflect on your progress and share your successes.

- **Example:** A content creator posts a milestone update, thanking their audience for helping them reach a specific goal.
- **Tip:** Use this phase to express gratitude and build a deeper connection with your community.

3. Emotional Connection with Your Audience

The Full Moon's emotional intensity encourages authentic and heartfelt content, fostering deeper connections with your audience.

- **Example:** A lifestyle blogger shares a vulnerable post about overcoming challenges, resonating with their audience on a personal level.
- **Tip:** Share stories or insights that evoke strong emotions, such as joy, inspiration, or resilience.

4. Gaining Clarity and Insight

The Full Moon illuminates both successes and areas for improvement, offering valuable insights for refining your strategy.

- **Example:** A podcaster reviews audience feedback during the Full Moon, identifying themes or topics to explore in future episodes.
- **Tip:** Use this phase to analyze your content performance and gather feedback.

Strategies for Harnessing Full Moon Energy

To fully leverage the Full Moon's potential, approach this phase with intention, focus, and celebration. Here are actionable strategies:

1. Time Major Releases for Maximum Impact

The Full Moon's energy enhances visibility, making it the ideal time for high-impact launches or announcements.

- **Action Plan:**
    - Schedule major releases, such as product launches, campaigns, or collaborations, during the Full Moon.
    - Use bold visuals, compelling headlines, and clear calls to action to capture attention.
    - Promote your content across multiple platforms to maximize reach.
- **Example:** An eCommerce brand launches a new product line during the Full Moon, pairing the release with a live event to engage their audience.

2. Celebrate and Reflect

The Full Moon is a time to acknowledge your achievements and assess your progress.

- **Action Plan:**
    - Share a milestone or success story with your audience, highlighting the journey that led to it.
    - Reflect on your recent projects, identifying what worked well and what could be improved.
    - Express gratitude to your audience, collaborators, or team for their support.
- **Example:** A content creator posts a heartfelt thank-you message after reaching a follower milestone, sharing behind-the-scenes insights about their journey.

3. Share Emotionally Resonant Content

The Full Moon's energy heightens emotions, making it a powerful time for storytelling and personal connections.

- **Action Plan:**
    - Create content that taps into universal emotions, such as hope, perseverance, or celebration.
    - Share personal stories or lessons learned, inviting your audience to reflect on their own experiences.

- Use visuals, music, or narratives that evoke strong feelings.
- **Example:** A filmmaker releases a short film about resilience during the Full Moon, using poignant storytelling to inspire their audience.

4. Engage Your Audience Actively

The Full Moon is an excellent time to interact with your audience, fostering engagement and community.

- **Action Plan:**
    - Host live events, such as Q&A sessions, webinars, or watch parties.
    - Encourage audience participation through polls, contests, or interactive content.
    - Respond to comments, messages, or feedback to strengthen connections.
- **Example:** A YouTuber hosts a live stream during the Full Moon, answering audience questions and sharing exclusive updates.

Content Ideas for the Full Moon

1. **Launch Content:** Announce new projects, products, or collaborations.
2. **Milestone Celebrations:** Share updates about achievements or progress.
3. **Emotional Storytelling:** Create posts or videos that evoke strong emotions or share personal experiences.
4. **Gratitude Posts:** Thank your audience, collaborators, or supporters.
5. **Live Events:** Host interactive sessions to connect directly with your audience.

Tools to Enhance Full Moon Content Creation

1. **Analytics Platforms:** Use tools like Google Analytics or YouTube Studio to evaluate engagement and identify high-performing content.
2. **Live Streaming Apps:** Platforms like Instagram Live, YouTube Live, or Twitch are perfect for Full Moon events.
3. **Social Media Scheduling Tools:** Tools like Buffer or Hootsuite help you schedule and promote your Full Moon content strategically.

Real-Life Applications of Full Moon Energy

- **Example 1:** A wellness influencer launches a guided meditation series during the Full Moon, aligning the content with themes of reflection and clarity.
- **Example 2:** A digital artist releases a special collection of prints, pairing the launch with a heartfelt blog post about their creative journey.

Potential Challenges and How to Overcome Them

1. Emotional Overload

The Full Moon's energy can feel overwhelming, leading to scattered focus or heightened stress.

- **Solution:** Ground yourself with mindfulness practices, such as meditation or journaling, before diving into your work.

2. Impulsivity

The heightened emotions of the Full Moon may lead to impulsive decisions or actions.

- **Solution:** Pause and reflect before making major choices, ensuring they align with your long-term goals.

3. Overcommitment

The Full Moon's energy may tempt you to take on too much, risking burnout.

- **Solution:** Prioritize a few high-impact tasks or projects, focusing on quality over quantity.

Final Thoughts

The Full Moon is a time of celebration, visibility, and emotional connection, offering content creators a powerful opportunity to amplify their impact and engage deeply with their audience. By aligning with its energy, you can release impactful content, reflect on your progress, and set the stage for future growth. Whether launching a major project, sharing a personal story, or celebrating milestones, the Full Moon encourages you to step into the spotlight and shine.

Chapter 28: Waxing Phases – Building Momentum in Creative Work

The waxing phases of the Moon, from the New Moon to the Full Moon, represent growth, progress, and building energy. In this part of the lunar cycle, the Moon gradually increases in light, symbolizing the expansion of ideas and the pursuit of goals. For content creators, the waxing phases are a time to harness this growing energy to nurture ideas, develop projects, and build momentum toward achieving their objectives.

This chapter explores the significance of the waxing phases in creative work, providing actionable strategies for aligning with this dynamic energy to enhance productivity, overcome challenges, and bring projects closer to fruition.

Understanding the Waxing Phases of the Moon

The waxing period includes three key phases, each carrying unique energetic qualities that guide the creative process:

1. **Waxing Crescent Moon:** A time for nurturing intentions and building initial momentum.
2. **First Quarter Moon:** A phase of decisive action and overcoming obstacles.
3. **Waxing Gibbous Moon:** A period of refinement, preparation, and attention to detail.

The Significance of the Waxing Phases

The waxing phases align with a natural process of growth and expansion, making them ideal for creators who want to advance their projects and lay the groundwork for success. Key qualities of these phases include:

- **Growth:** Each phase supports the steady progression of ideas and projects.
- **Action:** These phases encourage consistent effort and proactive decision-making.
- **Refinement:** The waxing energy helps creators perfect their work as they approach completion.
- **Momentum:** The increasing light of the Moon mirrors the building energy of creative work.

How the Waxing Phases Influence Content Creation

Each phase of the waxing Moon plays a distinct role in the creative process. Understanding these roles can help creators align their efforts with the lunar cycle for maximum impact.

1. Waxing Crescent Moon: Nurturing Ideas and Building Momentum

The Waxing Crescent Moon follows the New Moon, bringing a spark of inspiration and motivation to move forward. It's a time for nurturing your intentions and taking the first steps toward your goals.

- **Energy:** Optimistic, inspired, and exploratory.
- **Focus:** Building momentum, laying foundations, and gathering resources.
- **Content Strategy:**
    - Begin developing ideas outlined during the New Moon.
    - Research, plan, and organize the logistics of your projects.
    - Create teasers or preview content to spark curiosity.
- **Example:** A writer drafts the outline of a new book, focusing on themes and structure, while sharing snippets of their process on social media to engage their audience.

2. First Quarter Moon: Taking Decisive Action

The First Quarter Moon marks a turning point in the waxing cycle, bringing a surge of energy and the need for decisive action. This phase often presents challenges that require problem-solving and persistence.

- **Energy:** Focused, determined, and action-oriented.
- **Focus:** Making progress, addressing obstacles, and refining plans.
- **Content Strategy:**
    - Take tangible steps to execute your projects, such as drafting, filming, or designing.
    - Address any roadblocks or challenges with creative solutions.
    - Share updates with your audience to maintain engagement.
- **Example:** A content creator finalizes the script for a video series and begins filming, overcoming initial hurdles like technical glitches or scheduling conflicts.

3. Waxing Gibbous Moon: Refining and Perfecting

The Waxing Gibbous Moon leads up to the Full Moon, signaling a time for refinement and preparation. This phase is about polishing your work and ensuring it's ready for maximum impact.

- **Energy:** Focused, meticulous, and productive.
- **Focus:** Refining details, testing strategies, and preparing for launches.
- **Content Strategy:**
    - Edit and fine-tune your content, ensuring it aligns with your goals and audience expectations.
    - Test your strategies, gather feedback, and make necessary adjustments.

○ Plan promotional efforts to coincide with the Full Moon's peak energy.
- **Example:** A podcaster edits and schedules episodes while designing promotional graphics and testing audience engagement strategies.

Strategies for Harnessing Waxing Moon Energy

To make the most of the waxing phases, content creators should align their efforts with the Moon's growing energy, focusing on steady progress and preparation. Here are actionable strategies for each phase:

1. Waxing Crescent Phase

- **Set Milestones:** Break your goals into actionable steps and assign timelines for each.
- **Gather Resources:** Research tools, collaborators, or materials needed for your projects.
- **Engage Your Audience:** Share teasers or polls to build excitement and gather input.

2. First Quarter Phase

- **Take Bold Steps:** Focus on executing major tasks, such as drafting, filming, or designing.
- **Solve Challenges:** Address roadblocks with a problem-solving mindset.
- **Collaborate Effectively:** Work with team members or collaborators to ensure progress.

3. Waxing Gibbous Phase

- **Refine Your Work:** Edit and polish your content, paying attention to details.
- **Test Strategies:** Gather feedback from beta testers or collaborators.
- **Prepare for Launch:** Finalize your promotional materials and schedule releases for the Full Moon.

Content Ideas for the Waxing Phases

1. **Behind-the-Scenes Content:** Share your creative process with your audience, building anticipation for what's to come.
2. **Teasers and Previews:** Release snippets or trailers that give your audience a taste of your upcoming projects.
3. **Interactive Content:** Use polls, Q&A sessions, or surveys to engage your audience and refine your ideas.
4. **Work-in-Progress Updates:** Post progress updates that showcase your efforts and invite feedback.

Tools to Enhance Productivity During Waxing Phases

1. **Project Management Tools:** Use platforms like Trello, Asana, or Notion to track your progress and stay organized.
2. **Content Creation Software:** Leverage tools like Canva, Adobe Creative Suite, or Final Cut Pro to develop and refine your content.
3. **Analytics Platforms:** Use tools like Google Analytics or Instagram Insights to track audience engagement and gather feedback.

Real-Life Applications of Waxing Moon Energy

- **Example 1:** A wellness coach uses the Waxing Crescent phase to outline a new challenge, the First Quarter to film workout videos, and the Waxing Gibbous to refine their marketing strategy.
- **Example 2:** A fashion influencer plans a campaign during the Waxing Crescent, collaborates with a photographer during the First Quarter, and finalizes promotional materials during the Waxing Gibbous.

Potential Challenges and How to Overcome Them

1. Losing Momentum

The steady growth of the waxing phases requires consistent effort, which can be challenging to maintain.

- **Solution:** Set realistic goals and celebrate small victories to stay motivated.

2. Overwhelming Details

The Waxing Gibbous phase's focus on refinement may lead to perfectionism.

- **Solution:** Set clear boundaries for revisions and prioritize tasks that have the most impact.

3. Facing Obstacles

The First Quarter phase often brings challenges that require problem-solving and adaptability.

- **Solution:** Approach obstacles with flexibility and seek support from collaborators or mentors.

Final Thoughts

The waxing phases of the Moon offer a natural framework for building momentum, nurturing ideas, and advancing creative projects. By aligning with these phases, content creators can harness their energy to stay productive, overcome challenges, and refine their work for maximum impact.

Whether you're brainstorming during the Waxing Crescent, taking bold steps during the First Quarter, or perfecting your work during the Waxing Gibbous, the waxing Moon provides the inspiration and drive to bring your vision to life.

Chapter 29: Waning Phases – Reflecting and Refining Existing Content

The waning phases of the Moon, from the Full Moon to the New Moon, represent a period of reflection, release, and renewal. As the Moon's light diminishes, its energy encourages creators to slow down, assess progress, and refine their work. This phase is ideal for reviewing existing content, letting go of strategies that no longer serve, and preparing for the next cycle of creation.

In this chapter, we explore the significance of the waning phases in content creation, providing strategies to refine existing work, assess performance, and align with your long-term goals. This period of introspection and recalibration is essential for growth and sustainable success.

Understanding the Waning Phases of the Moon

The waning period includes three key phases, each offering unique opportunities for reflection and refinement:

1. **Waning Gibbous Moon:** A time for sharing insights, analyzing outcomes, and gathering feedback.
2. **Last Quarter Moon:** A phase of reassessment, release, and strategic adjustments.
3. **Waning Crescent Moon:** A period for rest, introspection, and preparation for the next cycle.

The Significance of the Waning Phases

The waning Moon aligns with a natural process of reflection and letting go, making it ideal for creators who want to refine their strategies and recharge. Key qualities of these phases include:

- **Reflection:** Assess the effectiveness of your efforts and identify areas for improvement.
- **Release:** Let go of outdated strategies, content, or projects that no longer align with your goals.
- **Preparation:** Use the quieter energy to restore and recalibrate for the next cycle.
- **Connection:** Deepen relationships with your audience by sharing insights or addressing feedback.

How the Waning Phases Influence Content Creation

Each phase of the waning Moon plays a specific role in helping creators refine their work and align with their vision.

1. Waning Gibbous Moon: Sharing and Reflecting

The Waning Gibbous Moon follows the Full Moon, bringing an energy of reflection and sharing. It's a time to analyze outcomes and gather feedback.

- **Energy:** Insightful, thoughtful, and collaborative.
- **Focus:** Sharing lessons, analyzing performance, and seeking input.
- **Content Strategy:**
    - Publish reflective content, such as case studies or lessons learned.
    - Review analytics to evaluate the performance of recent content.
    - Seek feedback from your audience or collaborators.
- **Example:** A content creator shares a blog post about their journey to achieve a recent milestone, inviting audience input on future directions.

2. Last Quarter Moon: Releasing and Reassessing

The Last Quarter Moon is a time of release and reassessment, encouraging creators to let go of what no longer serves and refine their strategies.

- **Energy:** Releasing, simplifying, and strategizing.
- **Focus:** Decluttering, revising, and realigning with your goals.
- **Content Strategy:**
    - Conduct a content audit to identify pieces that need updating or retiring.
    - Reevaluate your content pillars or focus areas to ensure alignment with your vision.
    - Simplify workflows or processes to enhance efficiency.
- **Example:** A blogger updates old posts with new information and better SEO practices, retiring outdated articles that no longer align with their niche.

3. Waning Crescent Moon: Restoring and Preparing

The Waning Crescent Moon signals the end of the cycle, encouraging rest, introspection, and preparation for the next phase of creation.

- **Energy:** Restorative, introspective, and preparatory.
- **Focus:** Resting, recharging, and setting intentions for the next cycle.
- **Content Strategy:**
    - Take a break from creating new content and focus on self-care.
    - Reflect on lessons learned during the lunar cycle.

◦ Begin outlining goals or themes for the upcoming New Moon.
- **Example:** A social media influencer pauses regular posting to focus on wellness, sharing a gratitude post with their audience and hinting at upcoming projects.

Strategies for Harnessing Waning Moon Energy

To make the most of the waning phases, content creators should embrace reflection, release, and renewal. Here are actionable strategies for each phase:

1. Waning Gibbous Phase

- **Analyze Performance:** Use analytics to evaluate the effectiveness of recent campaigns or content.
- **Engage Your Audience:** Share reflective or educational posts that invite interaction and feedback.
- **Collaborate:** Seek input from collaborators or mentors to refine your approach.

2. Last Quarter Phase

- **Declutter and Refine:** Conduct a content audit to identify what to update, repurpose, or retire.
- **Simplify Workflows:** Streamline processes and eliminate inefficiencies.
- **Realign Goals:** Reflect on whether your efforts align with your long-term vision and adjust as needed.

3. Waning Crescent Phase

- **Rest and Recharge:** Take time to focus on self-care and restoration.
- **Reflect on Lessons:** Journal about what worked well and what could be improved in the next cycle.
- **Prepare for the Future:** Begin setting intentions and brainstorming ideas for the upcoming New Moon.

Content Ideas for the Waning Phases

1. **Reflective Posts:** Share lessons learned, milestones achieved, or challenges overcome.
2. **Content Audits:** Update or repurpose older content to maintain relevance.
3. **Audience Engagement:** Ask for feedback or suggestions to shape future projects.
4. **Gratitude Posts:** Express appreciation for your audience, collaborators, or team.
5. **Behind-the-Scenes Content:** Share insights into your creative process or planning stages.

Tools to Enhance Reflection and Refinement

1. **Analytics Platforms:** Use tools like Google Analytics, YouTube Studio, or Instagram Insights to evaluate content performance.
2. **Content Management Systems:** Platforms like Notion or Trello can help you organize audits and updates.
3. **Journaling Apps:** Use apps like Day One or Penzu to document lessons learned and plan future goals.

Real-Life Applications of Waning Moon Energy

- **Example 1:** A fitness coach uses the Waning Gibbous phase to gather testimonials from their audience, the Last Quarter to refine their program offerings, and the Waning Crescent to reflect on their personal wellness journey.
- **Example 2:** A travel vlogger conducts a content audit during the Last Quarter, updating old videos with fresh thumbnails and descriptions to boost engagement.

Potential Challenges and How to Overcome Them

1. Resistance to Letting Go

It can be difficult to release content or strategies that you've invested time in, even if they're no longer effective.

- **Solution:** Focus on the long-term benefits of decluttering and realigning with your goals.

2. Overanalyzing

Reflection can lead to overanalyzing or second-guessing your decisions.

- **Solution:** Set boundaries for your review process and prioritize actionable insights.

3. Feeling Unproductive

The slower energy of the waning phases may feel unproductive compared to the waxing phases.

- **Solution:** Embrace this time as essential for restoration and strategic planning, knowing it supports future growth.

Final Thoughts

The waning phases of the Moon offer a powerful opportunity for reflection, refinement, and renewal. By aligning with this energy, content creators can assess their progress, release outdated strategies, and prepare for the next cycle of creation. Whether you're analyzing performance during the Waning Gibbous, decluttering during the Last Quarter, or resting during the Waning Crescent, these phases provide the space and insight needed for sustainable growth and success.

Chapter 30: Meteor Showers – Times of Inspiration and Fast Ideas

Meteor showers are awe-inspiring celestial events that capture humanity's imagination. In astrology and metaphysics, they symbolize bursts of inspiration, rapid ideas, and heightened creativity. Often associated with transformative energy, meteor showers offer moments when our minds are illuminated, akin to the streaks of light across the night sky. For content creators, these cosmic events signify windows of opportunity to embrace quick thinking, brainstorm bold ideas, and push creative boundaries.

In this chapter, we explore the symbolic significance of meteor showers, their influence on content creation, and how to harness their fleeting yet potent energy for impactful work. By aligning with the transformative energy of these events, creators can amplify their creativity, spark innovation, and seize inspiration as it strikes.

The Symbolism of Meteor Showers

Meteor showers are events where Earth passes through a comet's debris, causing fragments to burn brightly as they enter our atmosphere. This natural phenomenon is rich with symbolic meaning:

1. **Illumination:** Sudden flashes of insight and creativity, much like meteors lighting up the sky.
2. **Transformation:** A reminder that even fleeting moments of brilliance can leave lasting impressions.
3. **Momentum:** Meteor showers inspire quick action and dynamic movement.
4. **Magic and Wonder:** They evoke a sense of awe and possibility, encouraging creators to dream big and think outside the box.

For content creators, meteor showers are a metaphorical call to action: seize the moment, act on inspiration, and bring bold ideas to life.

How Meteor Showers Influence Content Creation

The energy of meteor showers can spark rapid bursts of creativity and innovation. Here's how these cosmic events influence the creative process:

1. Bursts of Inspiration

Meteor showers symbolize moments of clarity and inspiration, making them ideal for generating fresh ideas.

- **Example:** A creator suddenly envisions a unique concept for a new video series during a meteor shower, sketching out the idea in one sitting.
- **Tip:** Use this time to brainstorm without self-censorship, letting ideas flow freely.

2. Heightened Creativity

The dynamic energy of meteor showers encourages creators to push boundaries and experiment with new formats or styles.

- **Example:** A graphic designer experiments with bold, unconventional visuals inspired by the brilliance of meteors streaking across the sky.
- **Tip:** Embrace spontaneity and allow yourself to step outside your creative comfort zone.

3. Quick Thinking and Fast Execution

Meteor showers inspire urgency and momentum, making them perfect for acting on ideas quickly and efficiently.

- **Example:** A social media influencer capitalizes on a trending topic during a meteor shower, creating and posting content in real-time to maximize engagement.
- **Tip:** Focus on speed and agility, trusting your instincts to guide your decisions.

4. Transformative Breakthroughs

The energy of meteor showers often brings new perspectives and innovative solutions to long-standing challenges.

- **Example:** A writer finds the perfect plot twist to resolve a story conflict, inspired by the transformative energy of a meteor shower.
- **Tip:** Use this time to revisit stalled projects or brainstorm solutions to creative roadblocks.

Strategies for Harnessing Meteor Shower Energy

To fully leverage the dynamic energy of meteor showers, creators should embrace spontaneity, agility, and innovation. Here are actionable strategies:

1. Create a Brainstorming Ritual

Meteor showers are ideal for generating bold and unconventional ideas. Establish a ritual that sets the stage for creative exploration.

- **Action Plan:**
    ◦ Set aside dedicated time during the meteor shower to brainstorm.
    ◦ Create a stimulating environment with music, visuals, or lighting that evokes inspiration.
    ◦ Use tools like whiteboards, sticky notes, or brainstorming apps to capture your ideas.
- **Example:** A content creator watches a live stream of the meteor shower while sketching out concepts for a new series, drawing inspiration from the event's beauty.

2. Act on Impulses

The fleeting nature of meteor showers encourages quick action. Use this time to act on ideas that excite or challenge you.

- **Action Plan:**
    ◦ Identify one or two ideas to develop immediately, focusing on speed rather than perfection.
    ◦ Create rapid prototypes, drafts, or outlines to capture your vision.
    ◦ Share your work-in-progress with collaborators or your audience for feedback.
- **Example:** A photographer takes advantage of the meteor shower to shoot nighttime landscapes, editing and posting a gallery the same evening.

3. Experiment Boldly

Meteor showers are a time for breaking routines and exploring new creative territories. Embrace the unexpected and take risks.

- **Action Plan:**
    ◦ Experiment with a new format, medium, or style that you've been hesitant to try.
    ◦ Collaborate with other creators to blend perspectives and generate fresh ideas.
    ◦ Use the cosmic energy as a theme or inspiration for your work.

- **Example:** A musician creates an ambient track inspired by the meteor shower, incorporating celestial sounds and dynamic crescendos.

4. Reflect on Your Inspiration

While the energy of meteor showers is fast-paced, it's also important to reflect on the ideas and insights they spark.

- **Action Plan:**
    - Journal or record voice notes about the inspiration you received during the meteor shower.
    - Identify patterns or recurring themes in your ideas that align with your long-term goals.
    - Plan how to integrate your insights into future projects.
- **Example:** A blogger reflects on their brainstorming session during the meteor shower, identifying a recurring theme of transformation to guide their next series.

Content Ideas for Meteor Showers

1. **Cosmic-Themed Posts:** Create content inspired by the wonder and beauty of meteor showers, such as astrology insights or celestial-themed art.
2. **Real-Time Content:** Capture and share live moments of the meteor shower, inviting your audience to experience it with you.
3. **Quick Tutorials or Tips:** Share fast, actionable advice that aligns with the energetic momentum of a meteor shower.
4. **Inspirational Stories:** Highlight moments of transformation or serendipity in your life or creative process.
5. **Interactive Content:** Engage your audience with polls, questions, or challenges related to the theme of inspiration and rapid action.

Tools to Support Meteor Shower Creativity

1. **Brainstorming Apps:** Use tools like MindMeister or Miro to capture and organize fast ideas.
2. **Video and Photo Editing Tools:** Leverage apps like Adobe Premiere Pro or Lightroom to quickly edit and share content inspired by the event.
3. **Scheduling Tools:** Platforms like Buffer or Later can help you plan and release time-sensitive content efficiently.

Real-Life Applications of Meteor Shower Energy

- **Example 1:** A digital artist creates a limited-edition series of meteor-themed artwork during a meteor shower, sharing progress updates in real-time to build excitement.
- **Example 2:** A science communicator uses the meteor shower as an opportunity to host a live Q&A session, blending education with real-time observation.

Potential Challenges and How to Overcome Them
1. Feeling Overwhelmed by Fast Ideas
The rapid pace of inspiration can lead to scattered focus or difficulty prioritizing.

- **Solution:** Capture all ideas first, then sort and prioritize them based on feasibility and alignment with your goals.

2. Fear of Taking Risks
Bold experimentation can feel intimidating or risky.

- **Solution:** Start small by testing one idea or collaborating with others to share the creative load.

3. Burnout from High Energy
The intensity of meteor showers can lead to overexertion or creative fatigue.

- **Solution:** Balance quick action with moments of rest and reflection to sustain your energy.

Final Thoughts
Meteor showers offer fleeting yet powerful moments of inspiration and creativity, making them ideal for sparking bold ideas, experimenting with new approaches, and acting with urgency. By aligning with their energy, content creators can embrace spontaneity, push creative boundaries, and transform fleeting insights into impactful work. Whether brainstorming new projects, experimenting with unconventional formats, or sharing cosmic-themed content, meteor showers remind us of the beauty and power of rapid inspiration.

Chapter 31: Lunar Nodes – Finding Your Content's True Purpose

In astrology, the lunar nodes—**North Node** and **South Node**—represent the karmic axis, guiding individuals toward their life's purpose and illuminating lessons from past experiences. The North Node points to the path of growth, evolution, and destiny, while the South Node signifies comfort zones, inherited talents, and past patterns. For content creators, understanding the energy of the lunar nodes provides profound insight into aligning their work with their true purpose and creating content that resonates deeply with their audience.

This chapter delves into the astrological significance of the lunar nodes, their role in uncovering your creative purpose, and how to use their guidance to shape content that is authentic, impactful, and aligned with your long-term goals.

What Are the Lunar Nodes?

The lunar nodes are not physical celestial bodies but mathematical points where the Moon's orbit intersects the ecliptic, the Sun's apparent path through the sky. Their astrological significance lies in their symbolic representation of:

1. **North Node (Rahu):** Your direction for growth, destiny, and untapped potential.
2. **South Node (Ketu):** Your comfort zone, innate skills, and past patterns that may hold you back.

Together, the lunar nodes create a roadmap for personal and professional evolution, offering guidance on how to balance the lessons of the past (South Node) with the opportunities of the future (North Node).

The Influence of Lunar Nodes on Content Creation

The lunar nodes encourage creators to move beyond superficial goals, pushing them to align their content with their highest purpose. Here's how they influence the creative process:

1. North Node: Purpose-Driven Content

The North Node calls creators to embrace new challenges and align their work with their soul's growth. It often involves stepping outside of comfort zones and exploring uncharted territory.

- **Key Questions to Ask:**
    - What type of content feels purposeful and aligned with my long-term vision?
    - How can I use my platform to contribute meaningfully to my audience?
    - What topics or themes push me out of my comfort zone but feel deeply rewarding?
- **Example:** A travel influencer evolves their niche by focusing on sustainable travel practices, aligning their content with a broader purpose of environmental awareness.

2. South Node: Honoring Your Skills and Experience

The South Node represents your inherent strengths and the skills you've already mastered. While it's a source of stability, relying too heavily on it can lead to stagnation.

- **Key Questions to Ask:**
    - What skills or knowledge can I draw from to enhance my content?
    - Am I clinging to strategies or themes that feel safe but no longer resonate?
    - How can I use my expertise to support my growth toward the North Node?
- **Example:** A lifestyle blogger leverages their expertise in productivity to create content on time management while exploring deeper themes of work-life balance inspired by their North Node.

Balancing the North and South Nodes in Creative Work

Balancing the energies of the lunar nodes is essential for sustainable growth and authenticity in content creation. The South Node offers a foundation of skills and knowledge, while the North Node encourages creators to evolve and align with their purpose.

1. Step Outside Your Comfort Zone

The North Node often feels unfamiliar or intimidating, but its energy is essential for growth.

- **Action Plan:**
  - Identify one area of your work that feels challenging but aligns with your long-term goals.
  - Experiment with new formats, topics, or platforms that push your boundaries.
  - Embrace feedback and reflection as tools for growth.
- **Example:** A fitness influencer begins sharing personal stories of mental health challenges, stepping beyond their usual workout-focused content to connect more deeply with their audience.

2. Build on Your Strengths

The South Node provides a wealth of experience and skills that can support your growth toward the North Node.

- **Action Plan:**
  - Audit your past content to identify recurring strengths or themes.
  - Use your expertise to establish credibility while introducing new topics or approaches.
  - Avoid becoming too reliant on past successes, ensuring you stay open to evolution.
- **Example:** A graphic designer uses their technical skills to create visually stunning content while exploring storytelling to add emotional depth to their work.

Using Lunar Nodes to Align Your Content Strategy

The lunar nodes offer a blueprint for aligning your content with your higher purpose. Here's how to integrate their guidance into your strategy:

1. Discover Your Nodes

In astrology, the placement of the North and South Nodes in your natal chart provides specific insights into your life's purpose. For example:

- **North Node in Aries:** Focus on bold, independent content that emphasizes leadership.
- **North Node in Cancer:** Create emotionally resonant content that fosters connection and care.
- **North Node in Aquarius:** Innovate with technology or explore themes of social justice and community.
- **Action Plan:**
    - Research your nodes' placements using an astrology app or consultation.
    - Reflect on how their themes align with your creative journey.

2. Create Purpose-Driven Content

The North Node encourages creators to align their work with their personal mission and audience's needs.

- **Action Plan:**
    - Define your content's core purpose or mission statement.
    - Align your topics, tone, and style with this mission.
    - Regularly revisit your strategy to ensure it reflects your evolving goals.
- **Example:** A chef with a North Node in Virgo transitions from sharing general recipes to focusing on healthy meal prep, aligning their work with themes of wellness and practicality.

3. Release Old Patterns

The South Node highlights habits or strategies that may feel comfortable but limit growth.

- **Action Plan:**
    - Identify aspects of your work that feel stagnant or uninspired.
    - Gradually phase out outdated themes or methods, replacing them with content aligned with your North Node.
    - Reflect on what you've learned from past patterns and use those lessons to guide your evolution.
- **Example:** A beauty influencer transitions from tutorial-heavy content to exploring the psychology of beauty and self-expression, stepping into a more purposeful role.

Content Ideas Inspired by the Lunar Nodes

1. **North Node Content:** Share projects or topics that challenge you to grow, even if they feel intimidating.
2. **South Node Content:** Reflect on past successes, sharing lessons learned or skills honed along the way.
3. **Balance Pieces:** Combine expertise with new approaches, blending familiarity with innovation.
4. **Purpose-Driven Stories:** Create narratives that align with your mission and inspire your audience.

Tools to Align with Lunar Node Energy

1. **Astrology Platforms:** Use tools like AstroSeek or TimePassages to discover your lunar nodes and understand their themes.
2. **Content Planning Tools:** Use Notion or Trello to integrate purpose-driven goals into your content calendar.
3. **Reflection Apps:** Journaling tools like Day One can help you track your progress and insights as you align with your North Node.

Real-Life Applications of Lunar Node Energy

- **Example 1:** A travel vlogger with a North Node in Capricorn shifts from casual travel diaries to strategic content about career-building through remote work, aligning their content with themes of structure and achievement.
- **Example 2:** A musician with a South Node in Pisces draws on their innate creativity while focusing on building a structured release schedule to align with their North Node in Virgo.

Potential Challenges and How to Overcome Them

1. Fear of the Unknown

Moving toward the North Node can feel overwhelming or uncertain.

- **Solution:** Take small, manageable steps toward growth, celebrating progress along the way.

2. Over-Reliance on Comfort Zones

It's easy to lean on past successes, avoiding the challenges of the North Node.

- **Solution:** Regularly assess your work to ensure it aligns with your evolving goals and purpose.

3. Balancing Growth with Stability

Balancing the energy of the North and South Nodes can be challenging.

- **Solution:** Use your South Node skills as a foundation while gradually incorporating North Node themes.

Final Thoughts

The lunar nodes offer profound insights into aligning your content with your higher purpose, balancing the lessons of the past with the opportunities for growth. By embracing the North Node's energy, creators can evolve beyond comfort zones, crafting work that is authentic, impactful, and aligned with their destiny. Whether you're stepping into uncharted territory or building on your innate strengths, the lunar nodes provide a roadmap for meaningful and purposeful content creation.

Chapter 32: The North Node – Content That Brings Growth

The **North Node** in astrology represents the direction of growth, evolution, and life purpose. It is a guiding force that urges us to move beyond our comfort zones and embrace new challenges that lead to personal and professional fulfillment. For content creators, the North Node serves as a beacon, pointing toward the kind of work that brings meaningful progress and aligns with their highest potential. Creating content aligned with the energy of the North Node ensures not only growth for the creator but also impactful resonance with their audience.

This chapter explores the significance of the North Node, how it influences content creation, and actionable strategies to align your creative efforts with its energy. By focusing on purposeful and growth-oriented content, creators can expand their influence, deepen their connection with their audience, and achieve sustainable success.

Understanding the North Node

The North Node, often referred to as the "karmic destiny," symbolizes areas of life where we are meant to grow. It represents qualities, skills, and experiences that may initially feel unfamiliar or challenging but ultimately lead to fulfillment and purpose.

- **Themes of the North Node:**
    - **Growth:** Moving beyond the familiar to explore new possibilities.
    - **Purpose:** Aligning with your higher mission and long-term vision.
    - **Challenge:** Stepping into roles or themes that push you outside your comfort zone.
    - **Impact:** Creating work that inspires and uplifts others while fulfilling your own goals.

The energy of the North Node is aspirational, calling you to rise to your potential by embracing the unfamiliar and prioritizing long-term growth over short-term comfort.

How the North Node Influences Content Creation

For content creators, the North Node's energy can serve as a compass, guiding the types of projects, topics, and strategies that will lead to meaningful growth. Here's how it manifests in creative work:

1. Expanding Horizons

The North Node encourages creators to explore new formats, niches, or platforms that align with their mission.

- **Example:** A travel influencer with a North Node in Aquarius shifts from showcasing luxury getaways to exploring sustainable travel practices, aligning their content with themes of innovation and community.

2. Building Authentic Connections

Content aligned with the North Node resonates deeply because it reflects your true purpose and values.

- **Example:** A writer with a North Node in Cancer transitions from technical writing to storytelling that fosters emotional connection and healing.

3. Embracing Challenges

The North Node often requires stepping into uncomfortable territory, such as tackling complex topics or addressing personal vulnerabilities.

- **Example:** A lifestyle blogger with a North Node in Scorpio begins sharing transformative personal experiences, creating content that dives deep into themes of resilience and rebirth.

4. Delivering Impact

Content rooted in the North Node's energy is inherently impactful, inspiring both creators and their audiences to grow.

- **Example:** A fitness coach with a North Node in Virgo focuses on creating practical, habit-building guides rather than quick-fix solutions, helping their audience achieve lasting change.

Strategies for Creating Growth-Oriented Content

To fully harness the North Node's energy in your content creation, focus on aligning your efforts with growth, authenticity, and purpose. Here are actionable strategies:

1. Define Your North Node Mission

Understanding your North Node's placement in your natal chart provides clarity on the themes and areas of growth you're meant to pursue.

- **Action Plan:**
  - Use an astrology app or consult a professional astrologer to identify your North Node's sign and house placement.
  - Research the qualities and lessons associated with your North Node.
  - Reflect on how these themes align with your content and goals.
- **Example:** A creator with a North Node in Libra (themes of balance, partnership, and aesthetics) shifts their focus toward collaborative projects and content that promotes harmony and beauty.

2. Step Outside Your Comfort Zone

Growth requires moving beyond familiar patterns and experimenting with new approaches.

- **Action Plan:**
  - Identify one area of your content creation that feels stagnant or overly comfortable.
  - Brainstorm ways to incorporate fresh elements, such as new topics, formats, or platforms.
  - Take small, consistent steps toward embracing these changes.
- **Example:** A video creator accustomed to short-form content experiments with producing a documentary-style series, pushing their creative boundaries.

3. Align with Your Audience's Needs

The North Node's energy is not only about personal growth but also about contributing to the growth of others.

- **Action Plan:**
  - Conduct audience research to understand their challenges, aspirations, and preferences.
  - Create content that addresses these needs while aligning with your purpose.
  - Use analytics and feedback to refine your approach.

- **Example:** A career coach creates a series of workshops focused on navigating career transitions, addressing their audience's desire for guidance while aligning with their own North Node in Capricorn (themes of structure and achievement).

4. Focus on Long-Term Impact
The North Node encourages sustainable growth and meaningful contributions over quick wins or superficial success.

- **Action Plan:**
    - Prioritize projects that align with your long-term vision, even if they require more effort or time.
    - Avoid content that feels trendy but doesn't resonate with your core values or purpose.
    - Reflect regularly on how your work contributes to your audience and aligns with your goals.
- **Example:** A chef transitions from sharing quick, viral recipes to creating a course on culinary fundamentals, focusing on teaching foundational skills for lasting impact.

Content Ideas Inspired by the North Node

1. **Personal Growth Stories:** Share your journey of embracing challenges and stepping into your purpose.
2. **Educational Content:** Create guides, tutorials, or resources that empower your audience to grow.
3. **Collaborative Projects:** Partner with creators or organizations aligned with your North Node themes.
4. **Visionary Themes:** Explore forward-thinking topics that challenge norms or inspire change.
5. **Legacy Work:** Develop projects or series that align with your long-term vision and values.

Tools to Support North Node Content Creation

1. **Astrology Platforms:** Use tools like AstroSeek or TimePassages to explore your North Node's influence.
2. **Content Planning Tools:** Platforms like Notion or Trello can help you organize and prioritize growth-oriented projects.
3. **Analytics Platforms:** Use tools like Google Analytics or Instagram Insights to assess the impact and alignment of your content.

Real-Life Applications of North Node Energy

- **Example 1:** A mental health advocate with a North Node in Sagittarius (themes of truth and exploration) creates a podcast exploring global perspectives on mental health, expanding their content beyond individual experiences.
- **Example 2:** A digital artist with a North Node in Pisces (themes of imagination and spirituality) begins incorporating ethereal, dreamlike elements into their work, aligning with their creative and spiritual vision.

Potential Challenges and How to Overcome Them

1. Fear of Failure

Pursuing North Node goals often involves uncertainty and the possibility of failure.

- **Solution:** Embrace failure as a learning experience and focus on incremental progress.

2. Resistance to Change

Moving beyond comfort zones can feel intimidating or overwhelming.

- **Solution:** Start small by introducing one or two new elements to your content and build from there.

3. Balancing Old and New

It can be challenging to balance South Node expertise with North Node growth.

- **Solution:** Use your South Node skills as a foundation while gradually incorporating North Node themes.

Final Thoughts

The North Node offers a roadmap for creating content that not only drives personal growth but also resonates deeply with your audience. By aligning your efforts with its themes of purpose, challenge, and long-term impact, you can craft work that inspires and uplifts both yourself and others. Whether you're exploring new creative territories, addressing meaningful topics, or stepping into uncharted roles, the North Node reminds you that growth lies just beyond the familiar.

Chapter 33: The South Node – Revisiting and Repurposing Old Content

The **South Node** in astrology represents our comfort zone, innate skills, and past patterns. It symbolizes the talents and experiences we bring from the past, offering a strong foundation upon which we can build. However, while the South Node provides a sense of stability, relying too heavily on it can lead to stagnation. For content creators, the South Node invites a balance: honor your expertise and revisit old content while avoiding the trap of complacency. This phase is ideal for revisiting, refreshing, and repurposing existing work to align with evolving goals and audience needs.

In this chapter, we explore the significance of the South Node in content creation, offering strategies to repurpose old material, reflect on past successes, and use these insights to fuel future growth.

Understanding the South Node

The South Node, often referred to as the "karmic past," represents areas where we excel but may feel limited by familiarity. In content creation, it reflects the strengths and strategies that have served us well but may need updating to remain relevant.

- **Themes of the South Node:**
    - **Stability:** A foundation of skills and knowledge that provides a sense of security.
    - **Reflection:** Insights from past successes and challenges.
    - **Potential Pitfalls:** A tendency to over-rely on old methods, leading to creative stagnation.
    - **Repurposing:** Transforming existing content into fresh, impactful formats.

The South Node is a resource to draw from, not a place to stay. It invites creators to revisit their roots while evolving toward their North Node purpose.

How the South Node Influences Content Creation

The South Node encourages creators to reflect on their past work, drawing valuable lessons and leveraging existing material to support new goals. Here's how it manifests in creative work:

1. Honoring Your Expertise

The South Node highlights your natural skills and past achievements, providing a strong foundation for growth.

- **Example:** A content creator with a South Node in Virgo leverages their organizational expertise to repurpose detailed how-to guides into a comprehensive eBook.
- **Tip:** Use your past work to establish credibility and showcase your strengths.

2. Revisiting Old Content

The South Node encourages creators to revisit existing material, refreshing and repurposing it for current needs.

- **Example:** A blogger updates an old post on social media strategies with new examples, statistics, and insights.
- **Tip:** Regularly audit your content library to identify pieces with potential for repurposing.

3. Avoiding Stagnation

While the South Node offers a sense of security, over-reliance on it can limit creative growth and innovation.

- **Example:** A podcaster notices their episodes follow the same structure and decides to introduce a new interview format to keep their audience engaged.
- **Tip:** Balance revisiting old content with exploring new ideas aligned with your North Node.

4. Building Bridges Between Past and Future

The South Node acts as a bridge, connecting your past expertise to your evolving goals and audience expectations.

- **Example:** A fitness influencer transforms their old workout tutorials into a subscription-based program, aligning with their North Node in Capricorn's focus on structure and long-term impact.
- **Tip:** Use your South Node as a foundation while incorporating elements that reflect your growth.

Strategies for Revisiting and Repurposing Old Content

To harness the energy of the South Node, focus on revisiting and revitalizing past work in ways that align with your current goals. Here are actionable strategies:

1. Conduct a Content Audit

Revisiting your content library is the first step in identifying material with potential for repurposing or improvement.

- **Action Plan:**
    ◦ Review your content analytics to identify high-performing or evergreen pieces.
    ◦ Identify posts, videos, or projects that could benefit from updates or reformatting.
    ◦ Categorize content by theme, format, and relevance to your current goals.
- **Example:** A YouTuber analyzes their most-viewed videos and identifies opportunities to create updated versions with improved production quality.

2. Refresh and Update

Old content often holds timeless value but may require updates to remain relevant.

- **Action Plan:**
    ◦ Add current data, trends, or examples to existing content.
    ◦ Improve visuals, formatting, or SEO to enhance visibility and engagement.
    ◦ Align older pieces with your current branding or messaging.
- **Example:** A blogger revisits a popular post from three years ago, updating it with new statistics, a fresh design, and internal links to recent articles.

3. Repurpose Into New Formats

Transforming old content into new formats allows you to reach different audience segments and maximize its value.

- **Action Plan:**
    ◦ Convert blog posts into videos, infographics, or podcast episodes.
    ◦ Bundle related content into eBooks, guides, or courses.
    ◦ Extract quotes or highlights from long-form content for social media posts.
- **Example:** An educator compiles a series of webinars into a digital course, complete with downloadable worksheets and quizzes.

4. Reflect on Lessons Learned

The South Node encourages reflection on past successes and challenges to inform future strategies.

- **Action Plan:**
    ◦ Analyze what worked well in your most successful content and why.

- Identify recurring themes or patterns that resonate with your audience.
- Use insights from past failures to refine your approach moving forward.
- **Example:** A marketer reviews an underperforming campaign and realizes the messaging was too broad, using this insight to craft more targeted content.

5. Bridge Old and New Audiences

Repurposing content can help you connect with both loyal followers and new audiences.

- **Action Plan:**
  - Promote refreshed content to existing followers while optimizing it for discovery by new users.
  - Highlight the evolution of your work, sharing your journey from old content to current projects.
  - Use call-to-action strategies to engage both new and returning audience members.
- **Example:** A lifestyle influencer shares a "then and now" series, showcasing how their approach to wellness has evolved over time.

Content Ideas Inspired by the South Node

1. **Then-and-Now Posts:** Compare old and new projects to highlight your growth.
2. **Top Performers:** Revisit your most successful content and update it with fresh insights.
3. **Educational Series:** Transform older tutorials or guides into an updated series or course.
4. **Content Compilations:** Bundle related posts, videos, or episodes into a cohesive resource.
5. **Reflections:** Share lessons learned from your creative journey, using old content as a reference.

Tools for Revisiting and Repurposing Content

1. **Analytics Platforms:** Use tools like Google Analytics, YouTube Studio, or Instagram Insights to identify high-performing content.
2. **Content Management Tools:** Platforms like Notion or Airtable can help you organize and track updates to your content library.
3. **Creative Tools:** Leverage tools like Canva, Adobe Creative Suite, or Final Cut Pro to refresh and reformat old material.

Real-Life Applications of South Node Energy

- **Example 1:** A wellness coach revisits a blog post on stress management, transforming it into a three-part video series with updated techniques.
- **Example 2:** A digital artist repurposes an old sketchbook collection into a curated digital art book, available for purchase online.

- **Example 3:** A tech reviewer updates their "Top Gadgets of 2019" article to reflect the latest trends, rebranding it as "Top Gadgets Revisited: Then and Now."

Potential Challenges and How to Overcome Them

1. Over-Reliance on Old Content

Focusing too much on past work can limit innovation and growth.

- **Solution:** Balance repurposing with creating new, forward-thinking content.

2. Perfectionism in Updates

The desire to perfect old content may slow progress.

- **Solution:** Focus on meaningful improvements rather than complete overhauls.

3. Audience Fatigue

Reusing old content without clear updates or relevance may disengage your audience.

- **Solution:** Clearly communicate the value of refreshed content, emphasizing what's new and improved.

Final Thoughts

The South Node invites content creators to reflect on their past work, leveraging their expertise to enhance and repurpose old content while remaining open to growth and evolution. By revisiting successful material, updating it for relevance, and transforming it into new formats, creators can honor their roots while building momentum for the future. This balance between stability and innovation ensures that your work remains impactful, authentic, and aligned with your evolving vision.

Chapter 34: Celestial Events – Aligning Releases with Cosmic Timing

Celestial events, such as eclipses, solstices, equinoxes, meteor showers, planetary alignments, and retrogrades, hold significant astrological and symbolic meaning. These events mark shifts in energy, opportunities for transformation, and windows of heightened collective attention. For content creators, aligning content releases with these powerful cosmic moments can amplify impact, boost engagement, and resonate deeply with audiences drawn to the energy of the stars.

This chapter explores the significance of celestial events, how they influence collective moods and behaviors, and actionable strategies for timing your content releases to align with cosmic energy for maximum effectiveness.

The Power of Celestial Events

Celestial events are more than astronomical phenomena; they carry symbolic meanings rooted in ancient traditions and collective awareness. Aligning your content with these events can:

- **Resonate with Collective Energy:** Many people feel attuned to celestial events, making them more receptive to themes related to these occurrences.
- **Leverage Cosmic Themes:** Each event carries unique astrological meanings that can inspire specific content topics.
- **Boost Visibility:** These events often trend on social media, providing opportunities for increased reach and engagement.

Key Celestial Events and Their Influences on Content Creation
1. Eclipses – Transformation and Turning Points
Eclipses are powerful cosmic events that symbolize sudden changes, revelations, and accelerated growth.

- **Themes:** Transformation, closure, new beginnings, and heightened emotions.
- **Content Strategies:**
    - Use solar eclipses for launching new projects or campaigns.
    - Leverage lunar eclipses for reflective or transformational content, such as personal stories or lessons learned.
    - Create content that addresses themes of change, letting go, or stepping into a new phase.
- **Example:** A content creator releases a video on overcoming adversity during a lunar eclipse, aligning with the theme of transformation.

2. Solstices – Peaks of Energy
The solstices mark the longest (Summer Solstice) and shortest (Winter Solstice) days of the year, symbolizing culmination and renewal.

- **Themes:**
    - **Summer Solstice:** Celebration, abundance, and growth.
    - **Winter Solstice:** Reflection, rest, and preparation for new beginnings.
- **Content Strategies:**
    - Use the Summer Solstice for celebratory or expansive content, such as achievements or success stories.
    - Leverage the Winter Solstice for introspective content, such as gratitude posts or setting intentions for the future.
- **Example:** A lifestyle influencer releases a "Mid-Year Goals Review" during the Summer Solstice, celebrating accomplishments and setting goals for the remainder of the year.

3. Equinoxes – Balance and Harmony

The equinoxes occur when day and night are equal, symbolizing balance and transition.

- **Themes:** Balance, alignment, and harmony.
- **Content Strategies:**
    - Use the Spring Equinox for content about renewal, growth, or planting seeds for future success.
    - Leverage the Autumn Equinox for reflective content on finding balance or harvesting the fruits of your labor.
- **Example:** A wellness coach launches a mindfulness challenge during the Autumn Equinox, focusing on balancing physical, emotional, and mental well-being.

4. Meteor Showers – Inspiration and Quick Ideas

Meteor showers symbolize bursts of energy, fast-paced inspiration, and fleeting opportunities.

- **Themes:** Creativity, spontaneity, and rapid action.
- **Content Strategies:**
    - Share bold, creative content that pushes boundaries during meteor showers.
    - Highlight themes of transformation, inspiration, or wonder.
- **Example:** A photographer shares a time-lapse video of a meteor shower, accompanied by an inspiring story about capturing fleeting moments.

5. Planetary Alignments – Collective Shifts

Planetary alignments occur when multiple planets align in a straight line, symbolizing heightened energy and collaboration.

- **Themes:** Unity, breakthroughs, and collaborative efforts.
- **Content Strategies:**
    - Collaborate with other creators to release joint projects.
    - Focus on themes of alignment, synergy, or collective growth.
- **Example:** A team of creators launches a collaborative series on sustainability during a planetary alignment, emphasizing the power of working together for global impact.

6. Retrogrades – Reflection and Reassessment

Planetary retrogrades, particularly Mercury retrograde, symbolize periods of slowing down, revisiting the past, and rethinking strategies.

- **Themes:** Reflection, revision, and realignment.
- **Content Strategies:**
    - Use retrograde periods for revisiting and repurposing old content.
    - Share lessons learned or reflective pieces about past experiences.
    - Avoid launching new projects, focusing instead on refining existing work.
- **Example:** A writer republishes a refreshed version of a popular blog post during Mercury retrograde, incorporating updated insights.

Strategies for Aligning Content Releases with Celestial Events

To effectively align your content strategy with celestial events, follow these actionable steps:

1. Plan Ahead with an Astrology Calendar

Understanding the timing and significance of upcoming celestial events is essential for alignment.

- **Action Plan:**
    ◦ Use tools like astrology apps, calendars, or websites to track celestial events.
    ◦ Incorporate these dates into your content calendar, assigning themes and tasks based on each event's energy.
- **Example:** A creator schedules a gratitude campaign for the Winter Solstice and a bold launch for the next solar eclipse.

2. Tailor Content to Cosmic Themes

Each celestial event carries unique symbolism that can inspire your content topics and messaging.

- **Action Plan:**
    ◦ Identify the themes associated with an event and brainstorm content ideas that align with them.
    ◦ Use visuals, titles, and descriptions that evoke the energy of the event.
- **Example:** A fashion influencer creates a photo shoot inspired by the balance of light and dark for the Autumn Equinox, using natural settings and symbolic imagery.

3. Use Social Media Trends

Celestial events often trend on social media, offering opportunities to increase visibility and engagement.

- **Action Plan:**
    ◦ Use event-related hashtags to reach a wider audience (e.g., #LunarEclipse or #SummerSolstice).
    ◦ Create interactive content, such as polls, live streams, or Q&A sessions, tied to the event.
- **Example:** A tarot reader hosts a live stream during Mercury retrograde, answering audience questions about navigating this reflective period.

4. Align Launches with Energetic Peaks

Certain celestial events, such as eclipses and solstices, carry powerful energy for new beginnings and transformations.

- **Action Plan:**
    - Schedule major launches or announcements during high-energy events.
    - Use these moments to build anticipation and excitement among your audience.
- **Example:** A coach launches a transformational coaching program during a solar eclipse, emphasizing themes of growth and change.

5. Reflect and Recharge During Quiet Periods

Not all celestial events are suited for high-energy activities. Use reflective periods, such as retrogrades or the Waning Moon, for rest and preparation.

- **Action Plan:**
    - Focus on reviewing and refining your content during these quieter phases.
    - Share reflective pieces that resonate with the introspective energy of the time.
- **Example:** A wellness blogger publishes a "Lessons from the Past Year" post during the Waning Moon phase.

Content Ideas for Celestial Events

1. **Live Streams and Events:** Host real-time observations or discussions about celestial events.
2. **Inspirational Posts:** Share content inspired by the energy of the event, such as motivational quotes or stories.
3. **Collaborations:** Work with other creators to produce themed content for planetary alignments.
4. **Educational Pieces:** Teach your audience about the significance of celestial events and their symbolism.
5. **Interactive Activities:** Create challenges, polls, or Q&A sessions tied to the themes of the event.

Tools to Support Celestial Content Creation

1. **Astrology Calendars:** Tools like TimePassages or The Moon Calendar to track celestial events.
2. **Content Scheduling Platforms:** Use Buffer, Later, or Hootsuite to plan and schedule event-aligned content.
3. **Creative Tools:** Platforms like Canva or Adobe Creative Suite to design event-themed visuals and graphics.

Real-Life Applications of Celestial Timing

- **Example 1:** A meditation app releases a guided visualization during the Spring Equinox, focusing on renewal and growth.
- **Example 2:** A fashion brand launches a "Celestial Collection" during a planetary alignment, incorporating cosmic-inspired designs.
- **Example 3:** A wellness coach creates a gratitude journal for the Winter Solstice, aligning with themes of reflection and renewal.

Potential Challenges and How to Overcome Them
1. Overloading Your Schedule
Aligning with multiple celestial events can feel overwhelming.

- **Solution:** Prioritize events that resonate most with your brand or audience, focusing on quality over quantity.

2. Misalignment with Audience Interests
Not all audiences may connect with celestial themes.

- **Solution:** Incorporate celestial events subtly, tying them to universally relatable themes like change, growth, or balance.

3. Timing Logistics
Celestial events occur at specific times, which may not align with your schedule.

- **Solution:** Prepare content in advance and use scheduling tools to release it at the optimal time.

Final Thoughts
Aligning content releases with celestial events allows creators to tap into cosmic energy, resonate with collective awareness, and amplify their impact. By understanding the themes and timing of these events, creators can craft purposeful, timely, and engaging content that aligns with their audience's interests and the rhythms of the cosmos. Whether celebrating the light of the solstices, reflecting during retrogrades, or harnessing the transformative power of eclipses, celestial events offer endless opportunities for creative inspiration and meaningful connection.

Chapter 35: Stargazing for Creators – Finding New Ideas in the Night Sky

Stargazing has been a source of inspiration for countless creators throughout history. From poets and philosophers to artists and inventors, the night sky has ignited imaginations and opened minds to new ideas. For modern content creators, stargazing offers more than just awe-inspiring views; it provides a meditative and reflective practice to uncover fresh perspectives, connect with the cosmos, and channel creative energy.

In this chapter, we'll explore how stargazing can enhance your creativity, guide you in finding unique content ideas, and help you align your work with the mysteries of the universe. By embracing this timeless practice, you can unlock the power of the stars to inspire and inform your creative journey.

The Creative Power of Stargazing

Stargazing is more than just looking at the stars; it's an opportunity to connect with the vastness of the universe and tap into a deeper well of creativity. The night sky offers:

- **Perspective:** The stars remind us of the infinite possibilities beyond our immediate concerns, helping us think expansively.
- **Inspiration:** Patterns, constellations, and celestial phenomena spark ideas for themes, visuals, and narratives.
- **Reflection:** The stillness of the night fosters introspection, allowing creators to explore their inner thoughts and emotions.
- **Connection:** Stargazing links us to ancient traditions and shared human experiences, providing a sense of continuity and meaning.

How Stargazing Inspires Content Creation

The practice of stargazing can influence content creation in profound ways, sparking ideas and guiding new approaches. Here's how it can shape your creative process:

1. Discovering New Themes and Narratives

The stories and myths associated with constellations and celestial bodies provide rich material for content ideas.

- **Example:** A storyteller draws inspiration from the legend of Orion to create a series of short stories about a modern-day hero guided by the stars.
- **Tip:** Research myths and folklore associated with constellations to uncover narratives that resonate with your brand or audience.

2. Visual and Aesthetic Inspiration

The beauty of the night sky, from shimmering stars to the Milky Way's grandeur, inspires visuals and aesthetics.

- **Example:** A graphic designer creates a celestial-themed branding package inspired by the colors and patterns of a nebula.
- **Tip:** Use stargazing as a mood board for your visual projects, capturing the colors, textures, and moods of the night sky.

3. Meditative Problem-Solving

The act of stargazing clears the mind, creating space for insights and solutions to creative challenges.

- **Example:** A blogger struggling with writer's block finds clarity during a stargazing session, unlocking the perfect angle for their next post.
- **Tip:** Use stargazing as a form of meditation, allowing your thoughts to flow freely without judgment.

4. Connecting with Universal Themes

The stars evoke universal themes like wonder, exploration, and eternity, which resonate deeply with audiences.

- **Example:** A filmmaker uses the theme of stargazing to explore human connections and the search for meaning in their next project.
- **Tip:** Incorporate cosmic themes into your work to tap into shared emotions and aspirations.

Strategies for Stargazing as a Creative Practice

To fully harness the creative potential of stargazing, approach it as an intentional practice. Here are actionable strategies to get started:

1. Plan Your Stargazing Sessions

Choosing the right time and place for stargazing ensures a meaningful experience.

- **Action Plan:**
    - Use stargazing apps like Stellarium or Sky Guide to identify optimal viewing times and locations.
    - Select a dark-sky area away from city lights for the best visibility.
    - Schedule your sessions around celestial events like meteor showers, lunar eclipses, or planetary alignments.
- **Example:** A photographer plans a stargazing trip during the Perseids meteor shower, capturing breathtaking images to use in a creative campaign.

2. Bring Tools for Inspiration

Equipping yourself with the right tools enhances your stargazing experience and helps you capture ideas.

- **Action Plan:**
    - Bring a notebook or voice recorder to jot down thoughts and inspirations.
    - Use a telescope or binoculars to explore details of the night sky.
    - Bring a camera or smartphone for astrophotography to document the experience.
- **Example:** A visual artist sketches constellations and nebulae during a stargazing session, later incorporating them into a celestial-themed collection.

3. Reflect and Brainstorm

Stargazing offers an opportunity for reflection and idea generation.

- **Action Plan:**
    - Start your session with a question or challenge you want to explore creatively.
    - Spend time observing the sky in silence, allowing thoughts to arise naturally.
    - Use freewriting or mind-mapping techniques immediately after stargazing to capture insights.
- **Example:** A content strategist reflects on their brand's direction under the stars, uncovering a new tagline that aligns with their vision.

4. Use Celestial Phenomena as Content Themes
Align your content strategy with upcoming celestial events to create timely and relevant material.

- **Action Plan:**
    - Research upcoming celestial events and their symbolic meanings.
    - Develop content ideas that tie into these events, such as blogs, videos, or social media campaigns.
    - Use event-related hashtags to boost visibility and engagement.
- **Example:** A travel blogger writes a guide to the best stargazing destinations, timed to coincide with an upcoming meteor shower.

Content Ideas Inspired by Stargazing

1. **Cosmic-Themed Stories:** Create narratives inspired by constellations, myths, or the universe's mysteries.
2. **Astrophotography Galleries:** Share images of the night sky paired with personal reflections or stories.
3. **Meditative Content:** Develop guided visualizations or mindfulness exercises inspired by stargazing.
4. **Educational Pieces:** Teach your audience about constellations, celestial events, or the science of the stars.
5. **Inspirational Quotes:** Pair starry visuals with quotes about wonder, exploration, or creativity.

Tools for Stargazing and Creativity

1. **Stargazing Apps:** Stellarium, Sky Guide, and Star Walk to identify stars, constellations, and celestial events.
2. **Photography Tools:** DSLRs, telescopes with camera adapters, or astrophotography apps like NightCap Camera.
3. **Creative Tools:** Journaling apps like Day One or drawing apps like Procreate to capture inspirations.

Real-Life Applications of Stargazing Creativity

- **Example 1:** A musician composes a celestial-inspired album after spending nights under the stars, blending ambient sounds with astronomical themes.
- **Example 2:** A jewelry designer creates a constellation-themed collection, incorporating the shapes and symbolism of star patterns.
- **Example 3:** A wellness coach designs a stargazing meditation guide, helping clients connect with the cosmos for relaxation and insight.

Potential Challenges and How to Overcome Them
1. Weather and Light Pollution
Cloud cover or urban lighting can interfere with stargazing.

- **Solution:** Use weather apps to plan your sessions and seek out dark-sky reserves for optimal visibility.

2. Overwhelmed by Ideas
Stargazing can spark a flood of ideas, making it difficult to focus.

- **Solution:** Capture all ideas first, then sort and prioritize them based on relevance and feasibility.

3. Lack of Equipment
Not everyone has access to advanced stargazing tools.

- **Solution:** Start with simple tools like a smartphone and a stargazing app, gradually upgrading as needed.

Final Thoughts
Stargazing offers creators a unique and profound source of inspiration, connecting them to the vastness of the universe and sparking ideas that transcend the ordinary. By incorporating stargazing into your creative practice, you can uncover fresh perspectives, explore cosmic themes, and align your work with the wonder and mystery of the stars. Whether crafting stories, designing visuals, or reflecting on your creative journey, the night sky provides a boundless canvas for imagination and innovation.

Chapter 36: Aligning Your Brand with Your Astrological Chart

Astrology is not just a tool for personal growth—it can also be a powerful framework for shaping your brand's identity, strategy, and connection with your audience. By aligning your brand with your astrological chart, you can create a cohesive, purpose-driven identity that resonates deeply with your values, mission, and audience. Your astrological chart offers insights into your creative strengths, challenges, and opportunities, helping you make informed decisions about how to structure and present your brand.

This chapter explores how to use your astrological chart to align your brand with cosmic principles, offering actionable strategies to infuse your brand with purpose, authenticity, and a touch of celestial magic.

The Role of Astrology in Branding

Astrology provides a map of your personality, values, and unique energy, which can be translated into your brand's identity. Key elements of your natal chart—such as your Sun, Moon, Rising Sign, and Midheaven—offer insights into:

- **Core Values:** What drives your brand and its mission.
- **Emotional Resonance:** How to connect with your audience on a deeper level.
- **Communication Style:** How you express your brand's message.
- **Growth Opportunities:** Areas to expand or evolve your brand's reach and impact.

Aligning your brand with your astrological chart ensures that your work is authentic, purpose-driven, and in harmony with your natural strengths.

Key Astrological Chart Elements for Branding

1. The Sun Sign: Your Brand's Core Identity

The Sun represents your essence, purpose, and vitality. In branding, it reflects your brand's core identity and mission.

- **Questions to Consider:**
    - What does your brand stand for?
    - What unique qualities set your brand apart?
    - How can your brand inspire and energize your audience?
- **Example:** A brand with a Leo Sun may emphasize creativity, boldness, and self-expression, positioning itself as a vibrant leader in its niche.

2. The Moon Sign: Emotional Connection

The Moon governs emotions, intuition, and inner needs. For branding, it reflects how your brand connects with your audience on an emotional level.

- **Questions to Consider:**
    - How does your brand make people feel?
    - What emotional needs does your brand fulfill for your audience?
    - How can your brand foster trust and loyalty?
- **Example:** A brand with a Cancer Moon might focus on creating nurturing, empathetic content that fosters a sense of community and care.

3. The Rising Sign: Your Brand's First Impression

The Rising Sign, or Ascendant, represents how others perceive you at first glance. It reflects your brand's outward appearance and initial impression.

- **Questions to Consider:**
    - What image or vibe does your brand project?
    - How does your branding (logo, colors, design) reflect this energy?
    - What first impression do you want your audience to have?
- **Example:** A brand with an Aquarius Rising might adopt futuristic designs, innovative messaging, and a unique aesthetic to stand out.

4. The Midheaven (MC): Professional Goals

The Midheaven represents career, public image, and long-term aspirations. It aligns with your brand's overarching goals and reputation.

- **Questions to Consider:**
  - What legacy do you want your brand to create?
  - How do you want your brand to be remembered or recognized?
  - What professional milestones align with your vision?
- **Example:** A brand with a Capricorn Midheaven might prioritize building a solid reputation, focusing on professionalism, structure, and long-term success.

5. Mercury: Communication Style

Mercury governs communication, intellect, and messaging. It reflects how your brand expresses its voice and interacts with its audience.

- **Questions to Consider:**
  - What tone and style should your brand adopt in its messaging?
  - How does your audience prefer to receive information?
  - What platforms align best with your communication strengths?
- **Example:** A brand with Mercury in Gemini might focus on quick, engaging content like social media posts, memes, or interactive stories.

6. Venus: Aesthetic and Values

Venus governs beauty, harmony, and values. It reflects your brand's aesthetic and the principles it prioritizes.

- **Questions to Consider:**
  - What visual style best represents your brand?
  - How can your brand create a sense of harmony and connection?
  - What values does your brand uphold?
- **Example:** A brand with Venus in Libra might emphasize elegant designs, balanced layouts, and collaborative values.

7. Mars: Energy and Drive

Mars represents action, energy, and ambition. It reflects how your brand takes initiative and pursues its goals.

- **Questions to Consider:**
    - What motivates your brand's actions and strategies?
    - How does your brand approach challenges and competition?
    - What energizes your creative process?
- **Example:** A brand with Mars in Aries might adopt a bold, assertive approach, launching campaigns with confidence and speed.

Strategies for Aligning Your Brand with Your Chart
1. Conduct a Natal Chart Analysis
Understanding your full astrological chart is the first step in aligning your brand with cosmic energy.

- **Action Plan:**
    - Use astrology tools like AstroSeek or TimePassages to generate your natal chart.
    - Identify key placements (Sun, Moon, Rising, Midheaven, Mercury, Venus, Mars).
    - Reflect on how these placements align with your brand's mission, values, and goals.

2. Define Your Brand's Cosmic Identity
Translate your chart's insights into a cohesive brand identity.

- **Action Plan:**
    - Write a mission statement inspired by your Sun and Midheaven placements.
    - Choose a communication style aligned with Mercury's energy.
    - Develop a visual brand identity that reflects Venus and Rising Sign influences.
- **Example:** A creator with a Taurus Sun and Pisces Rising develops a brand identity focused on sensual aesthetics, calm tones, and a nurturing approach.

3. Align Content with Cosmic Themes
Create content that reflects your chart's energy and aligns with its strengths.

- **Action Plan:**
    - Use your Moon placement to craft emotionally resonant stories.
    - Leverage your Mars placement to set an energetic pace for content releases.
    - Incorporate Midheaven goals into long-term content strategies.
- **Example:** A brand with a Sagittarius Moon focuses on inspirational, adventurous storytelling, resonating with themes of exploration and growth.

4. Leverage Planetary Transits
Align your content strategy with real-time planetary movements that influence your chart.

- **Action Plan:**
    - Track major transits and how they interact with your natal placements.
    - Schedule launches, collaborations, or campaigns during favorable transits.
    - Use retrograde periods for revisiting and refining existing content.
- **Example:** A creator with a Virgo Midheaven schedules a content audit during Mercury retrograde, aligning with the transit's reflective energy.

Content Ideas for Astrological Branding

1. **Cosmic Mission Statements:** Share how astrology inspires your brand's purpose and vision.
2. **Astrological Themes:** Create content tied to your natal chart's strengths (e.g., storytelling for a Gemini Mercury).
3. **Celestial Aesthetics:** Develop a visual identity inspired by your Rising Sign or Venus placement.
4. **Audience Engagement:** Share insights from your chart and invite your audience to explore theirs.

Tools for Astrological Branding

1. **Astrology Platforms:** AstroSeek, TimePassages, or Chani to analyze your chart.
2. **Design Tools:** Canva or Adobe Creative Suite to incorporate celestial aesthetics.
3. **Content Planning Tools:** Trello or Notion to align branding goals with astrological insights.

Real-Life Applications of Astrological Branding

- **Example 1:** A wellness coach with a Pisces Moon integrates intuitive, healing content into their brand, creating meditative videos and nurturing blog posts.
- **Example 2:** A tech entrepreneur with an Aquarius Rising adopts a futuristic brand identity, incorporating sleek designs and forward-thinking messaging.
- **Example 3:** A fashion brand with Venus in Leo emphasizes bold, luxurious aesthetics and a confident tone.

Potential Challenges and How to Overcome Them
1. Misalignment Between Chart and Brand
Your chart may highlight traits that feel disconnected from your current brand.

- **Solution:** Reflect on how to bridge your chart's energy with your brand's evolving goals, blending past expertise with future aspirations.

2. Overemphasis on Astrology
Focusing too much on astrology may alienate certain audiences.

- **Solution:** Subtly integrate astrological insights into your brand, ensuring they enhance rather than overshadow your core identity.

3. Resistance to Change
Adapting your brand based on astrological insights may feel daunting.

- **Solution:** Start small, experimenting with one or two elements (e.g., messaging style or visual identity) to ease the transition.

Final Thoughts
Aligning your brand with your astrological chart offers a powerful way to create a purpose-driven identity that resonates deeply with your audience. By understanding your chart's key elements and incorporating their energy into your brand strategy, you can craft content, messaging, and visuals that reflect your unique strengths and aspirations. Whether tapping into your Sun's purpose, your Moon's emotional depth, or your Rising Sign's outward persona, astrology provides a cosmic blueprint for building a brand that shines as brightly as the stars.

Chapter 37: The Power of Rising Signs in Audience Appeal

In astrology, the **Rising Sign**, or Ascendant, represents how you present yourself to the world and the first impression you make. It is the "mask" you wear when interacting with others and determines how others perceive you. For content creators, understanding the energy of the Rising Sign can be a game-changer in crafting a brand identity, resonating with your audience, and maximizing your appeal.

This chapter explores the significance of Rising Signs in audience engagement, offering insights into how each Ascendant influences branding, content style, and communication strategies. By aligning with your Rising Sign's traits, you can create a powerful and authentic connection with your audience.

Understanding the Rising Sign

Your Rising Sign is the zodiac sign that was rising on the eastern horizon at the moment of your birth. Unlike the Sun or Moon Signs, which reflect your core self and emotions, the Rising Sign governs:

1. **First Impressions:** How others initially perceive you or your brand.
2. **Persona:** The "face" or outward identity you show to the world.
3. **Communication Style:** How you approach and interact with your audience.
4. **Aesthetic:** The visual and thematic elements that resonate with your Rising Sign's energy.

In content creation, the Rising Sign influences your brand's aesthetic, tone, and how you establish trust and rapport with your audience.

How the Rising Sign Shapes Audience Appeal

Your Rising Sign directly impacts how your audience experiences your content and brand. Here's how it plays a role:

1. Establishing First Impressions

Your Rising Sign governs the initial impression your content and branding create. It sets the tone for how audiences perceive your authenticity, style, and energy.

2. Shaping Visual Identity

The Rising Sign influences the aesthetic elements of your brand, from color palettes and fonts to imagery and design.

3. Guiding Engagement Strategies

Each Rising Sign has a unique way of connecting with people, shaping how you engage with your audience through messaging, interaction, and storytelling.

4. Building Trust and Resonance

Your Rising Sign helps you align with audience expectations and emotional needs, making your brand more relatable and approachable.

The Rising Signs and Their Influence on Branding

Each Rising Sign brings a unique energy and style to branding and audience engagement. Let's explore how each Ascendant shapes your brand's appeal:

Aries Rising: Bold and Energetic

- **First Impression:** Dynamic, confident, and action-oriented.
- **Visual Style:** Bright, bold colors and sharp designs that convey energy.
- **Engagement Strategy:** Use direct, impactful messaging that inspires action.
- **Audience Appeal:** Appeals to audiences seeking motivation, leadership, and innovation.
- **Example:** A fitness influencer with Aries Rising uses high-energy workout videos and bold visuals to inspire followers to push their limits.

Taurus Rising: Grounded and Luxurious

- **First Impression:** Stable, reliable, and aesthetically pleasing.
- **Visual Style:** Earthy tones, elegant designs, and a focus on sensory appeal.
- **Engagement Strategy:** Build trust with consistent, high-quality content and a nurturing tone.
- **Audience Appeal:** Resonates with those seeking comfort, stability, and indulgence.
- **Example:** A lifestyle brand with Taurus Rising showcases serene imagery, luxurious product recommendations, and calming tones in its messaging.

Gemini Rising: Witty and Versatile

- **First Impression:** Curious, playful, and communicative.
- **Visual Style:** Bright, dynamic designs with varied and engaging elements.
- **Engagement Strategy:** Use humor, quick-witted messaging, and interactive content like polls or Q&A sessions.
- **Audience Appeal:** Attracts audiences who value versatility, humor, and intellectual stimulation.
- **Example:** A tech reviewer with Gemini Rising incorporates clever puns and rapid-fire comparisons into their videos, keeping their audience entertained and informed.

Cancer Rising: Nurturing and Emotional

- **First Impression:** Caring, empathetic, and emotionally resonant.
- **Visual Style:** Soft colors, comforting imagery, and warm, heartfelt designs.
- **Engagement Strategy:** Use personal storytelling and emotionally evocative content to build deep connections.
- **Audience Appeal:** Appeals to audiences seeking authenticity, care, and emotional support.

- **Example:** A mental health advocate with Cancer Rising shares vulnerable and relatable posts, creating a safe and nurturing space for their audience.

Leo Rising: Charismatic and Creative

- **First Impression:** Confident, magnetic, and expressive.
- **Visual Style:** Bold colors, eye-catching designs, and an emphasis on individuality.
- **Engagement Strategy:** Use dramatic storytelling, vibrant visuals, and engaging performances to captivate your audience.
- **Audience Appeal:** Attracts audiences drawn to confidence, creativity, and inspiration.
- **Example:** A fashion influencer with Leo Rising showcases bold outfits and shares their personal journey of self-expression, inspiring others to embrace their uniqueness.

Virgo Rising: Practical and Detail-Oriented

- **First Impression:** Analytical, organized, and helpful.
- **Visual Style:** Clean, minimalistic designs with a focus on clarity and structure.
- **Engagement Strategy:** Provide actionable tips, step-by-step guides, and reliable information.
- **Audience Appeal:** Resonates with those seeking organization, practicality, and value.
- **Example:** A productivity coach with Virgo Rising creates detailed tutorials and templates to help their audience achieve their goals.

Libra Rising: Harmonious and Charming

- **First Impression:** Balanced, elegant, and approachable.
- **Visual Style:** Sophisticated designs with a focus on symmetry and beauty.
- **Engagement Strategy:** Foster a sense of collaboration and community, emphasizing fairness and connection.
- **Audience Appeal:** Appeals to those drawn to aesthetics, relationships, and diplomacy.
- **Example:** A relationship coach with Libra Rising creates visually stunning content and hosts live discussions on fostering harmony in personal relationships.

Scorpio Rising: Intense and Transformative

- **First Impression:** Mysterious, powerful, and deeply compelling.
- **Visual Style:** Dark, dramatic designs with rich colors and intriguing imagery.
- **Engagement Strategy:** Share transformative stories and delve into deep, thought-provoking topics.
- **Audience Appeal:** Attracts audiences seeking depth, mystery, and empowerment.

- **Example:** A documentary filmmaker with Scorpio Rising explores hidden truths and powerful narratives, captivating their audience with intense storytelling.

Sagittarius Rising: Adventurous and Optimistic

- **First Impression:** Free-spirited, enthusiastic, and inspiring.
- **Visual Style:** Vibrant, expansive designs with themes of exploration and growth.
- **Engagement Strategy:** Share uplifting, adventurous content that encourages curiosity and self-discovery.
- **Audience Appeal:** Resonates with those seeking inspiration, adventure, and optimism.
- **Example:** A travel vlogger with Sagittarius Rising shares their global journeys with infectious energy and uplifting messages.

Capricorn Rising: Professional and Ambitious

- **First Impression:** Disciplined, trustworthy, and success-oriented.
- **Visual Style:** Polished, professional designs with muted, sophisticated tones.
- **Engagement Strategy:** Highlight expertise, reliability, and long-term value in your messaging.
- **Audience Appeal:** Attracts audiences seeking guidance, structure, and results.
- **Example:** A financial advisor with Capricorn Rising creates professional, data-driven content that helps their audience achieve long-term goals.

Aquarius Rising: Innovative and Unique

- **First Impression:** Visionary, unconventional, and socially conscious.
- **Visual Style:** Futuristic designs with bold, quirky elements.
- **Engagement Strategy:** Share innovative ideas, champion causes, and create content that challenges norms.
- **Audience Appeal:** Appeals to audiences who value originality, progress, and inclusivity.
- **Example:** A tech entrepreneur with Aquarius Rising shares cutting-edge innovations and socially conscious solutions, engaging their forward-thinking audience.

Pisces Rising: Dreamy and Inspirational

- **First Impression:** Creative, intuitive, and ethereal.
- **Visual Style:** Soft, whimsical designs with flowing, dreamlike elements.
- **Engagement Strategy:** Use storytelling, art, and emotive content to inspire your audience.
- **Audience Appeal:** Resonates with those seeking creativity, spirituality, and imagination.
- **Example:** An artist with Pisces Rising shares enchanting, otherworldly visuals and poetic captions, creating a deeply inspiring experience for their audience.

Strategies for Leveraging Your Rising Sign
1. Identify Your Rising Sign

- Use an astrology app or consult an astrologer to determine your Rising Sign.
- Reflect on how its energy aligns with your current branding and content style.

2. Align Your Visual Identity

- Choose colors, designs, and imagery that reflect your Rising Sign's aesthetic.
- Ensure consistency across your platforms to create a cohesive brand presence.

3. Craft Messaging Around First Impressions

- Develop a tone and style that aligns with your Rising Sign's strengths.
- Use your unique energy to make your content stand out and resonate deeply.

4. Engage Your Audience Authentically

- Tailor your engagement strategies to match your Rising Sign's approach.
- Reflect its energy in how you interact, respond, and connect with your audience.

Final Thoughts

Your Rising Sign is a key to unlocking your brand's appeal, guiding how you present yourself and connect with your audience. By embracing its energy, you can create a strong first impression, build trust, and cultivate a brand identity that resonates on a profound level. Whether bold and dynamic like Aries or nurturing and emotional like Cancer, your Rising Sign provides a celestial blueprint for capturing your audience's attention and heart.

Chapter 38: Midheaven Sign – Career Path Insights for Content Creators

The **Midheaven**, also known as the **Medium Coeli (MC)**, is the highest point in your natal chart and represents your public image, career aspirations, and ultimate life direction. In astrology, the Midheaven is a guiding star for professional growth and reputation, offering valuable insights into your ideal career path and how you are perceived in the public eye. For content creators, under-standing your Midheaven Sign provides clarity on your niche, branding, and long-term goals.

In this chapter, we explore the significance of the Midheaven in shaping your career path as a content creator. We'll uncover how each Midheaven Sign influences your professional journey and offer actionable strategies to align your creative efforts with its guidance.

What Is the Midheaven?

The Midheaven is located at the cusp of the tenth house in your natal chart and symbolizes:

- **Career Aspirations:** Your ultimate professional goals and ambitions.
- **Public Image:** How you are perceived by your audience and society.
- **Legacy:** The lasting impact and contributions you aim to make in your field.
- **Professional Style:** Your natural approach to work and achievement.

For content creators, the Midheaven provides a blueprint for crafting a career that aligns with your higher purpose and resonates with your audience.

How the Midheaven Shapes Career Paths

The Midheaven influences multiple aspects of your professional life as a content creator:

1. Choosing Your Niche

Your Midheaven Sign reflects the themes, topics, and industries where you are most likely to thrive.

2. Building Your Brand

It shapes your public persona and the message you convey to your audience.

3. Setting Career Goals

The Midheaven guides your long-term vision and the milestones you aim to achieve.

4. Navigating Challenges

It highlights potential obstacles and areas of growth in your professional journey.

Midheaven Signs and Career Insights for Content Creators
Each Midheaven Sign carries unique qualities and preferences that influence your career path and branding as a content creator.
Aries Midheaven: The Trailblazer

- **Key Traits:** Ambitious, bold, and action-oriented.
- **Ideal Career Path:** Leadership roles, entrepreneurship, or pioneering content in a niche.
- **Content Style:** Dynamic, high-energy, and motivational.
- **Challenges:** Avoiding burnout and balancing impulsiveness with strategy.
- **Example:** A fitness coach with an Aries Midheaven creates adrenaline-pumping workout videos and launches innovative fitness challenges, inspiring audiences to take action.

Taurus Midheaven: The Builder

- **Key Traits:** Practical, reliable, and focused on quality.
- **Ideal Career Path:** Luxury branding, wellness, or content emphasizing beauty and stability.
- **Content Style:** Grounded, visually appealing, and centered on long-term value.
- **Challenges:** Overcoming resistance to change and embracing innovation.
- **Example:** A lifestyle blogger with a Taurus Midheaven crafts serene, aesthetic content about sustainable living and self-care routines.

Gemini Midheaven: The Communicator

- **Key Traits:** Versatile, curious, and engaging.
- **Ideal Career Path:** Writing, teaching, or creating diverse content across multiple platforms.
- **Content Style:** Informative, witty, and fast-paced.
- **Challenges:** Maintaining focus and avoiding spreading too thin.
- **Example:** A tech reviewer with a Gemini Midheaven creates lively, informative videos comparing the latest gadgets, pairing humor with in-depth analysis.

Cancer Midheaven: The Nurturer

- **Key Traits:** Empathetic, intuitive, and emotionally resonant.
- **Ideal Career Path:** Family, wellness, or emotionally-driven content.
- **Content Style:** Personal, heartfelt, and nurturing.
- **Challenges:** Setting boundaries and balancing personal vulnerability with professionalism.
- **Example:** A mental health advocate with a Cancer Midheaven shares deeply personal stories and creates a safe, supportive space for their audience.

Leo Midheaven: The Performer

- **Key Traits:** Charismatic, creative, and inspiring.
- **Ideal Career Path:** Entertainment, personal branding, or any niche that allows self-expression.
- **Content Style:** Bold, theatrical, and visually striking.
- **Challenges:** Avoiding over-reliance on validation and staying grounded.
- **Example:** A fashion influencer with a Leo Midheaven creates vibrant, trend-setting content that showcases their unique sense of style.

Virgo Midheaven: The Strategist

- **Key Traits:** Detail-oriented, analytical, and service-driven.
- **Ideal Career Path:** Education, organization, or practical content that solves problems.
- **Content Style:** Clear, structured, and helpful.
- **Challenges:** Avoiding perfectionism and embracing creativity.
- **Example:** A productivity coach with a Virgo Midheaven produces meticulous guides and tools to help audiences streamline their lives.

Libra Midheaven: The Harmonizer

- **Key Traits:** Diplomatic, aesthetic, and relationship-focused.
- **Ideal Career Path:** Art, design, or content centered on beauty, balance, and collaboration.
- **Content Style:** Elegant, refined, and relationship-driven.
- **Challenges:** Making decisive choices and asserting individuality.
- **Example:** A relationship coach with a Libra Midheaven creates visually stunning videos about fostering harmony in personal and professional connections.

Scorpio Midheaven: The Transformer

- **Key Traits:** Intense, passionate, and deeply insightful.
- **Ideal Career Path:** Psychology, mystery, or transformative content that delves into complex topics.
- **Content Style:** Intriguing, powerful, and emotionally impactful.
- **Challenges:** Managing intensity and maintaining transparency.
- **Example:** A documentarian with a Scorpio Midheaven creates in-depth explorations of untold stories, uncovering hidden truths and challenging perceptions.

Sagittarius Midheaven: The Explorer

- **Key Traits:** Inspirational, adventurous, and philosophical.
- **Ideal Career Path:** Travel, education, or content that inspires growth and exploration.
- **Content Style:** Uplifting, expansive, and thought-provoking.
- **Challenges:** Staying focused and balancing ambition with practical steps.
- **Example:** A travel vlogger with a Sagittarius Midheaven shares transformative journeys that inspire their audience to explore the world and embrace new perspectives.

Capricorn Midheaven: The Achiever

- **Key Traits:** Ambitious, disciplined, and results-driven.
- **Ideal Career Path:** Business, finance, or content that emphasizes success and achievement.
- **Content Style:** Professional, authoritative, and goal-oriented.
- **Challenges:** Balancing work with personal fulfillment and avoiding overwork.
- **Example:** A financial advisor with a Capricorn Midheaven creates data-driven content to help audiences build wealth and achieve long-term success.

Aquarius Midheaven: The Visionary

- **Key Traits:** Innovative, unconventional, and socially conscious.
- **Ideal Career Path:** Technology, activism, or content that promotes progress and inclusivity.
- **Content Style:** Futuristic, creative, and collaborative.
- **Challenges:** Balancing idealism with practicality and staying grounded.
- **Example:** A tech entrepreneur with an Aquarius Midheaven creates forward-thinking tutorials and shares socially-conscious innovations.

Pisces Midheaven: The Dreamer

- **Key Traits:** Imaginative, spiritual, and intuitive.
- **Ideal Career Path:** Art, spirituality, or content that evokes inspiration and emotion.
- **Content Style:** Ethereal, emotive, and deeply creative.
- **Challenges:** Staying organized and translating vision into actionable steps.
- **Example:** A visual artist with a Pisces Midheaven creates mesmerizing, dreamlike visuals that inspire their audience's imagination.

Strategies for Aligning Your Career with Your Midheaven
1. Discover Your Midheaven Sign

- Use an astrology tool like AstroSeek or TimePassages to identify your Midheaven Sign.
- Reflect on how its traits align with your professional goals and current content.

2. Define Your Career Vision

- Write a mission statement inspired by your Midheaven's qualities.
- Set short-term and long-term goals that reflect your aspirations and audience's needs.

3. Develop a Brand Identity

- Align your visual and messaging strategies with your Midheaven's energy.
- Ensure consistency across platforms to reinforce your brand image.

4. Tailor Your Content Strategy

- Choose themes, formats, and platforms that align with your Midheaven's strengths.
- Reflect on how your content contributes to your legacy and professional growth.

5. Embrace Challenges

- Use your Midheaven Sign's potential challenges as growth opportunities.
- Reflect on how these lessons can shape your content and career direction.

Final Thoughts

Your Midheaven Sign serves as a celestial compass, guiding your career path and professional legacy as a content creator. By aligning with its energy, you can create a brand that reflects your highest aspirations, resonates with your audience, and leaves a lasting impact. Whether you're a bold Aries trailblazer, a nurturing Cancer storyteller, or a visionary Aquarius innovator, your Midheaven provides the roadmap to fulfilling your creative and professional potential.

Chapter 39: Personal Planet Combinations – Customizing Your Content Strategy

Astrology is a dynamic interplay of celestial energies, and your **personal planets**—Sun, Moon, Mercury, Venus, and Mars—hold the key to your unique personality, creative style, and how you approach life. Each planet governs a specific aspect of your identity and expression, and their interactions in your natal chart (known as **planetary combinations**) shape your strengths, challenges, and opportunities as a content creator.

This chapter explores the role of personal planet combinations in customizing your content strategy. By understanding how these planets interact, you can align your creative efforts with your unique energy, maximize your impact, and resonate more deeply with your audience.

The Role of Personal Planets in Content Creation

Each personal planet governs a fundamental aspect of your personality and creative process:

- **Sun:** Your core identity and creative purpose.
- **Moon:** Your emotional needs and intuitive connection with your audience.
- **Mercury:** Your communication style and how you convey your message.
- **Venus:** Your aesthetic preferences and values.
- **Mars:** Your drive, ambition, and approach to taking action.

The combinations of these planets create a personalized blueprint for crafting content that reflects your authentic self and aligns with your strengths.

Key Personal Planet Combinations and Their Influence
1. Sun-Moon Combination: Identity and Emotional Connection
The Sun represents your core identity, while the Moon reflects your emotional world and intuitive connection. Together, they shape the tone and emotional depth of your content.

- **Harmonious Combination (e.g., Sun in Leo, Moon in Aries):** Bold, confident content that inspires and energizes your audience.
- **Challenging Combination (e.g., Sun in Gemini, Moon in Virgo):** Balancing intellectual versatility with emotional grounding.

Example: A creator with Sun in Leo and Moon in Cancer combines bold self-expression with nurturing storytelling, creating content that feels both inspiring and heartfelt.
Content Strategy Tips:

- Highlight themes that reflect your Sun's purpose and your Moon's emotional resonance.
- Balance authenticity with emotional relatability to connect deeply with your audience.

2. Mercury-Venus Combination: Communication and Aesthetics
Mercury governs your communication style, while Venus influences your sense of beauty and harmony. Together, they shape the tone, style, and visual appeal of your content.

- **Harmonious Combination (e.g., Mercury in Libra, Venus in Taurus):** Balanced, elegant messaging paired with visually appealing content.
- **Challenging Combination (e.g., Mercury in Scorpio, Venus in Aquarius):** Finding harmony between intense communication and unconventional aesthetics.

Example: A creator with Mercury in Gemini and Venus in Leo produces witty, engaging posts with a bold, eye-catching design.
Content Strategy Tips:

- Use your Mercury placement to craft clear, engaging messages.
- Align visuals and themes with your Venus placement for a cohesive aesthetic.

3. Sun-Mars Combination: Purpose and Action

The Sun reflects your purpose, while Mars represents your drive and how you take action. Together, they determine your creative momentum and work ethic.

- **Harmonious Combination (e.g., Sun in Aries, Mars in Sagittarius):** High-energy, adventurous content with a bold and optimistic tone.
- **Challenging Combination (e.g., Sun in Pisces, Mars in Capricorn):** Balancing dreamy aspirations with disciplined execution.

Example: A creator with Sun in Virgo and Mars in Cancer uses meticulous planning and a nurturing approach to create impactful, heartfelt content.

Content Strategy Tips:

- Use your Sun's placement to identify your core themes and your Mars placement to drive execution.
- Balance ambition with rest to sustain your creative energy.

4. Moon-Venus Combination: Emotional Connection and Aesthetic Appeal

The Moon governs emotions, while Venus influences beauty and values. Together, they shape how you evoke feelings and create visually resonant content.

- **Harmonious Combination (e.g., Moon in Pisces, Venus in Cancer):** Dreamy, emotionally evocative content with a nurturing aesthetic.
- **Challenging Combination (e.g., Moon in Aries, Venus in Capricorn):** Balancing emotional expression with structured, goal-oriented design.

Example: A creator with Moon in Scorpio and Venus in Libra produces deeply emotional narratives paired with elegant visuals.

Content Strategy Tips:

- Use your Moon placement to craft emotionally resonant themes.
- Leverage your Venus placement to enhance your content's visual and aesthetic appeal.

5. Mercury-Mars Combination: Communication and Execution

Mercury shapes how you communicate, while Mars governs how you act. Together, they influence your ability to execute ideas effectively.

- **Harmonious Combination (e.g., Mercury in Aquarius, Mars in Aries):** Innovative, forward-thinking content delivered with dynamic energy.
- **Challenging Combination (e.g., Mercury in Taurus, Mars in Leo):** Balancing methodical thinking with bold action.

Example: A creator with Mercury in Virgo and Mars in Scorpio produces precise, detail-oriented content with a transformative edge.

Content Strategy Tips:

- Align your communication strategy (Mercury) with your action plan (Mars).
- Use Mars' energy to propel creative execution and overcome procrastination.

Integrating Personal Planet Combinations into Your Content Strategy
1. Analyze Your Natal Chart
Identify the placements of your Sun, Moon, Mercury, Venus, and Mars to understand your personal planet combinations.

- **Action Plan:**
    - Use astrology tools like AstroSeek or TimePassages to generate your natal chart.
    - Reflect on how each combination influences your strengths and challenges in content creation.

2. Craft Content That Reflects Your Unique Energy
Align your themes, visuals, and messaging with the qualities of your personal planet combinations.

- **Action Plan:**
    - Use Sun-Moon insights to set the emotional tone of your content.
    - Leverage Mercury-Venus combinations to balance communication with aesthetic appeal.
    - Execute plans with the focus and energy of Sun-Mars and Mercury-Mars combinations.

3. Balance Strengths and Challenges
Each combination brings both strengths and potential challenges. Use astrology as a guide to balance these dynamics.

- **Action Plan:**
    - Identify areas where your combinations complement each other.
    - Focus on overcoming challenges, such as balancing emotional depth (Moon) with clarity in communication (Mercury).

4. Create a Content Calendar Aligned with Your Planets
Use insights from your personal planet combinations to structure a content strategy that reflects your unique energy.

- **Action Plan:**
    - Schedule content creation around themes inspired by your Sun and Moon.
    - Use Mercury's placement to guide your communication style in each piece of content.
    - Plan high-energy tasks during favorable Mars transits.

Examples of Personal Planet Content Strategies

- **Example 1:** A creator with Sun in Leo, Moon in Pisces, and Mercury in Gemini combines bold storytelling, dreamy visuals, and witty messaging to craft engaging, emotionally resonant content.
- **Example 2:** A content strategist with Venus in Taurus and Mars in Capricorn emphasizes elegant design and disciplined execution, creating high-value, polished content.
- **Example 3:** A podcaster with Mercury in Aquarius and Moon in Scorpio delivers thought-provoking discussions with emotional depth and a transformative perspective.

Potential Challenges and How to Overcome Them

1. Conflicting Energies

Certain planet combinations may create internal tension, such as balancing emotional intuition with logical analysis.

- **Solution:** Use each placement in its domain (e.g., rely on Moon for emotional themes and Mercury for logical structure).

2. Overemphasis on One Planet

Focusing too heavily on one planet's traits may limit your versatility.

- **Solution:** Integrate insights from all your personal planets to create a balanced strategy.

3. Difficulty in Execution

Mars' placement may affect your ability to act on ideas.

- **Solution:** Use Mars transits or align content creation with high-energy days to overcome inertia.

Final Thoughts

Your personal planet combinations offer a celestial blueprint for creating content that aligns with your authentic self and connects deeply with your audience. By understanding how these planets interact, you can craft a customized content strategy that reflects your strengths, overcomes challenges, and brings your creative vision to life. Whether balancing the emotional depth of your Moon, the aesthetic flair of Venus, or the dynamic drive of Mars, your personal planets are the key to unlocking your full potential as a content creator.

Chapter 40: Yearly and Monthly Transits – Planning Your Content Calendar

Astrological transits are the movements of celestial bodies as they interact with the planets in your natal chart. These transits influence the energy, opportunities, and challenges you face, making them a powerful tool for content creators to align their strategies with cosmic rhythms. By understanding yearly and monthly transits, you can plan your content calendar to optimize productivity, engagement, and growth while staying attuned to universal energies.

This chapter explores how to use yearly and monthly astrological transits to structure your content calendar, schedule launches, and navigate challenges with precision and creativity.

What Are Transits?

In astrology, **transits** refer to the current positions of planets as they move through the zodiac and interact with the placements in your natal chart. They provide insights into:

1. **Themes of the Year:** Long-term influences from outer planets (e.g., Jupiter, Saturn).
2. **Monthly Shifts:** Short-term changes influenced by inner planets (e.g., Mercury, Venus, Mars).
3. **Opportunities and Challenges:** How planetary aspects (conjunctions, trines, squares) impact your personal and professional life.

For content creators, tracking transits allows you to align your work with cosmic energy, making your efforts more effective and resonant.

The Role of Yearly and Monthly Transits in Content Planning

Transits influence your content strategy by:

1. **Highlighting Key Themes:** Outer planets bring overarching themes that guide your year's focus.
2. **Timing Content Releases:** Monthly transits of faster-moving planets influence short-term energy and productivity.
3. **Navigating Challenges:** Retrogrades and difficult aspects highlight periods for reflection and adjustment.
4. **Maximizing Opportunities:** Favorable transits offer windows for launches, collaborations, and creative breakthroughs.

Yearly Transits: Outer Planets and Long-Term Strategy
Outer planets move slowly, shaping overarching themes and long-term goals. These planets include:

1. Jupiter: Expansion and Growth

- **Cycle:** Spends about one year in each sign.
- **Influence:** Highlights areas of growth, abundance, and opportunity in your life and career.
- **Content Strategy:**
    ◦ Plan major launches, collaborations, or educational content during Jupiter's favorable transits.
    ◦ Focus on niches aligned with Jupiter's current sign (e.g., travel, education, or philosophy when in Sagittarius).
- **Example:** During Jupiter in Aries, a content creator might focus on bold, pioneering projects that emphasize leadership and innovation.

2. Saturn: Discipline and Structure

- **Cycle:** Spends about 2.5 years in each sign.
- **Influence:** Encourages long-term planning, discipline, and mastering challenges.
- **Content Strategy:**
    ◦ Build systems and frameworks for consistent content creation.
    ◦ Use Saturn's energy to tackle ambitious, long-term projects.
- **Example:** During Saturn in Aquarius, a digital entrepreneur might focus on building a community-driven platform or exploring tech innovations.

3. Uranus: Innovation and Change

- **Cycle:** Spends about 7 years in each sign.
- **Influence:** Brings sudden changes, breakthroughs, and opportunities for innovation.
- **Content Strategy:**
    ◦ Experiment with new formats, platforms, or technologies during Uranus transits.
    ◦ Embrace themes of freedom and transformation in your content.
- **Example:** During Uranus in Taurus, a content creator might explore sustainability, personal finance, or innovative approaches to material resources.

4. Neptune: Imagination and Spirituality

- **Cycle:** Spends about 14 years in each sign.
- **Influence:** Enhances creativity, intuition, and spiritual exploration.
- **Content Strategy:**
    - Create emotionally resonant, imaginative content during Neptune's favorable aspects.
    - Avoid overpromising or losing focus during challenging Neptune transits.
- **Example:** During Neptune in Pisces, a filmmaker might craft dreamy, otherworldly narratives that inspire deep reflection.

5. Pluto: Transformation and Power

- **Cycle:** Spends 12-31 years in each sign.
- **Influence:** Represents transformation, power dynamics, and profound growth.
- **Content Strategy:**
    - Focus on content that explores deep, transformative themes.
    - Use Pluto transits to redefine your brand or niche.
- **Example:** During Pluto in Capricorn, a business coach might emphasize strategies for personal empowerment and long-term success.

Monthly Transits: Inner Planets and Short-Term Strategy

Inner planets move quickly, influencing your day-to-day activities and short-term goals. These planets include:

1. Sun: Monthly Themes

- **Cycle:** Moves through one sign each month.
- **Influence:** Highlights the themes of the month, influencing collective energy.
- **Content Strategy:**
    - Align your topics with the Sun's sign (e.g., focus on adventure during Sagittarius season or introspection during Scorpio season).

2. Moon: Weekly Energy Shifts

- **Cycle:** Moves through all 12 signs in about 28 days.
- **Influence:** Governs emotional energy and intuitive timing.
- **Content Strategy:**
    - Use the New Moon for brainstorming and intention setting.
    - Launch projects during the Full Moon for maximum visibility.

3. Mercury: Communication and Ideas

- **Cycle:** Moves through a sign in 15-60 days (except during retrogrades).
- **Influence:** Influences communication, learning, and planning.
- **Content Strategy:**
    - Schedule writing, editing, and negotiations during direct Mercury periods.
    - Use Mercury retrograde to revisit and refine old content.

4. Venus: Aesthetics and Relationships

- **Cycle:** Moves through a sign in about 23-60 days (except during retrogrades).
- **Influence:** Impacts creativity, beauty, and relationship dynamics.
- **Content Strategy:**
    - Focus on visual design and relationship-building during favorable Venus transits.
    - Avoid rebranding during Venus retrograde.

5. Mars: Energy and Action

- **Cycle:** Moves through a sign in about 6-7 weeks (except during retrogrades).
- **Influence:** Drives action, ambition, and physical energy.
- **Content Strategy:**
    - Schedule high-energy tasks and launches during direct Mars transits.

○ Reflect and reorganize during Mars retrograde.

Creating a Transit-Based Content Calendar
1. Identify Key Yearly Transits

- Use an astrology calendar to track outer planet transits and their aspects to your natal chart.
- Highlight periods of growth (Jupiter transits), restructuring (Saturn transits), and transformation (Pluto transits).

2. Track Monthly Shifts

- Align your content themes with the Sun's zodiac sign and the Moon's phases.
- Plan short-term goals around Mercury, Venus, and Mars transits.

3. Align Launches with Favorable Transits

- Use Jupiter and Mars transits for launches and expansion.
- Schedule promotions and relationship-building during favorable Venus transits.

4. Reflect During Retrogrades

- Revisit and repurpose old content during Mercury or Venus retrograde.
- Use retrogrades for introspection, fine-tuning, and resolving past challenges.

Tools for Transit Planning

1. **Astrology Apps:** Use tools like TimePassages, AstroSeek, or Chani for transit insights.
2. **Content Calendars:** Integrate transit themes into platforms like Notion, Trello, or Google Calendar.
3. **Journals:** Track how transits influence your energy, creativity, and audience engagement.

Real-Life Applications of Transit-Based Content Strategy

- **Example 1:** A wellness influencer plans a mindfulness campaign during Neptune's trine to their Venus, emphasizing imagination and emotional connection.
- **Example 2:** A tech entrepreneur schedules a major product launch during Jupiter's transit through their Midheaven, leveraging expansion energy.
- **Example 3:** A content creator uses Mercury retrograde to revisit and enhance their best-performing blog posts, optimizing them for SEO and relevance.

Potential Challenges and How to Overcome Them
1. Overloading Your Schedule

- **Solution:** Focus on major transits and prioritize quality over quantity.

2. Navigating Difficult Transits

- **Solution:** Use challenging transits for introspection and refinement, rather than pushing forward aggressively.

3. Adapting to Retrogrades

- **Solution:** Embrace retrogrades as opportunities for review and growth, avoiding new commitments.

Final Thoughts

Yearly and monthly transits provide a celestial roadmap for planning your content calendar, aligning your creative efforts with the flow of cosmic energy. By integrating outer planet influences for long-term strategy and inner planet transits for day-to-day planning, you can optimize your productivity, enhance your engagement, and navigate challenges with confidence. Whether leveraging Jupiter's expansion, Saturn's discipline, or the Moon's intuitive timing, aligning with transits empowers you to create content that resonates deeply and authentically.

Appendix

Appendix A: Quick Zodiac Reference for Content Planning

Astrology offers invaluable insights for content creators, helping to align themes, aesthetics, and strategies with the energy of each zodiac sign. This quick-reference guide serves as a toolkit for planning content based on the zodiac's unique characteristics. Whether you're creating seasonal campaigns, tapping into cosmic trends, or aligning your brand with celestial energies, this appendix ensures you stay inspired and on track.

The Zodiac Signs and Their Creative Energy

Each zodiac sign brings a distinct energy, which can be harnessed to craft meaningful and impactful content. Here's a breakdown of all 12 signs, their key traits, and how to integrate their energy into your content planning.

1. Aries (March 21 - April 19) – The Trailblazer

- **Element:** Fire
- **Ruling Planet:** Mars
- **Key Traits:** Bold, energetic, adventurous, competitive, pioneering.
- **Content Ideas:**
    ◦ Launch bold campaigns or new projects.
    ◦ Create motivational content that inspires action.
    ◦ Use dynamic visuals with vibrant reds and bold contrasts.
    ◦ Share stories of courage, leadership, or breaking boundaries.

Example: Launch a high-energy fitness challenge or an entrepreneurial guide.

2. Taurus (April 20 - May 20) – The Builder

- **Element:** Earth
- **Ruling Planet:** Venus
- **Key Traits:** Grounded, luxurious, sensual, practical, patient.
- **Content Ideas:**
    ◦ Highlight themes of stability, self-care, and indulgence.
    ◦ Create visually rich, aesthetic content with earthy tones and textures.
    ◦ Share guides on sustainable living or mindful spending.
    ◦ Focus on sensory appeal, like food, fashion, or interior design.

Example: A serene self-care routine video with soothing visuals.

3. Gemini (May 21 - June 20) – The Communicator

- **Element:** Air
- **Ruling Planet:** Mercury
- **Key Traits:** Curious, witty, versatile, talkative, intellectual.
- **Content Ideas:**
    - Produce engaging, fast-paced content like quick tips or tutorials.
    - Use humor and clever wordplay in messaging.
    - Host Q&A sessions, interactive polls, or live streams.
    - Cover diverse topics to appeal to a wide audience.

Example: A tech blogger shares a "Top 5 Gadgets You Need" video.

4. Cancer (June 21 - July 22) – The Nurturer

- **Element:** Water
- **Ruling Planet:** Moon
- **Key Traits:** Emotional, intuitive, caring, nostalgic, family-oriented.
- **Content Ideas:**
    - Share personal stories or emotionally resonant narratives.
    - Focus on home, family, or traditions.
    - Use soft, warm visuals with calming colors.
    - Offer tips for creating comfort or fostering connections.

Example: A heartfelt blog post on creating holiday memories.

5. Leo (July 23 - August 22) – The Performer

- **Element:** Fire
- **Ruling Planet:** Sun
- **Key Traits:** Charismatic, creative, bold, dramatic, self-expressive.
- **Content Ideas:**
    - Showcase your personality with vibrant, confident content.
    - Create campaigns that highlight individuality and uniqueness.
    - Use golds, yellows, and striking visuals.
    - Share stories of triumph, creativity, or leadership.

Example: A vibrant social media campaign celebrating self-expression.

6. Virgo (August 23 - September 22) – The Strategist

- **Element:** Earth
- **Ruling Planet:** Mercury
- **Key Traits:** Analytical, detail-oriented, helpful, practical, methodical.
- **Content Ideas:**
    - Offer step-by-step guides, tutorials, or checklists.
    - Focus on organization, productivity, or health topics.
    - Use clean, minimalist visuals with muted tones.
    - Emphasize clarity and precision in your messaging.

Example: A productivity coach shares a "Monthly Planner Setup" video.

7. Libra (September 23 - October 22) – The Harmonizer

- **Element:** Air
- **Ruling Planet:** Venus
- **Key Traits:** Charming, balanced, diplomatic, aesthetic, relationship-focused.
- **Content Ideas:**
    - Highlight themes of beauty, balance, and partnership.
    - Use elegant visuals with soft pastels and symmetrical designs.
    - Collaborate with other creators or promote relationship-building.
    - Share content about fairness, justice, or interpersonal dynamics.

Example: A fashion influencer creates a "Wardrobe Essentials for Every Season" series.

8. Scorpio (October 23 - November 21) – The Transformer

- **Element:** Water
- **Ruling Planet:** Pluto (and Mars)
- **Key Traits:** Intense, mysterious, passionate, transformative, resilient.
- **Content Ideas:**
    - Dive into deep, thought-provoking topics.
    - Use dramatic visuals with dark, moody tones.
    - Focus on transformation, empowerment, or uncovering truths.
    - Share personal or collective journeys of resilience and growth.

Example: A documentary exploring hidden stories or taboos.

9. Sagittarius (November 22 - December 21) – The Explorer

- **Element:** Fire
- **Ruling Planet:** Jupiter
- **Key Traits:** Adventurous, optimistic, philosophical, expansive, curious.
- **Content Ideas:**
    - Focus on travel, exploration, or personal growth.
    - Create uplifting, inspiring content with vibrant visuals.
    - Share philosophical musings or lessons from life experiences.
    - Encourage your audience to embrace adventure and open-mindedness.

Example: A travel vlogger showcases a "Bucket List Destinations" series.

10. Capricorn (December 22 - January 19) – The Achiever

- **Element:** Earth
- **Ruling Planet:** Saturn
- **Key Traits:** Ambitious, disciplined, practical, resourceful, responsible.
- **Content Ideas:**
    - Highlight themes of success, structure, and perseverance.
    - Use professional, polished visuals with neutral tones.
    - Share goal-setting techniques or career advice.
    - Focus on long-term value and credibility in your messaging.

Example: A financial expert shares a "Year-End Financial Planning Guide."

11. Aquarius (January 20 - February 18) – The Visionary

- **Element:** Air
- **Ruling Planet:** Uranus
- **Key Traits:** Innovative, unconventional, socially conscious, forward-thinking.
- **Content Ideas:**
    - Create futuristic or tech-focused content.
    - Use bold, unconventional designs and messaging.
    - Promote social causes or highlight progressive ideas.
    - Encourage collaboration and community-building.

Example: A tech innovator shares a series on "The Future of AI in Everyday Life."

12. Pisces (February 19 - March 20) – The Dreamer

- **Element:** Water
- **Ruling Planet:** Neptune
- **Key Traits:** Imaginative, intuitive, spiritual, empathetic, creative.
- **Content Ideas:**
  - Focus on creativity, art, or spirituality.
  - Use dreamy, ethereal visuals with soft colors.
  - Share content about emotional healing or imaginative storytelling.
  - Encourage introspection and connection with the subconscious.

Example: An artist launches a "Dream-Inspired Art" collection.

How to Use This Guide

1. **Plan by Zodiac Season:** Align your content themes with the energy of the Sun's zodiac sign for the month.
2. **Incorporate Personal Placements:** Use your own zodiac placements (e.g., Sun, Moon, Rising) to create content that feels authentic and aligned.
3. **Tap Into Trends:** Use trending astrological themes (e.g., Venus retrograde, eclipses) to craft timely and relevant content.

Final Thoughts

This quick-reference guide is your go-to resource for aligning content creation with the unique energy of each zodiac sign. By understanding the traits and strengths of the zodiac, you can craft content that resonates deeply with your audience and stays in harmony with the cosmos. Whether you're planning bold Aries launches, serene Taurus aesthetics, or introspective Cancer reflections, let the zodiac guide your creative journey.

Appendix B: Planetary Influence Guide for Beginners

Astrology revolves around the movements and energies of celestial bodies, each of which exerts a unique influence on our personalities, emotions, and life paths. Understanding the roles of the planets in astrology is essential for harnessing their energies effectively in your personal and professional life, including content creation. This beginner-friendly guide provides a comprehensive overview of the planetary influences, their astrological meanings, and how to incorporate them into your creative strategies.

The Planets in Astrology

In astrology, planets symbolize distinct energies that shape our motivations, relationships, communication, and more. Each planet governs specific areas of life, and its placement in your natal chart provides insights into your strengths, challenges, and opportunities.

Planets are categorized into two groups:

1. **Personal Planets:** Faster-moving planets that influence your personality and day-to-day experiences (e.g., Sun, Moon, Mercury, Venus, Mars).
2. **Outer Planets:** Slower-moving planets that influence societal trends, long-term themes, and generational traits (e.g., Jupiter, Saturn, Uranus, Neptune, Pluto).

Personal Planets
1. The Sun – Core Identity and Purpose

- **Represents:** Ego, vitality, creative essence, and life purpose.
- **Zodiac Ruler:** Leo
- **Key Themes:** Self-expression, leadership, individuality.
- **Influence in Content Creation:** Reflects your unique voice and the core themes of your content.
- **Questions to Ask:**
    - What drives your creativity?
    - How can your content showcase your individuality?

Example: A creator with the Sun in Taurus may focus on themes of luxury, stability, and nature, producing content that reflects these values.

2. The Moon – Emotions and Intuition

- **Represents:** Emotional world, instincts, and inner needs.
- **Zodiac Ruler:** Cancer
- **Key Themes:** Nurturing, comfort, intuition, cycles.
- **Influence in Content Creation:** Shapes the emotional tone of your work and your connection with your audience.
- **Questions to Ask:**
    - How does your content resonate emotionally with your audience?
    - What themes feel most intuitive to explore?

Example: A creator with the Moon in Pisces might produce dreamy, emotionally resonant content that inspires empathy and imagination.

3. Mercury – Communication and Thought Processes

- **Represents:** Communication, intellect, and adaptability.
- **Zodiac Ruler:** Gemini and Virgo
- **Key Themes:** Learning, messaging, curiosity, versatility.
- **Influence in Content Creation:** Governs how you convey ideas and interact with your audience.
- **Questions to Ask:**
    - How can you communicate your ideas clearly and effectively?
    - What platforms or formats align with your communication style?

Example: A creator with Mercury in Sagittarius may focus on inspirational, big-picture topics, delivering content in a storytelling format.

4. Venus – Beauty and Relationships

- **Represents:** Aesthetics, values, and connections.
- **Zodiac Ruler:** Taurus and Libra
- **Key Themes:** Harmony, attraction, creativity, love.
- **Influence in Content Creation:** Shapes your visual identity and your approach to building relationships.
- **Questions to Ask:**
    - What aesthetic best represents your brand?
    - How do you foster connections with your audience?

Example: A creator with Venus in Leo might adopt a bold, glamorous aesthetic and focus on themes of self-expression and creativity.

5. Mars – Drive and Action

- **Represents:** Energy, ambition, and initiative.
- **Zodiac Ruler:** Aries
- **Key Themes:** Motivation, courage, conflict, passion.
- **Influence in Content Creation:** Drives your productivity, execution, and approach to challenges.
- **Questions to Ask:**
    - How can you channel your energy into impactful content?
    - What strategies keep you motivated and focused?

Example: A creator with Mars in Capricorn may approach projects with discipline and a focus on achieving long-term success.

Social Planets

6. Jupiter – Growth and Abundance

- **Represents:** Expansion, optimism, and wisdom.
- **Zodiac Ruler:** Sagittarius
- **Key Themes:** Opportunity, growth, learning, generosity.
- **Influence in Content Creation:** Encourages exploring new opportunities and expanding your reach.
- **Questions to Ask:**
    - How can you grow your audience or skill set?
    - What new opportunities align with your long-term goals?

Example: A creator with Jupiter in Aquarius might focus on innovative, community-driven content that inspires collective growth.

7. Saturn – Discipline and Structure

- **Represents:** Responsibility, structure, and long-term goals.
- **Zodiac Ruler:** Capricorn
- **Key Themes:** Discipline, ambition, resilience, authority.
- **Influence in Content Creation:** Guides consistent effort and mastery in your work.
- **Questions to Ask:**
    - What systems or routines support your content creation?
    - How do you balance creativity with discipline?

Example: A creator with Saturn in Virgo may emphasize practical, detail-oriented content and build a reputation for reliability.

Outer Planets

8. Uranus – Innovation and Change

- **Represents:** Revolution, individuality, and technology.
- **Zodiac Ruler:** Aquarius
- **Key Themes:** Innovation, freedom, progress, originality.
- **Influence in Content Creation:** Encourages experimenting with new formats, platforms, and ideas.
- **Questions to Ask:**
    - How can you stand out by being unconventional?
    - What innovative approaches can you try in your content?

Example: A creator with Uranus in Taurus might explore sustainability or create tech-driven solutions for practical problems.

9. Neptune – Imagination and Spirituality

- **Represents:** Creativity, intuition, and dreams.
- **Zodiac Ruler:** Pisces
- **Key Themes:** Inspiration, compassion, illusion, spirituality.
- **Influence in Content Creation:** Fuels artistic expression and emotional depth.
- **Questions to Ask:**
    - How can your content inspire or uplift your audience?
    - What themes of imagination or spirituality resonate with you?

Example: A creator with Neptune in Pisces might focus on art, healing, or storytelling with ethereal and emotional undertones.

10. Pluto – Transformation and Power

- **Represents:** Transformation, power, and rebirth.
- **Zodiac Ruler:** Scorpio
- **Key Themes:** Depth, empowerment, renewal, intensity.
- **Influence in Content Creation:** Encourages tackling profound, transformative topics.
- **Questions to Ask:**
    - How can your content empower or transform your audience?
    - What deeper truths are you ready to explore?

Example: A creator with Pluto in Capricorn may focus on themes of personal and professional empowerment through structure and discipline.

How to Use Planetary Influences in Content Creation
1. Plan Around Planetary Transits

- Track current planetary movements to align your content with the energy of the moment. For example:
    ◦ Use Mercury retrograde to revisit and refine old content.
    ◦ Leverage Jupiter transits for launches or collaborations.

2. Reflect on Your Natal Chart

- Identify how each planet's placement influences your creative style and challenges.
- Focus on leveraging your strengths while balancing any challenges.

3. Align Themes with Planetary Energy

- Integrate planetary themes into your content. For example:
    ◦ Venus for beauty and design.
    ◦ Mars for energy-driven campaigns.

4. Balance Inner and Outer Planet Energies

- Use personal planets to guide daily content strategies.
- Use outer planets to align with long-term trends and transformations.

Final Thoughts

Understanding planetary influences is like having a cosmic toolkit for content creation. By aligning your efforts with the energy of the planets, you can create content that feels authentic, purposeful, and impactful. Whether tapping into the bold drive of Mars, the aesthetic sensibilities of Venus, or the expansive energy of Jupiter, the planets offer endless inspiration for crafting meaningful work.

This guide is a starting point for exploring astrology's rich layers and integrating its wisdom into your creative journey. For deeper insights, refer to your natal chart and track current transits to align your content with the stars.

Appendix C: Lunar Calendar with Phases and Key Dates for the Year

The Moon's phases play a powerful role in shaping energy, mood, and productivity. For content creators, aligning your efforts with the lunar cycle can amplify creativity, focus, and audience engagement. This appendix provides a detailed lunar calendar for the year, explaining each phase's significance and highlighting key lunar events to help you optimize your content strategy.

The Lunar Phases and Their Influences

Each lunar phase carries a distinct energy that can be harnessed for specific creative and strategic purposes:

1. New Moon – Beginnings and Intention Setting

- **Energy:** Quiet, introspective, ideal for planning and goal setting.
- **Activities:** Brainstorm ideas, set intentions, and prepare for new projects.
- **Content Ideas:** Announce new projects, share your vision, or create reflective content.

2. Waxing Crescent – Building Momentum

- **Energy:** Optimistic, motivating, perfect for taking the first steps.
- **Activities:** Start working on plans, refine ideas, and seek inspiration.
- **Content Ideas:** Share behind-the-scenes looks at your creative process or tease upcoming projects.

3. First Quarter – Action and Overcoming Challenges

- **Energy:** Active, dynamic, focused on problem-solving and execution.
- **Activities:** Tackle challenges, make decisions, and take significant action.
- **Content Ideas:** Post tutorials, practical guides, or content showing progress toward goals.

4. Waxing Gibbous – Refinement and Preparation

- **Energy:** Determined, meticulous, ideal for fine-tuning and adjusting.
- **Activities:** Review work, prepare for launches, and ensure readiness.
- **Content Ideas:** Publish previews, provide updates, or share lessons learned during preparation.

5. Full Moon – Completion and Visibility

- **Energy:** Intense, celebratory, ideal for showcasing work and reaping rewards.
- **Activities:** Launch projects, share results, and engage with your audience.
- **Content Ideas:** Host live events, release major announcements, or publish impactful stories.

6. Waning Gibbous – Reflection and Sharing

- **Energy:** Gratifying, thoughtful, focused on teaching and celebrating achievements.
- **Activities:** Reflect on successes, share insights, and express gratitude.
- **Content Ideas:** Post thank-you messages, share case studies, or publish thought leadership pieces.

7. Last Quarter – Release and Letting Go

- **Energy:** Transitional, introspective, focused on clearing and simplifying.
- **Activities:** Wrap up loose ends, release what's not working, and reassess goals.
- **Content Ideas:** Share lessons learned, refine strategies, or post reflective content.

8. Waning Crescent – Rest and Rejuvenation

- **Energy:** Restorative, calm, ideal for introspection and healing.
- **Activities:** Pause, recharge, and plan for the next cycle.
- **Content Ideas:** Publish soothing or inspirational content, such as meditations or affirmations.

Key Lunar Events for the Year

Below is a lunar calendar for the current year, highlighting New Moons, Full Moons, eclipses, and other key lunar events.

January

- **January 11:** New Moon in Capricorn
- **January 18:** First Quarter Moon in Aries
- **January 25:** Full Moon in Leo
- **January 31:** Last Quarter Moon in Scorpio

Content Focus: Start the year with goal-setting content during the New Moon, followed by bold, creative launches during the Full Moon in Leo.

February

- **February 10:** New Moon in Aquarius
- **February 17:** First Quarter Moon in Taurus
- **February 24:** Full Moon in Virgo

Content Focus: Highlight innovation and community themes during the New Moon in Aquarius and focus on practical, detail-oriented launches around the Full Moon in Virgo.

March

- **March 9:** New Moon in Pisces
- **March 16:** First Quarter Moon in Gemini
- **March 23:** Full Moon in Libra
- **March 30:** Last Quarter Moon in Capricorn

Content Focus: Dive into imaginative storytelling during the New Moon in Pisces and emphasize balance and harmony in collaborations around the Full Moon in Libra.

April

- **April 8:** New Moon in Aries
- **April 15:** First Quarter Moon in Cancer
- **April 22:** Full Moon in Scorpio

Content Focus: Use the New Moon in Aries for bold beginnings and tackle transformative topics around the Full Moon in Scorpio.

May

- **May 7:** New Moon in Taurus
- **May 14:** First Quarter Moon in Leo
- **May 21:** Full Moon in Sagittarius
- **May 28:** Last Quarter Moon in Aquarius

Content Focus: Focus on luxury and sustainability themes during the New Moon in Taurus and explore adventurous, big-picture ideas around the Full Moon in Sagittarius.

June

- **June 6:** New Moon in Gemini
- **June 13:** First Quarter Moon in Virgo
- **June 20:** Full Moon in Capricorn
- **June 27:** Last Quarter Moon in Pisces

Content Focus: Communicate diverse ideas during the New Moon in Gemini and emphasize structure and discipline during the Full Moon in Capricorn.

July

- **July 5:** New Moon in Cancer
- **July 12:** First Quarter Moon in Libra
- **July 19:** Full Moon in Aquarius

Content Focus: Nurture your audience with heartfelt content during the New Moon in Cancer and explore innovative, community-focused ideas around the Full Moon in Aquarius.

August

- **August 4:** New Moon in Leo
- **August 11:** First Quarter Moon in Scorpio
- **August 18:** Full Moon in Pisces

Content Focus: Showcase your creativity and individuality during the New Moon in Leo and lean into dreamy, emotional narratives around the Full Moon in Pisces.

September

- **September 3:** New Moon in Virgo
- **September 10:** First Quarter Moon in Sagittarius
- **September 17:** Full Moon in Aries

Content Focus: Focus on organization and productivity during the New Moon in Virgo and share bold, high-energy content during the Full Moon in Aries.

October

- **October 2:** New Moon in Libra
- **October 9:** First Quarter Moon in Capricorn
- **October 16:** Full Moon in Taurus

Content Focus: Highlight themes of balance and beauty during the New Moon in Libra and share grounded, practical content around the Full Moon in Taurus.

November

- **November 1:** New Moon in Scorpio
- **November 8:** First Quarter Moon in Aquarius
- **November 15:** Full Moon in Gemini

Content Focus: Explore deep, transformative topics during the New Moon in Scorpio and focus on storytelling and communication during the Full Moon in Gemini.

December

- **December 1:** New Moon in Sagittarius
- **December 8:** First Quarter Moon in Pisces
- **December 15:** Full Moon in Cancer

Content Focus: Share inspiring, expansive ideas during the New Moon in Sagittarius and nurture your audience with heartfelt, family-focused themes during the Full Moon in Cancer.

How to Use This Lunar Calendar

1. **Plan Content Around Lunar Phases:** Align brainstorming, creation, and launches with the corresponding lunar energy.
2. **Leverage Key Lunar Events:** Use New Moons for fresh starts and Full Moons for visibility and audience engagement.
3. **Monitor Personal Reactions:** Track how lunar phases and signs influence your mood and productivity to fine-tune your strategy.

Final Thoughts

The Moon's cycles provide a natural rhythm for content planning, encouraging intentionality and alignment with cosmic energy. Use this lunar calendar as a guide to craft meaningful, resonant content throughout the year. By aligning your efforts with the Moon's phases, you can create a powerful, intuitive connection with your audience and achieve greater creative flow.

Appendix D: Step-by-Step Guide to Creating a Personalized Content Calendar Based on Transits

Astrological transits provide a roadmap for aligning your content strategy with the energy of the cosmos. By integrating transits into your planning process, you can optimize creativity, productivity, and audience engagement. This appendix offers a detailed, step-by-step guide to crafting a personalized content calendar that reflects your unique astrological blueprint and current planetary influences.

Step 1: Understand Your Natal Chart

Your natal chart serves as the foundation for customizing your content calendar. The planets' positions at the time of your birth reveal your strengths, challenges, and creative tendencies.

How to Analyze Your Chart:

1. **Generate Your Natal Chart:** Use free tools like AstroSeek, TimePassages, or Chani to create your chart.
2. **Identify Key Placements:**
     ◦ **Sun Sign:** Core identity and purpose.
     ◦ **Moon Sign:** Emotional tone and connection with your audience.
     ◦ **Mercury Sign:** Communication style.
     ◦ **Venus Sign:** Aesthetic preferences.
     ◦ **Mars Sign:** Action and motivation.
     ◦ **Midheaven (MC):** Career direction and public persona.
3. **Note House Placements:** Look at the house positions of your planets to understand which areas of life they influence.

Application to Content Creation:

- Use your Sun and Midheaven to define your brand's identity and purpose.
- Leverage your Moon for crafting emotionally resonant content.
- Align your communication strategy with Mercury's energy.

Step 2: Track Current Transits

Astrological transits reflect the movement of planets in real-time and how they interact with your natal chart. These influences shape your creative energy and opportunities.

How to Track Transits:

1. **Use Transit Tools:** Platforms like Astro.com, The Moon Calendar app, or Planet Watcher provide daily transit updates.
2. **Monitor Personal and Collective Energy:**
    ◦ **Personal Transits:** Look at how transiting planets aspect your natal chart.
    ◦ **Collective Transits:** Consider broader influences like Jupiter in Taurus or Mercury retrograde.
3. **Identify Key Events:**
    ◦ New and Full Moons
    ◦ Retrogrades
    ◦ Major planetary aspects (e.g., conjunctions, trines, squares)

Application to Content Creation:

• Align launches and high-visibility projects with supportive transits like Jupiter trines or Full Moons.
• Use retrogrades for reviewing and refining content.

Step 3: Map Out Lunar Phases

The Moon's phases create a natural rhythm for planning and executing projects. Incorporate these cycles into your calendar for an intuitive, flow-based approach.

Lunar Phases and Their Focus:

1. **New Moon:** Set intentions and brainstorm ideas.
2. **Waxing Crescent:** Begin work on new projects.
3. **First Quarter:** Take decisive action and overcome obstacles.
4. **Waxing Gibbous:** Refine and prepare for launches.
5. **Full Moon:** Showcase, launch, or celebrate.
6. **Waning Gibbous:** Reflect on progress and share insights.
7. **Last Quarter:** Release outdated ideas and strategies.
8. **Waning Crescent:** Rest, recharge, and plan for the next cycle.

Application to Content Creation:

• Schedule brainstorming sessions during the New Moon.

- Launch major projects during the Full Moon for maximum visibility.

Step 4: Align Content Themes with Planetary Energies
Each planet governs specific themes that can inspire your content. By aligning your topics with planetary transits, you can create relevant, resonant material.
Planetary Influences and Content Themes:

- **Sun:** Identity, leadership, and creative expression.
- **Moon:** Emotions, intuition, and nurturing.
- **Mercury:** Communication, learning, and technology.
- **Venus:** Beauty, relationships, and values.
- **Mars:** Action, ambition, and conflict resolution.
- **Jupiter:** Expansion, growth, and opportunities.
- **Saturn:** Discipline, structure, and responsibility.
- **Uranus:** Innovation, freedom, and change.
- **Neptune:** Creativity, spirituality, and dreams.
- **Pluto:** Transformation, empowerment, and deep exploration.

Application to Content Creation:

- Create content about self-care and nurturing during a Moon transit.
- Focus on aesthetics and beauty during Venus transits.
- Highlight transformative stories during Pluto aspects.

Step 5: Integrate Retrogrades into Your Calendar
Retrogrades are ideal for reflection, review, and refinement. While they may slow progress on new initiatives, they offer valuable opportunities for growth.
How to Work with Retrogrades:

1. **Mercury Retrograde:**
   - Review and update old content.
   - Double-check communications and technical setups.
2. **Venus Retrograde:**
   - Reassess branding and aesthetic elements.
   - Reflect on relationship-building strategies.
3. **Mars Retrograde:**
   - Refine action plans and conserve energy.
4. **Outer Planet Retrogrades (Jupiter, Saturn, Uranus, Neptune, Pluto):**
   - Focus on long-term adjustments and internal growth.

Application to Content Creation:

- Revisit high-performing posts during Mercury retrograde and enhance them for renewed impact.
- Use Venus retrograde to refine your brand's visual identity.

Step 6: Plan Seasonal Campaigns with Zodiac Energy
Each zodiac sign carries unique energy that influences collective themes. Incorporate these traits into your seasonal content planning.
Zodiac Energy and Content Focus:

- **Aries Season (March-April):** Bold, motivational, action-oriented.
- **Taurus Season (April-May):** Grounded, aesthetic, focused on stability.
- **Gemini Season (May-June):** Versatile, curious, communication-driven.
- **Cancer Season (June-July):** Nurturing, emotional, family-focused.
- **Leo Season (July-August):** Creative, expressive, and bold.
- **Virgo Season (August-September):** Organized, practical, detail-oriented.
- **Libra Season (September-October):** Harmonious, aesthetic, relationship-focused.
- **Scorpio Season (October-November):** Intense, transformative, deeply emotional.
- **Sagittarius Season (November-December):** Adventurous, optimistic, expansive.
- **Capricorn Season (December-January):** Ambitious, disciplined, goal-oriented.
- **Aquarius Season (January-February):** Innovative, community-driven, unconventional.
- **Pisces Season (February-March):** Dreamy, spiritual, imaginative.

Application to Content Creation:

- Align launches and campaigns with zodiac themes. For example, focus on innovation and tech during Aquarius season or nurturing and family during Cancer season.

Step 7: Create a Visual Content Calendar

Compile all your astrological insights into a visual content calendar for easy reference and execution.

How to Build Your Calendar:

1. **Choose a Tool:** Use platforms like Trello, Notion, or Google Calendar.
2. **Include Key Dates:**
   - New and Full Moons
   - Retrogrades
   - Major planetary transits and aspects
3. **Color Code by Theme:**
   - Use different colors for brainstorming, launches, reviews, and rest periods.
4. **Add Reminders:**
   - Set alerts for important transits and deadlines.

Step 8: Review and Adjust Regularly

Astrology is dynamic, and so is your content strategy. Regularly review your calendar to adapt to shifting energies and new insights.

Tips for Reviewing:

- Reflect on how recent transits affected your productivity and engagement.
- Adjust future plans based on observed trends and results.
- Stay updated on upcoming transits and align accordingly.

Example: Content Calendar Snapshot

Here's an example of how your calendar might look for a single month:

Date	Astrological Event	Content Focus	Actions
March 9	New Moon in Pisces	Imagination, storytelling	Brainstorm dreamy, creative content ideas
March 16	First Quarter Moon in Gemini	Communication, collaboration	Launch an engaging Q&A series
March 23	Full Moon in Libra	Harmony, balance, relationships	Publish a collaborative project
March 30	Last Quarter Moon in Capricorn	Discipline, completion	Reflect on progress and refine strategy

Final Thoughts

Creating a personalized content calendar based on transits allows you to align your creative efforts with cosmic energy, maximizing productivity and impact. By integrating your natal chart, lunar phases, planetary transits, retrogrades, and zodiac seasons, you can craft a strategy that feels both intentional and inspired. Use this guide as a template to build your celestial content calendar and watch your creative projects flourish in harmony with the stars.

Appendix E: Astrological Glossary – Terms Every Content Creator Should Know

Astrology offers a vast lexicon of terms and concepts that may feel overwhelming at first. For content creators leveraging astrology in their strategies, understanding key terms is essential for applying cosmic insights effectively. This glossary provides clear, detailed definitions of essential astrological terms, focusing on how they relate to content planning, audience engagement, and creative inspiration.

Astrological Basics

Astrology

The study of how the positions and movements of celestial bodies influence human behavior, emotions, and events on Earth.

- **Application:** Use astrological insights to align your content themes with cosmic energies for greater resonance with your audience.

Natal Chart (Birth Chart)

A map of the sky at the exact moment and location of your birth, showing the positions of the planets in the zodiac signs and houses.

- **Application:** Analyze your natal chart to understand your creative strengths, challenges, and ideal career direction.

Zodiac

A band of 12 constellations through which the Sun, Moon, and planets move, forming the basis for astrological signs.

- **Application:** Align your content themes with the energy of the Sun's zodiac sign during each season.

Sun Sign

The zodiac sign where the Sun was at the time of your birth, representing your core identity and creative purpose.

- **Application:** Use your Sun Sign to shape your brand's voice and overarching mission.

Moon Sign

The zodiac sign where the Moon was at the time of your birth, representing your emotions and intuition.

- **Application:** Craft emotionally resonant content that connects with your audience's feelings, guided by your Moon Sign.

Rising Sign (Ascendant)

The zodiac sign that was rising on the eastern horizon at the time of your birth, representing your outward persona and first impressions.

- **Application:** Build your visual branding and public image based on the traits of your Rising Sign.

Planets and Their Influences

Sun

Represents identity, vitality, and purpose.

- **Application:** Align your content with the core themes of self-expression and authenticity.

Moon

Represents emotions, intuition, and cycles.

- **Application:** Schedule content releases around the Moon's phases to harness its energy.

Mercury

Represents communication, intellect, and technology.

- **Application:** Plan writing, speaking, and marketing tasks during favorable Mercury transits.

Venus

Represents beauty, relationships, and values.

- **Application:** Focus on visual aesthetics and relationship-building during Venus transits.

Mars

Represents energy, ambition, and action.

- **Application:** Use Mars transits to drive high-energy campaigns or overcome creative blocks.

Jupiter

Represents growth, abundance, and opportunities.

- **Application:** Plan expansion efforts, collaborations, or launches during Jupiter transits.

Saturn

Represents discipline, structure, and responsibility.

- **Application:** Build long-term content strategies and structures under Saturn's influence.

Uranus
Represents innovation, freedom, and change.

  - **Application:** Experiment with new formats, platforms, or ideas during Uranus transits.

Neptune
Represents creativity, spirituality, and dreams.

  - **Application:** Create emotionally resonant and imaginative content during Neptune transits.

Pluto
Represents transformation, empowerment, and depth.

  - **Application:** Explore transformative or taboo topics aligned with Pluto's energy.

Lunar Phases
New Moon
The beginning of the lunar cycle, representing fresh starts and intention setting.

  - **Application:** Use this phase to brainstorm ideas and plan upcoming projects.

Full Moon
The midpoint of the lunar cycle, representing completion, visibility, and celebration.

  - **Application:** Schedule launches or high-profile content releases during the Full Moon.

Waxing Phases
The Moon is growing in light, representing growth and momentum.

  - **Application:** Work on building and expanding your projects during these phases.

Waning Phases
The Moon is decreasing in light, representing reflection and release.

  - **Application:** Use these phases for revising, completing, or letting go of outdated content strategies.

Astrological Aspects
Conjunction
When two planets align in the same zodiac sign, amplifying their combined energy.

- **Application:** Use conjunctions for starting projects or tackling bold ideas.

Trine
When two planets form a harmonious 120-degree angle, promoting ease and flow.

- **Application:** Schedule creative or collaborative efforts during trines for smooth execution.

Square
When two planets form a challenging 90-degree angle, creating tension.

- **Application:** Address challenges and refine strategies during square transits.

Opposition
When two planets are directly opposite each other, representing balance and conflict.

- **Application:** Focus on finding harmony between opposing forces in your projects or brand.

Sextile
When two planets form a cooperative 60-degree angle, promoting opportunity.

- **Application:** Explore new ideas or partnerships during sextile transits.

Retrogrades
Retrograde
When a planet appears to move backward in the sky, signaling a period of reflection and review.

- **Mercury Retrograde:** Reflect on communication strategies and revisit old content.
- **Venus Retrograde:** Reassess branding and aesthetics.
- **Mars Retrograde:** Refine action plans and conserve energy.
- **Application:** Use retrogrades to revisit, revise, and refine your content strategies.

Astrological Houses

The natal chart is divided into 12 houses, each representing different areas of life. Planets in these houses influence specific aspects of your career and content creation.

1st House: Identity and appearance.

- **Focus:** Personal branding and first impressions.

2nd House: Finances and values.

- **Focus:** Monetization and value-driven content.

3rd House: Communication and learning.

- **Focus:** Writing, speaking, and networking.

4th House: Home and family.

- **Focus:** Personal storytelling and nurturing themes.

5th House: Creativity and self-expression.

- **Focus:** Art, entertainment, and innovation.

6th House: Work and health.

- **Focus:** Productivity and work-life balance.

7th House: Partnerships and relationships.

- **Focus:** Collaborations and community-building.

8th House: Transformation and shared resources.

- **Focus:** Deep, transformative topics.

9th House: Expansion and higher learning.

- **Focus:** Educational content and global themes.

10th House: Career and public image.

- **Focus:** Long-term goals and reputation.

11th House: Social networks and innovation.

- **Focus:** Community-driven projects and tech-savvy strategies.

12th House: Intuition and spirituality.

- **Focus:** Emotional depth and introspection.

Key Astrological Events
Solar Eclipse
Occurs during a New Moon, amplifying its energy for transformation and new beginnings.

- **Application:** Launch transformative projects or rebrand your content.

Lunar Eclipse
Occurs during a Full Moon, representing endings and revelations.

- **Application:** Reflect on your progress and let go of outdated strategies.

Final Thoughts
This astrological glossary provides a foundational understanding of key terms every content creator should know. By familiarizing yourself with these concepts, you can align your creative process with cosmic energies, enhancing the relevance and impact of your work. Let this glossary serve as your quick reference guide as you navigate the celestial roadmap to success!

Appendix F: Resource List – Best Apps and Tools for Astrological Tracking

Astrology offers a rich framework for planning and aligning your creative efforts with the cosmos, but to make the most of it, you need the right tools. This appendix provides a curated list of the best apps, websites, and tools for tracking astrological transits, analyzing natal charts, and integrating astrology into your content strategy. Whether you're a beginner or a seasoned astrologer, these resources will empower you to stay connected to cosmic energies and optimize your creative process.

Top Astrology Apps for Tracking Transits and Natal Charts

1. TimePassages

- **Features:**
  - Detailed natal chart generation with easy-to-understand explanations.
  - Real-time transit tracking and personalized insights.
  - Aspects and house placements with interpretations.
- **Best For:** Beginners and intermediate users who want a comprehensive yet user-friendly tool.
- **Platform:** iOS, Android
- **Pricing:** Free basic version; premium features available for purchase.

2. Astro.com (Astrodienst)

- **Features:**
  - Accurate natal chart calculations and advanced tools for professional astrologers.
  - Transit calendars, progressions, and solar return charts.
  - Access to an extensive library of articles and resources.
- **Best For:** Advanced users and those who prefer desktop tools.
- **Platform:** Web-based
- **Pricing:** Free; premium reports available.

3. The Pattern

- **Features:**
  - Focuses on personal growth and relationship dynamics based on astrology.
  - Provides daily insights and "patterns" tied to transits.
  - Customizable with friends' charts for relational insights.
- **Best For:** Those interested in understanding the emotional and psychological influences of astrology.
- **Platform:** iOS, Android
- **Pricing:** Free; optional in-app purchases.

4. Co–Star

- **Features:**
  - Minimalist interface with daily personalized horoscopes.
  - Real-time transit updates and natal chart insights.
  - Allows social connections to compare charts with friends.
- **Best For:** Beginners who want simple, modern astrology insights.
- **Platform:** iOS, Android
- **Pricing:** Free; in-app purchases available.

5. Chani App

- **Features:**
  - Weekly and daily horoscopes tailored to your chart.
  - Personalized rituals, meditations, and affirmations based on transits.
  - Insightful content on astrology for self-improvement and mindfulness.
- **Best For:** Creators who want astrology-based self-care and productivity tools.
- **Platform:** iOS, Android
- **Pricing:** Monthly subscription.

6. Moonly

- **Features:**
  - Lunar phase tracking with spiritual guidance and rituals.
  - Daily affirmations, meditations, and moon-based insights.
  - Focused on emotional and spiritual well-being.
- **Best For:** Creatives who want to align their content with lunar cycles.
- **Platform:** iOS, Android
- **Pricing:** Free; premium subscription available.

Best Websites for Astrology Insights
1. AstroSeek (Astro-Seek.com)

* **Features:**
    ◦ Accurate natal chart calculations with advanced customization.
    ◦ Transit charts, compatibility calculators, and solar/lunar calendars.
    ◦ Extensive library of astrological tools and resources.
* **Best For:** All levels, especially for detailed chart calculations and tools.
* **Website:** www.astro-seek.com

2. Cafe Astrology

* **Features:**
    ◦ Free natal chart and compatibility reports.
    ◦ Comprehensive articles on astrology basics and advanced topics.
    ◦ Monthly and yearly horoscopes.
* **Best For:** Beginners looking for clear, in-depth explanations.
* **Website:** www.cafeastrology.com

3. AstroStyle

* **Features:**
    ◦ Trendy, easy-to-read horoscopes and compatibility guides.
    ◦ Focus on lifestyle and astrology integration.
    ◦ Resources for using astrology in everyday life.
* **Best For:** Creatives who want stylish astrology advice.
* **Website:** www.astrostyle.com

4. The Astrology Podcast

* **Features:**
    ◦ Weekly podcasts covering transit forecasts, astrology news, and deep dives into astrological concepts.
    ◦ Expert interviews and accessible discussions for all levels.
* **Best For:** Audio learners and those seeking in-depth astrology education.
* **Website:** www.theastrologypodcast.com

5. Astrology Zone by Susan Miller

- **Features:**
    - ◦ Monthly horoscopes with detailed forecasts.
    - ◦ Special focus on career and financial astrology.
    - ◦ Practical advice for planning events and projects.
- **Best For:** Content creators seeking actionable guidance for business growth.
- **Website:** www.astrologyzone.com

Tools for Lunar Tracking

1. The Moon Calendar

- **Features:**
    - ◦ Tracks moon phases, zodiac signs, and major lunar events.
    - ◦ Offers personalized reminders and rituals.
- **Best For:** Creators planning content around the lunar cycle.
- **Platform:** iOS, Android
- **Pricing:** Free; premium version available.

2. Deluxe Moon

- **Features:**
    - ◦ Detailed moon phase tracking with astrological insights.
    - ◦ Interactive lunar calendars and recommendations for activities.
- **Best For:** Advanced lunar tracking for emotional and creative alignment.
- **Platform:** iOS, Android
- **Pricing:** Paid app.

3. My Moon Phase

- **Features:**
    - ◦ Simplified lunar calendar for tracking moon phases.
    - ◦ Focused on visual aesthetics and user-friendly design.
- **Best For:** Beginners and those who want quick lunar insights.
- **Platform:** iOS, Android
- **Pricing:** Free; in-app purchases available.

Astrology and Productivity Tools
1. Notion

- **Features:**
    ◦ Highly customizable templates for content calendars and astrology tracking.
    ◦ Integrate transit tracking, lunar cycles, and goal-setting.
- **Best For:** Content creators who want an all-in-one organizational tool.
- **Platform:** iOS, Android, Desktop
- **Pricing:** Free; premium plans available.

2. Google Calendar

- **Features:**
    ◦ Add astrological transits, lunar phases, and retrogrades as calendar events.
    ◦ Sync with astrology apps for real-time updates.
- **Best For:** Simple, seamless integration into existing workflows.
- **Platform:** Web, iOS, Android
- **Pricing:** Free.

3. Trello

- **Features:**
    ◦ Visual task management with boards for transit-based content planning.
    ◦ Color-code cards for different phases, transits, or zodiac seasons.
- **Best For:** Visual planners who want an intuitive way to align tasks with astrology.
- **Platform:** iOS, Android, Web
- **Pricing:** Free; premium version available.

Books and Educational Resources

1. "The Only Astrology Book You'll Ever Need" by Joanna Martine Woolfolk

- **Features:** Comprehensive guide to astrology, covering natal charts, transits, and interpretations.
- **Best For:** Beginners seeking a thorough understanding of astrology.

2. "Planets in Transit" by Robert Hand

- **Features:** Detailed explanations of transits and their effects on the natal chart.
- **Best For:** Intermediate to advanced users who want in-depth transit insights.

3. "Lunar Abundance" by Ezzie Spencer

- **Features:** Explores the Moon's phases as a tool for intentional living and goal-setting.
- **Best For:** Creators aligning with the lunar cycle for productivity and creativity.

Final Thoughts

Using these apps, websites, and tools can revolutionize the way you approach content creation, helping you align your efforts with astrological energies for maximum impact. Whether you're a beginner seeking simple insights or an experienced astrologer looking for advanced tools, this resource list has everything you need to track, plan, and execute your cosmic content strategy. Let the stars guide your way!

Appendix G: Tips for Adapting to Retrogrades and Celestial Shifts

Astrological retrogrades and celestial shifts are periods of transformation, introspection, and reevaluation. While they may seem challenging, these cosmic events can also offer unique opportunities for growth and recalibration when approached with awareness and strategy. This appendix provides detailed tips for adapting to retrogrades and celestial shifts, helping content creators maintain balance and productivity while harnessing the transformative power of these periods.

Understanding Retrogrades

In astrology, a planet is said to be in **retrograde** when it appears to move backward in its orbit from our perspective on Earth. Retrogrades often symbolize a slowing down of the planet's usual energy, encouraging reflection and reassessment.

Key Retrogrades to Watch:

1. **Mercury Retrograde** (3–4 times/year, ~3 weeks): Communication, technology, and travel disruptions.
2. **Venus Retrograde** (every 18 months, ~6 weeks): Reassessment of relationships, values, and aesthetics.
3. **Mars Retrograde** (every 2 years, ~2.5 months): Reconsideration of actions, goals, and energy.
4. **Outer Planet Retrogrades** (Jupiter, Saturn, Uranus, Neptune, Pluto): Longer retrogrades (4–6 months), influencing collective themes and personal introspection.

General Tips for Navigating Retrogrades
1. Slow Down and Reflect
Retrogrades are not the time to rush into new ventures. Instead:

- Revisit old projects or ideas.
- Reflect on your current strategies and their alignment with your goals.
- Focus on refining and improving existing content rather than creating something entirely new.

2. Double-Check Details
During retrogrades, especially Mercury retrograde:

- Review contracts, emails, and communications carefully.
- Back up your data and ensure your technology is functioning properly.
- Avoid signing major agreements or launching new projects unless absolutely necessary.

3. Embrace Patience
Retrogrades often bring delays or unexpected challenges. Cultivate patience by:

- Allowing extra time for tasks and deadlines.
- Reframing setbacks as opportunities to learn and adapt.
- Practicing mindfulness to stay grounded during uncertainty.

Retrograde-Specific Strategies
1. Mercury Retrograde: Rethink Communication

- **Do:** Edit and update existing content, revisit old topics, and refine messaging.
- **Don't:** Start new marketing campaigns or rely heavily on technology without backups.
- **Example:** Use this time to optimize your website or rework evergreen blog posts.

2. Venus Retrograde: Reassess Aesthetics and Relationships

- **Do:** Reevaluate your brand's visual identity, pricing strategy, or partnerships.
- **Don't:** Launch new branding efforts, collaborations, or product lines.
- **Example:** Conduct a branding audit to identify areas for improvement.

3. Mars Retrograde: Conserve Energy

- **Do:** Reflect on your goals and streamline your efforts.
- **Don't:** Initiate aggressive campaigns or make impulsive decisions.
- **Example:** Focus on long-term planning and tie up loose ends in ongoing projects.

4. Outer Planet Retrogrades: Internal Growth

- **Jupiter:** Reflect on areas of expansion and opportunity.
- **Saturn:** Reassess structures, commitments, and responsibilities.
- **Uranus:** Contemplate innovation and embrace unexpected changes.
- **Neptune:** Reconnect with intuition and creativity.
- **Pluto:** Examine power dynamics and personal transformation.

Adapting to Celestial Shifts
Celestial shifts, such as eclipses, planetary ingresses (when a planet moves into a new sign), and major aspects, often bring sudden changes and heightened energy.

Eclipses: Turning Points

Eclipses signify endings, beginnings, and revelations. They often highlight areas of life that need transformation.

- **Do:** Reflect on significant life changes and be open to shifts in direction.
- **Don't:** Force decisions or take hasty actions.
- **Example:** Use eclipses to brainstorm long-term goals or let go of unproductive habits.

Planetary Ingresses: New Themes

When a planet enters a new zodiac sign, it shifts the collective focus to different themes.

- **Do:** Align your content with the themes of the planet's new sign.
- **Don't:** Resist changes or cling to outdated strategies.
- **Example:** During Venus in Libra, emphasize beauty, harmony, and relationships in your content.

Major Aspects: Intense Energy

Conjunctions, oppositions, and squares can bring challenges, while trines and sextiles foster ease and opportunity.

- **Do:** Use harmonious aspects to initiate projects and challenging aspects to refine strategies.
- **Don't:** Avoid issues or conflicts; instead, address them constructively.
- **Example:** A Mars-Uranus conjunction might inspire bold, innovative content, while a Saturn square could help refine and structure your ideas.

Practical Tips for Content Creators
1. Adjust Your Content Calendar

- Mark retrogrades, eclipses, and major transits on your calendar.
- Schedule reflective tasks during retrogrades and launches during harmonious aspects.

2. Use Retrogrades for Repurposing

- Revisit high-performing content and give it a fresh update.
- Turn old blog posts into social media posts or repurpose videos into shorter clips.

3. Engage with Your Audience Thoughtfully

- Retrogrades often heighten emotions and introspection. Use this time to:
    - Share personal reflections or behind-the-scenes stories.
    - Host Q&A sessions or polls to understand your audience's needs.

4. Focus on Mindfulness and Self-Care

- Use celestial shifts as reminders to pause and recharge.
- Practice mindfulness techniques like journaling or meditation to navigate emotional intensity.

Tools for Navigating Retrogrades and Shifts
1. Astrology Apps

- **TimePassages:** Provides detailed retrograde and transit insights.
- **Chani App:** Offers actionable advice for navigating celestial events.

2. Journaling

- Reflect on how retrogrades and shifts affect your creativity, productivity, and mood.

3. Content Management Tools

- Use Trello or Notion to track tasks and adjust your calendar based on retrograde and transit periods.

Examples of Retrograde Success

- **Mercury Retrograde:** A creator revisits old blog posts and optimizes them for SEO, leading to increased organic traffic.
- **Venus Retrograde:** A lifestyle brand conducts a survey to understand audience preferences, using the insights to refine its product line.
- **Mars Retrograde:** A business coach focuses on backend improvements, such as updating workflows and organizing files, during a lull in client work.

Final Thoughts
Retrogrades and celestial shifts are not obstacles but opportunities for growth, recalibration, and deeper alignment with your creative purpose. By embracing these periods with awareness and adaptability, you can turn challenges into stepping stones for success. Use the tips and strategies in this guide to navigate cosmic changes confidently, ensuring your content remains intentional, impactful, and attuned to the rhythms of the universe.

<u>Message from the Author:</u>

I hope you enjoyed this book, I love astrology and knew there was not a book such as this out on the shelf. I love metaphysical items as well. Please check out my other books:

-Life of Government Benefits

-My life of Hell

-My life with Hydrocephalus

-Red Sky

-World Domination:Woman's rule

-World Domination:Woman's Rule 2: The War

-Life and Banishment of Apophis: book 1

-The Kidney Friendly Diet

-The Ultimate Hemp Cookbook

-Creating a Dispensary(legally)

-Cleanliness throughout life: the importance of showering from childhood to adulthood.

-Strong Roots: The Risks of Overcoddling children

-Hemp Horoscopes: Cosmic Insights and Earthly Healing

- Celestial Hemp Navigating the Zodiac: Through the Green Cosmos

-Astrological Hemp: Aligning The Stars with Earth's Ancient Herb

-The Astrological Guide to Hemp: Stars, Signs, and Sacred Leaves

-Green Growth: Innovative Marketing Strategies for your Hemp Products and Dispensary

-Cosmic Cannabis

-Astrological Munchies

-Henry The Hemp

-Zodiacal Roots: The Astrological Soul Of Hemp

- Green Constellations: Intersection of Hemp and Zodiac

-Hemp in The Houses: An astrological Adventure Through The Cannabis Galaxy

-Galactic Ganja Guide

Heavenly Hemp

Zodiac Leaves

Doctor Who Astrology

Cannastrology

Stellar Satvias and Cosmic Indicas

<u>Celestial Cannabis: A Zodiac Journey</u>

AstroHerbology: The Sky and The Soil: Volume 1

AstroHerbology:Celestial Cannabis:Volume 2

Cosmic Cannabis Cultivation

The Starry Guide to Herbal Harmony: Volume 1

The Starry Guide to Herbal Harmony: Cannabis Universe: Volume 2

Yugioh Astrology: Astrological Guide to Deck, Duels and more

Nightmare Mansion: Echoes of The Abyss

Nightmare Mansion 2: Legacy of Shadows

Nightmare Mansion 3: Shadows of the Forgotten

Nightmare Mansion 4: Echoes of the Damned

The Life and Banishment of Apophis: Book 2

Nightmare Mansion: Halls of Despair

<u>Healing with Herb: Cannabis and Hydrocephalus</u>

<u>Planetary Pot: Aligning with Astrological Herbs: Volume 1</u>

Fast Track to Freedom: 30 Days to Financial Independence Using AI, Assets, and Agile Hustles

<u>Cosmic Hemp Pathways</u>

How to Become Financially Free in 30 Days: 10,000 Paths to Prosperity

Zodiacal Herbage: Astrological Insights: Volume 1

Nightmare Mansion: Whispers in the Walls

The Daleks Invade Atlantis

Henry the hemp and Hydrocephalus

10X The Kidney Friendly Diet

Cannabis Universe: Adult coloring book

Hemp Astrology: The Healing Power of the Stars

Zodiacal Herbage: Astrological Insights: Cannabis Universe: Volume 2

<u>Planetary Pot: Aligning with Astrological Herbs: Cannabis Universes: Volume 2</u>

Doctor Who Meets the Replicators and SG-1: The Ultimate Battle for Survival

Nightmare Mansion: Curse of the Blood Moon

<u>The Celestial Stoner: A Guide to the Zodiac</u>

Cosmic Pleasures: Sex Toy Astrology for Every Sign

Hydrocephalus Astrology: Navigating the Stars and Healing Waters

Lapis and the Mischievous Chocolate Bar

Celestial Positions: Sexual Astrology for Every Sign

Apophis's Shadow Work Journal: : A Journey of Self-Discovery and Healing

Kinky Cosmos: Sexual Kink Astrology for Every Sign

Digital Cosmos: The Astrological Digimon Compendium

Stellar Seeds: The Cosmic Guide to Growing with Astrology

Apophis's Daily Gratitude Journal

Cat Astrology: Feline Mysteries of the Cosmos
The Cosmic Kama Sutra: An Astrological Guide to Sexual Positions
Unleash Your Potential: A Guided Journal Powered by AI Insights
Whispers of the Enchanted Grove

Cosmic Pleasures: An Astrological Guide to Sexual Kinks
369, 12 Manifestation Journal
Whisper of the nocturne journal(blank journal for writing or drawing)
The Boogey Book
Locked In Reflection: A Chastity Journey Through Locktober
Generating Wealth Quickly:
How to Generate $100,000 in 24 Hours
Star Magic: Harness the Power of the Universe
The Flatulence Chronicles: A Fart Journal for Self-Discovery
The Doctor and The Death Moth
Seize the Day: A Personal Seizure Tracking Journal
The Ultimate Boogeyman Safari: A Journey into the Boogie World and Beyond
Whispers of Samhain: 1,000 Spells of Love, Luck, and Lunar Magic: Samhain Spell Book
Apophis's guides:
Witch's Spellbook Crafting Guide for Halloween
<u>Frost & Flame: The Enchanted Yule Grimoire of 1000 Winter Spells</u>
<u>The Ultimate Boogey Goo Guide & Spooky Activities for Halloween Fun</u>
Harmony of the Scales: A Libra's Spellcraft for Balance and Beauty
The Enchanted Advent: 36 Days of Christmas Wonders

Nightmare Mansion: The Labyrinth of Screams
Harvest of Enchantment: 1,000 Spells of Gratitude, Love, and Fortune for Thanksgiving
The Boogey Chronicles: A Journal of Nightly Encounters and Shadowy Secrets
The 12 Days of Financial Freedom: A Step-by-Step Christmas Countdown to Transform Your Finances
Sigil of the Eternal Spiral Blank Journal
A Christmas Feast: Timeless Recipes for Every Meal
Holiday Stress-Free Solutions: A Survival Guide to Thriving During the Festive Season
Yu-Gi-Oh! Holiday Gifting Mastery: The Ultimate Guide for Fans and Newcomers Alike
Holiday Harmony: A Hydrocephalus Survival Guide for the Festive Season
Celestial Craft: The Witch's Almanac for 2025 – A Cosmic Guide to Manifestations, Moons, and Mystical Events
Doctor Who: The Toymaker's Winter Wonderland
Tulsa King Unveiled: A Thrilling Guide to Stallone's Mafia Masterpiece
Pendulum Craft: A Complete Guide to Crafting and Using Personalized Divination Tools
Nightmare Mansion: Santa's Eternal Eve

Starlight Noel: A Cosmic Journey through Christmas Mysteries
The Dark Architect: Unlocking the Blueprint of Existence
Surviving the Embrace: The Ultimate Guide to Encounters with The Hugging Molly
The Enchanted Codex: Secrets of the Craft for Witches, Wiccans, and Pagans
Harvest of Gratitude: A Complete Thanksgiving Guide
Yuletide Essentials: A Complete Guide to an Authentic and Magical Christmas
Celestial Smokes: A Cosmic Guide to Cigars and Astrology
Living in Balance: A Comprehensive Survival Guide to Thriving with Diabetes Insipidus
Cosmic Symbiosis: The Venom Zodiac Chronicles
The Cursed Paw of Ambition
Cosmic Symbiosis: The Astrological Venom Journal
Celestial Wonders Unfold: A Stargazer's Guide to the Cosmos (2024-2029)
The Ultimate Black Friday Prepper's Guide: Mastering Shopping Strategies and Savings
Cosmic Sales: The Astrological Guide to Black Friday Shopping
Legends of the Corn Mother and Other Harvest Myths
Whispers of the Harvest: The Corn Mother's Journal
The Evergreen Spellbook
The Doctor Meets the Boogeyman
The White Witch of Rose Hall's SpellBook
The Gingerbread Golem's Shadow: A Study in Sweet Darkness
The Gingerbread Golem Codex: An Academic Exploration of Sweet Myths
The Gingerbread Golem Grimoire: Sweet Magicks and Spells for the Festive Witch
The Curse of the Gingerbread Golem
10-minute Christmas Crafts for kids
<u>Christmas Crisis Solutions: The Ultimate Last-Minute Survival Guide</u>
Gingerbread Golem Recipes: Holiday Treats with a Magical Twist
The Infinite Key: Unlocking Mystical Secrets of the Ages
Enchanted Yule: A Wiccan and Pagan Guide to a Magical and Memorable Season
Dinosaurs of Power: Unlocking Ancient Magick
Astro-Dinos: The Cosmic Guide to Prehistoric Wisdom
Gallifrey's Yule Logs: A Festive Doctor Who Cookbook
The Dino Grimoire: Secrets of Prehistoric Magick
The Gift They Never Knew They Needed
The Gingerbread Golem's Culinary Alchemy: Enchanting Recipes for a Sweetly Dark Feast
A Time Lord Christmas: Holiday Adventures with the Doctor
Krampusproofing Your Home: Defensive Strategies for Yule
Silent Frights: A Collection of Christmas Creepypastas to Chill Your Bones
Santa Raptor's Jolly Carnage: A Dino-Claus Christmas Tale
Prehistoric Palettes: A Dino Wicca Coloring Journey
The Christmas Wishkeeper Chronicles
The Starlight Sleigh: A Holiday Journey

Elf Secrets: The True Magic of the North Pole

Candy Cane Conjurations

Cooking with Kids: Recipes Under 20 Minutes

Doctor Who: The TARDIS Confiscation

The Anxiety First Aid Kit: Quick Tools to Calm Your Mind

Frosty Whispers: A Winter's Tale

The Infinite Key: Unlocking the Secrets to Prosperity, Resilience, and Purpose

The Grasping Void: Why You'll Regret This Purchase

Astrology for Busy Bees: Star Signs Simplified

The Instant Focus Formula: Cut Through the Noise

The Secret Language of Colors: Unlocking the Emotional Codes

Sacred Fossil Chronicles: Blank Journal

The Christmas Cottage Miracle

Feeding Frenzy: Graboid-Inspired Recipes

Manifest in Minutes: The Quick Law of Attraction Guide

The Symbiote Chronicles: Doctor Who's Venomous Journey

Think Tiny, Grow Big: The Minimalist Mindset

The Energy Key: Unlocking Limitless Motivation

New Year, New Magic: Manifesting Your Best Year Yet

Unstoppable You: Mastering Confidence in Minutes

Infinite Energy: The Secret to Never Feeling Drained

Lightning Focus: Mastering the Art of Productivity in a Distracted World

Saturnalia Manifestation Magick: A Guide to Unlocking Abundance During the Solstice

Graboids and Garland: The Ultimate Tremors-Themed Christmas Guide

12 Nights of Holiday Magic

The Power of Pause: 60-Second Mindfulness Practices

The Quick Reset: How to Reclaim Your Life After Burnout

The Shadow Eater: A Tale of Despair and Survival

The Micro-Mastery Method: Transform Your Skills in Just Minutes a Day

Reclaiming Time: How to Live More by Doing Less

Chronovore: The Eternal Nexus

The Mind Reset: Unlocking Your Inner Peace in a Chaotic World

Confidence Code: Building Unshakable Self-Belief

Baby the Vampire Terrier

Baby the Vampire Terrier's Christmas Adventure

If you want solar for your home go here: https://www.harborsolar.live/apophisenterprises/

Get Some Tarot cards: https://www.makeplayingcards.com/sell/apophis-occult-shop

Get some shirts: https://www.bonfire.com/store/apophis-shirt-emporium/

Instagrams:
@apophis_enterprises,
@apophisbookemporium,
@apophisscardshop
Twitter: @apophisenterpr1
Tiktok:@apophisenterprise
Youtube: @sg1fan23477, @FiresideRetreatKingdom
Hive: @sg1fan23477
CheeLee: @SG1fan23477

Podcast: Apophis Chat Zone: https://open.spotify.com/show/5zXbr-CLEV2xzCp8ybrfHsk?si=fb4d4fdbdce44dec

Newsletter: https://apophiss-newsletter-27c897.beehiiv.com/

If you want to support me or see posts of other projects that I have come over to: **buymeacof-fee.com/mpetchinskg**
I post there daily several times a day

Get your Dinowicca or Christmas themed digital products, especially Santa Raptor songs and other musics. Here: **https://sg1fan23477.gumroad.com**

Apophis Yuletide Digital has not only digital Christmas items, but it will have all things with Dinowicca as well as other Digital products.

www.ingramcontent.com/pod-product-compliance
Lightning Source LLC
Chambersburg PA
CBHW080713120726
48001CB00010B/2995